THE BATTLEFIELDS THAT NEARLY WERE

DEFENDED ENGLAND 1940

THE
BATTLEFIELDS
THAT NEARLY WERE

DEFENDED ENGLAND 1940

WILLIAM FOOT

TEMPUS

This book is dedicated to my late parents who knew many of these places both before and after they were touched by war.

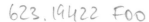

First published 2006

Tempus Publishing Limited
The Mill, Brimscombe Port,
Stroud, Gloucestershire, GL5 2QG
www.tempus-publishing.com

British Library Cataloguing in Publication Data.
A catalogue record for this book is available from the British Library.

ISBN 0 7524 3849 2

Typesetting and origination by Tempus Publishing Limited
Printed in Great Britain

CONTENTS

ACKNOWLEDGEMENTS

My thanks to the many people who helped with this book, both those who appear in its pages and many others who supplied invaluable information. Thanks also to the staff of all the research institutions I describe, in particular those of The National Archives, the National Monuments Record, and the Imperial War Museum. The latter have been particularly generous with their help, and I owe a special debt to Stephen Walton of the Department of Documents at Duxford (who appears here) and Neil Young of the Research and Information Department in London (who does not).

English Heritage generously allowed me to use many of the research materials from their Defence Areas Project on which this account is based, and also were kind enough to read through and comment on parts of the typescript. Any errors which may appear here, however, are mine alone as are the various interpretations of documentary and field evidence.

Finally, I must thank the Council for British Archaeology, which administered this project as well as the Defence of Britain Project, for allowing me to utilise data and maps for which they hold the copyright, and for their encouragement.

All the photographs were taken by me during the course of the fieldwork, and the sketch maps drawn shortly afterwards. It is hoped that these sketch maps will prove a useful accompaniment to the text. (See the Appendix for details of the relevant modern Ordnance Survey sheets.)

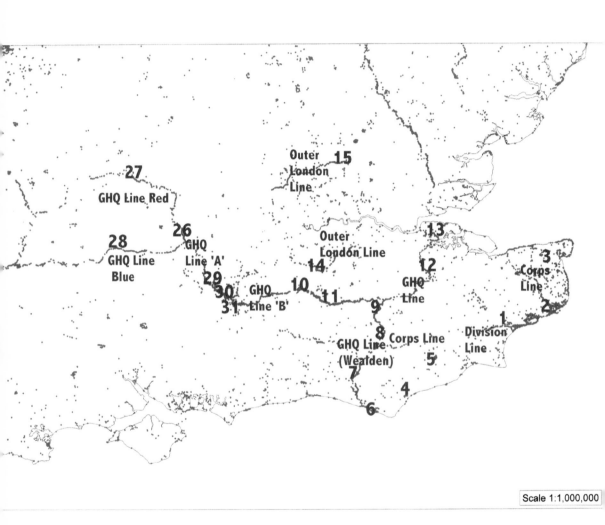

The following labels appear on the map:

Outer London Line 15

27

GHQ Line Red

28
GHQ Line Blue

26
GHQ Line 'A'

Outer London Line
14

13

3
Corps Line

12

29
30 GHQ Line 'B'
31

10
11

GHQ Line

9

2

8 Corps Line
GHQ Line (Wealden)

1

Division Line

5

7

4

6

Scale 1:1,000,000

1 Map of the South-East of England showing the positions of the areas described in the book in relation to the overall 1940 defence strategy. *Key to numbers:* 1 Royal Military Canal, Bilsington–Ruckinge; 2 Farthingloe, Dover; 3 Sarre; 4 Pevensey Castle; 5 Cripp's Corner; 6 Cuckmere Haven; 7 Barcombe Mills; 8 Old Lodge Warren; 9 Penshurst; 10 Dorking Gap; 11 Sidlow Bridge; 12 River Medway, Maidstone; 13 Deangate Ridge, Hoo; 14 Drift Bridge; 15 Cheshunt; 26 Sulham Valley; 27 Frilford – Fyfield; 28 Dunmill Lock; 29 Chequers Bridge; 30 Ewshot; 31 Waverley Abbey. *The background spot data indicating the structure of defence was produced from anti-invasion sites recorded by the Defence of Britain Project © Council for British Archaeology*

ABBREVIATIONS

AA	Anti-Aircraft
AP	Air Photograph
BL	British Library
Emp	Emplacement
FDL	Forward Defended Locality
GHQ	General Headquarters
GSGS	Geographical Section, General Staff
HER (SMR)	Historic Environment Record
	(replacing Sites and Monuments Record – SMR)
HAA	Heavy Anti-Aircraft
in	Inch e.g. 6in (calibre of gun barrel)
IWM	Imperial War Museum
LMG	Light Machine Gun
MMG	Medium Machine Gun
LAA	Light Anti-Aircraft
NMR	National Monuments Record
OP	Observation Post
PB	Pillbox
pdr	Pounder e.g. 2pdr (weight of gun shell)
RB	Roadblock
SM	Spigot mortar
TNA	The National Archives
	(formerly Public Record Office – PRO)

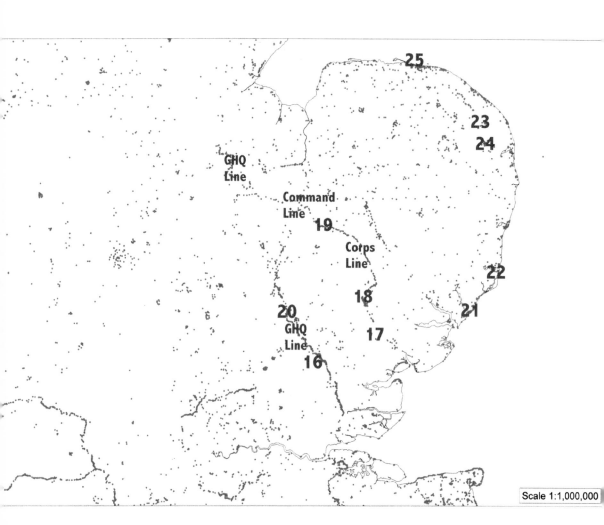

Scale 1:1,000,000

2 Map of the East of England showing the positions of the areas described in the book in relation to the overall 1940 defence strategy. *Key to numbers:* 16 Hartford End; 17 Wakes Colne; 18 Sudbury; 19 Jude's Ferry Bridge; 20 Audley End; 21 Bawdsey Point; 22 Walberswick; 23 Ludham Bridge; 24 Acle; 25 Weybourne. *The background spot data indicating the structure of defence was produced from anti-invasion sites recorded by the Defence of Britain Project © Council for British Archaeology*

1
EAST KENT: ROYAL MILITARY CANAL

First light. 17 September 1940. A smudging of grey across the blackened landscape, slowly revealing the shape of bridge and parapet, road, posts, and tangles of barbed wire. Now the line of the canal can be seen like a dark seam crossing the flat grass fields.

The breeze moves amongst the reeds on the canal bank. The great orb of the sky pales from darkness, gaining substance with the gathering light. The last stars look down with whitened eyes. The air is grey and full of the smell of the earth. Silence, long, drifting silence, as the day slowly strengthens.

A harsh cry, and a great white bird rises from the water, disappearing across the fields, its wings beating frantically at the air. The sound of shod feet on the bridge. Three steel-helmeted soldiers with slung rifles, their shapes like silhouettes against the growing light, pass along the road towards the line of the ridge beyond, now emerging from the dark. A rhythmic pulse of light from the hills, and then another, and darkness again. Now there is the sound of voices, and men stirring, and a clatter of metal, and a laugh, cut short. Above a long, flat-topped mound by the bridge can be seen more helmeted heads, and the black shapes of rifles held forward.

STAND TO!

The tense, watching silence is broken suddenly by a distant muffled crash, and a series of bright flashes that split the sea horizon, followed by a great rushing sound overhead. The soldiers' eyes are turned upwards. More crashes, now sharper, continuous, and a growing noise in the sky, the beating drone of aeroplanes coming closer. Their dark crossed shapes can now be seen above. The jangling sharp ring of a telephone. Shouts, movement. The bridge erupts in a fountain of dust. More roars and flashes, and the higher screaming howl of diving aircraft. The earth shakes as the bombs begin to fall.

Above the hills, the sky is sprouting white shapes that drift to earth. From close at hand, a stuttering rattle begins like a man beating a tattoo on a drum. Red spurts of fire flash on the ridge, like fireworks on bonfire night. And from the distance, borne on the breeze, from right to left, the sound of bells ringing out from the marshland churches.

As I stood by the bridge over the Royal Military Canal south of the Kent village of Bilsington in the early light of a spring morning, this scene came to mind. For here, 65 years ago, would have been one of the major points of attack by the 35th Division of the German 16th Army had Operation Sealion (the invasion of England) taken place. It very nearly did happen. For a few weeks in the summer of 1940, the outcome of history was balanced on a razor edge. The merest feather-touch of fate to alter the balance of history, and the battlefields to decide the destiny of the world might have been on English soil.

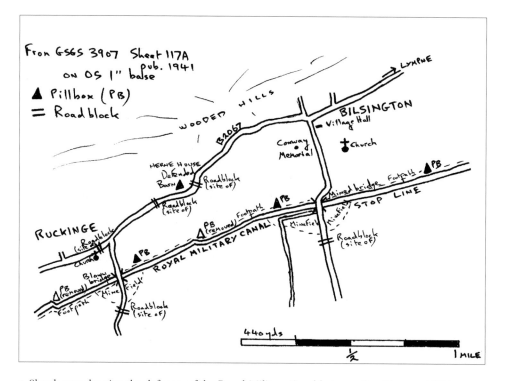

3 Sketch map showing the defences of the Royal Military Canal between Ruckinge and Bilsington

The German plans for Operation Sealion are known. They were amongst documents captured by Allied forces at the end of the war, and brought back to England to be examined by the Historical Section of the Cabinet Office. The documentation includes maps that show the first German assault objectives. One of these was the crossing of the Royal Military Canal in the area of Bilsington with the aim of taking the higher land beyond between Tenterden and Ashford. To the north, the German 17th Division would have attacked through Hythe to join up with their 7th Parachute Division, dropped at dawn on the ridge of the North Downs.

I'm holding a copy of a German map at the scale 1:25,000 (the same scale as my modern Ordnance Survey 'Explorer' sheet). The Germans took pre-war Ordnance Survey sheets and printed on them the British defence works they had spotted through air reconnaissance. Many of these maps are now held by the Imperial War Museum and the British Library in London (see Chapter 3). Both my 1940 map, and its modern equivalent, show the line of the Royal Military Canal running west from Hythe at the head of Romney Marsh, all the way to Rye, and then beyond, to a point near Pett where the canal rejoined the coast.

4 Royal Military Canal west of Ruckinge Bridge

The canal was built in the first years of the nineteenth century as a defence against the invasion threat of the French armies of Napoleon. In 1940, it was brought back into military use as an anti-tank barrier against German invasion. On my German map along its north bank there are many small triangles. This is the German map symbol for 'Klein-Kampfanlage' (a small concrete defence work, or pillbox). In the period June to July 1940, these were built at every 'flank' (staggered bend) of the canal, so that each length could be covered by enfilading machine-gun fire.

From the Bilsington Bridge, a footpath (part of the officially designated Royal Military Canal Path) runs along the north bank of the canal. I began by following it towards the east, heading for one pillbox that I knew survived at the first flank a few hundred yards from the bridge. As I walked across the dew-wet grass, I looked to my left across a broad grass field towards a low line of hills in the distance. Beneath these hills lies the village of Bilsington. Centuries ago, before Romney Marsh had been drained, the village had been at the edge of the dry land, overlooking a landscape of marshy islands and reed-fringed lagoons. Earlier still, in the Roman period, this area had probably once been open sea, and galleys had sailed where I now walked beside the canal. Even in the late medieval period, sea-going ships had still picked their way through twisting river channels to Appledore and Tenterden, and around the Isle of Oxney. A network of ditches and sewers now drained the land. In 1940, there had been plans to open the sea sluices in the event of invasion to re-flood vast tracts of the Marsh.

After some 800yds I spotted the pillbox that I was seeking, standing rather forlornly alongside a marshy, overgrown patch of land above the canal. It was set on a concrete base edged with concreted sandbags on the earth mound of the canal's former rampart. The pillbox was a small concrete-faced hexagonal example, known as a Type 22 from its plan as designated by the War Department's Directorate of Fortification and Works. It was in poor condition, its base now undermined by erosion and its walls cracked. An attached brick entry porch (or exterior blast wall) was also in danger of collapse. I peered inside. It had small, square embrasures, or loopholes (the terms are interchangeable, but I generally prefer embrasure) with the fitting points for wooden shelves beneath them. On these shelves the soldiers firing light machine guns (Brens: see Chapter 4) or rifles through the embrasures would place spare magazines, ammunition clips, or other equipment. The steel frames (mountings) into which machine guns were clamped so that they could be fired on fixed lines (predetermined sighting lines where fire could be laid down under battle conditions of smoke and darkness) were also screwed against the shelves.

Missing in this pillbox was the anti-ricochet wall, a central, usually Y-shaped, column of brick or concrete reaching from floor to ceiling that was designed to stop any bullets that might enter the pillbox from ricocheting around. It was also intended to protect the soldiers, or some of them at least, from blast should a grenade, or other explosive charge, be hurled in through the entrance or an embrasure.

There are a great number of misconceptions about pillboxes, and this might be the place, at the very beginning of our journey through the 1940 prepared battlefields, to correct some of these. An army in the field did not fight from pillboxes as if they were fixed defences, such as, from another age, a castle keep. Pillboxes were temporary fieldworks, hardened gun shelters designed to protect the weapons of an infantry section (usually six to eight men) from enemy fire. They were not small forts, standing in isolation, intended to be defended by a garrison at all costs. They were useful in a defensive role and formed part of the field defences of the British Army defending its homeland in 1940 in the same way that the German Army, later in the war, made use of them, for example, in Italy and France when operating in defence against Allied attacks.

Each pillbox was generally surrounded by its own defences, for example, an all-round barbed-wire perimeter and fire trenches, and linked with other components of defence, such as an anti-tank barrier. But you did not win battles by shutting yourself up behind concrete, and the British High Command was concerned in case too much reliance was placed on them. Many were soon abandoned and filled with barbed wire to prevent their possible use by enemy troops. Others, on the other hand, in key areas were strengthened, with thickened walls and roofs, so as to be able to withstand shell fire. From the late autumn of 1940, once the first invasion danger period had passed, orders were issued in many areas prohibiting the construction of any more.

Just one more note on pillboxes while we are having our first look at them. When did they originate and where did the name 'pillbox' come from? Concrete emplacements were constructed by the British on the Western Front battlefields of the First World War, following the model begun by the Germans. These structures were often large and of all sorts of shapes, designed to fit the ground of the battlefield. However, lines of concrete gun positions were also built during the First World War in East Anglia and Kent as part of the provisions for Home Defence. Many of these were of a cylindrical design with a circular overlapping roof, in fact just like one of the boxes in which pills were then dispensed. The name seems to have caught on fast, by both civilians and the military alike, and has continued in use until the present day. At the time of the Second World War, however, the much more typical shape was not circular, but hexagonal.

I had a copy of another map, a British one this time, which I had found amongst documents at The National Archives at Kew (formerly the Public Record Office). The map had been made by the 1st Battalion of the Royal Ulster Rifles in October 1940. This regiment had defended the line of the

Royal Military Canal during this time of critical invasion danger, and its War Diariy includes this most detailed map showing the positions of 'A' Company at Bilsington. The pillbox we have been looking at is shown; it was marked as 'unmanned', which shows that by this date the first defence provision of June to July, based purely on the front-edge linear defence of the canal itself as an anti-tank obstacle, had been supplemented by a much greater defence in depth back through Bilsington village to the higher ground beyond.

Most defence positions shown on the map, along the line of the lane from Bilsington Bridge to the village, and around Hill Farm to the north, would have been earthworks (section posts, weapon pits, and slit trenches) for light and medium machine-gun fire, and for mortars. Field artillery would also have been ranged on the canal from positions further inland. On the southern side of Bilsington Bridge was an extensive minefield continuing parallel with the canal for several hundred yards, and probably surrounded by barbed wire. A roadblock, formed in part at least by concrete 'dragon's teeth' (truncated concrete pyramids, known more officially as pimples or tetrahedra), was positioned on the lane at the south edge of the minefield.

I walked back from the pillbox towards the bridge, pondering on the defence positions the map showed. To my left across the canal was the minefield, and ahead would have been barbed wire at the bridge, which was prepared with explosives for demolition to be blown in the actual event of invasion. To my right I would have been closely observed by soldiers from their sandbagged posts: there was a platoon defence locality next to Quince Cottage on the bend in the lane north of the bridge, and weapon pits around Court Lodge Farm a little further to the north.

Back at the bridge, with its new steel span supported by what looked like the original brick piers, I looked over the expanses of Romney Marsh to the south, lit intermittently by the fleeting spring sunlight. A chilly breeze sweeping in from the sea made me pull my coat more tightly around me. I thought again of the scene here in 1940, with the silver shapes of aircraft wheeling in the sky as the Battle of Britain was fought out overhead, and the puffs of smoke from anti-aircraft fire and the distant sound of cannon fire. And I thought of the German Army, poised on the French coast only 20 or so miles away, and the scene that so nearly was – the landing barges grinding up on the shingle beaches, and the soldiers in their coal-scuttle helmets pouring ashore, the parachute troops descending over the downland to the north, and the flights of Stuka dive bombers beginning their screaming descent, the earth rocking with explosions, the green landscape being torn apart.

Of course, the positions of 'A' Company of the 1st Battalion Royal Ulster Rifles were just one component of a complicated scheme of defence across Romney

Marsh set in place from 1940-1; for the invasion danger did not disappear with the winning of the Battle of Britain in 1940, but was resumed in the spring of 1941, and only diminished with the news of Hitler's attack on Russia in June that year. The shoreline itself around the Romney Marsh peninsula, from Hythe to Dungeness and to the broad sandy beaches at Camber, was heavily defended. Pillboxes, and concrete anti-tank blocks and steel scaffolding, lined the beaches, with infantry platoon localities, ringed with barbed wire and surrounded by minefields, behind these defences, covering the shore with interlocking fire. Inland, the sewers and drains were widened and deepened as anti-tank ditches. All across the flat fields of the Marsh, concrete and wooden posts were set up to stop the landing of enemy transport aircraft and gliders.

Romney Marsh was part of 'A' Sub-Area (South), defended by XII Corps (from April 1941, under the command of the future Field Marshal Montgomery). More specifically, the area between Ruckinge and Bilsington north of the Royal Military Canal lay in 'Z' Sector, with 'T' Sector to the south. Other parts of Romney Marsh were designated as 'R' and 'S' Sectors. The system of defence was precisely referenced, both in the documents that implemented it and on the defence works themselves. Each 100yd section of beach had its own reference, e.g. 'C28': pillboxes and other defence works were numbered, and sometimes these numbers still survive stencilled on the walls inside. We shall see examples later in our travels.

I now walked west from Bilsington Bridge, following the footpath on the north bank of the canal. After a short distance I came to a second pillbox, also a Type 22, this time well dug into the old rampart of the canal so it had a low profile, and partly overgrown. It stood at a point where a drain flowed into the canal. A glance inside showed that, unlike the first pillbox I had seen, its brick anti-ricochet wall was present, but its entrance way was in danger of collapse. I inspected the outside walls. There was damage to the east face and around its embrasure as if it had been attacked by some madman wielding a sledgehammer. I didn't think this was a likely location for the more Herculean form of vandalism you can find on some sites, so it was possible the damage had been done during the war. My Royal Ulster Rifles map showed this pillbox had been manned in October 1940, probably by an infantry section of five or six men. Sometimes, later in the war, pillboxes were used for training in infantry assault, and were damaged by explosives or pot-marked by bullets. Heavier emplacements were also used to test the penetrative power of new weapons. Again, we shall find examples in our travels.

I was approaching the bridge south of Ruckinge. This had not merely been prepared for demolition, but had actually been blown up in August 1940. As at the Bilsington Bridge, there were extensive minefields alongside the lane to the south of the bridge and a roadblock formed of dragon's teeth. Here also on the flank of the canal just east of the bridge was another Type 22 concrete-faced pillbox, standing to the right of the path in a field behind barbed wire so I could not get to it to examine it closely. Viewed from a short distance, however, it seemed to be in excellent condition, the best of the three we have seen on this walk, although the entry porch was once more in danger of collapse (*colour plate 1*).

These pillboxes are concrete-faced because they were built with shuttering made of wooden planks. You can often see the marks of the planks in the concrete, usually laid horizontally, but sometimes as well vertically. However, pillboxes were also shuttered with other materials, of which, in the South and East of the country, brick was the most common. Brick, in fact, was much more generally available in 1940 than wood, which was in short supply. So bricks were used in areas such as the Weald of Kent, Surrey, and Sussex, or the Fens and East Anglia, where there were substantial brick industries. When the pillboxes were complete, the shuttering was left in place as it could not be used again (unlike wood) and it helped in any event with camouflage, another subject we shall be coming to. The brick-faced pillboxes you see, therefore, are not all-brick (although there are a few of these), but have a reinforced concrete core to their walls, sometimes as thick as 42in.

When I reached Ruckinge, I had completed my objective of walking a section of the stop line (I shall explain stop lines presently) formed by the Royal Military Canal. I had left my car in Bilsington village, and at first thought I would return by the same route I had just followed. But, looking at my maps, I decided to walk into Ruckinge village and take the B2067 road that connects with Bilsington. The 1940 map showed that 'A' Company of the Royal Ulster Rifles had been positioned around the church in Ruckinge, but nothing survives of those defences today. My map also told me that there had also been a heavy concentration of defences around Herne House to the east of the village, with two roadblocks on the road I was about to follow. Would I be able to find any evidence of these?

I set out warily down the winding, tree-lined road, with the occasional fast-moving car approaching me like a bullet and with no pavement to escape to. It did not take me long to reach the farm at Herne House. I was looking for remains of the roadblocks: sometimes you find dragon's teeth or other concrete blocks amongst undergrowth at the side of the road. At first I could not see anything, but suddenly I noticed that in the end wall of a stone barn facing the road was an embrasure (a loophole for machine gun or rifle fire) that had been blocked with brick. There was no doubting it. The barn had been turned into a pillbox. It had formed what was termed a defended building, a fairly frequent defence provision. Such fortification was easier and quicker than constructing a free-standing pillbox, and came with its own ready-made camouflage.

5 Defended barn near Bilsington

I looked at my Royal Ulster Rifles map again. Sure enough a pillbox was marked at this point. I had expected it to be one of the type we have just viewed on the canal, long since destroyed. But, no, here was the clear evidence of a defended building, almost certainly commanding one of the long-vanished roadblocks. I felt elated by my discovery, and, after recording and photographing it, skipped through the last mile back to my car in Bilsington.

I had left the car on the lane opposite the 50ft-high Cosway Memorial standing in a field overlooking Romney Marsh. Sir William Cosway was a local philanthropist, killed in 1834 in a runaway coaching accident. The memorial had been built the next year to his memory. Had there been any attempt to disguise it during the war, I wondered, for it was a prominent landmark? Local residents would probably know. They might be able to tell me as well more about the wartime defences. For one of the greatest sources of information about the home landscape during the war still resides with local people, some mere youngsters at the time, but with their memories bright. In the professional research world this is known as oral history. It is a most important but sometimes neglected resource. Imagine excavating a Roman fort and learning that there were still people alive who had seen the Roman soldiers there. To gain every syllable of what they had to tell would become the most critical task of all. And yet when the evidence is of our own age, we don't seem to bother so much, until, of course, it is too late.

On the other side of the lane from the Cosway Memorial is the village hall, a long building rather like an army hut with a corrugated-iron roof. Whatever the origins of the building, it had certainly been used by the Army in 1940. A document at The National Archives states that 30 other ranks were accommodated there. The headquarters of 'A' Company, Royal Ulster Rifles were also in the village, but the document did not give the exact location. This is where I needed a resident to help me, but there was no one about. Apart from the occasional passing car, Bilsington seemed a ghost village this spring morning. Knowing I had no time to seek anyone out, regretfully I drove away.

I was pleased with my early morning's work, and thought I would reward myself with a greasy bacon butty at a roadside cafe by the A20.

'On a trip?' asked the proprietor conversationally. They all stopped here – truck drivers, commercial travellers, and cars laden with booze and kids.

'No. Working I'm afraid.'

'What line is that?'

This was the moment, universally dreaded from hairdressing salons to cocktail parties, not that I went to many of the latter.

'I'm an archaeologist. I'm recording Second World War defence works; pillboxes, you know.'

'Don't worry mate. Someone has to.'

I thought, he's right. Someone has to do this. And that someone now is me. Perhaps not a job of world-shattering importance, unlike this café man feeding the cold and the ravenous, but one in which there is a considerable public interest. I know that to be true, and it is the reason why I'm writing this book. So this is a good point at which to tell you how it all came about, and what exactly I was doing visiting these out-of-the-way remains of the 1940 anti-invasion defences.

In fact, this was the job *they* had all wanted.

Who are they? Well, the whole rather strange and sometimes unfathomable world of people interested in the military archaeology of the twentieth century, and in particular of the Second World War. It has only been relatively recently that professional archaeologists have taken the subject seriously. Until that time, it was the interested amateur who largely led the way in recording and researching the scattered remains of the military's presence in the home landscape across the period of two world wars.

The standard of study has varied considerably. Airfields have arguably been the sites that have been explored most extensively, with much good work done by bodies such as the Airfield Research Group. Many books have been written about the history of airfields, describing their sites and layout and what survives today, in particular the excellent 'Action Stations' series published in the 1980s. But research into the subject that many find the most compelling of all (the anti-invasion defences of 1940-1) has been very scattered and uncoordinated, and, because of problems with the surviving documentation and the interpretation of the period (as we shall see), it remained wide open for a full, professional analysis to be made.

It is hard to define the fascination cast by the 1940 defences. Mention a pillbox to many people, and in an unlikely group, from camouflage-jacketed, crop-haired men driving ex-military Land Rovers to elderly moustachioed gentlemen in blue regimental blazers; from young women with bare mid-riffs and pierced ears to middle-aged village ladies in twin sets and pearls, eyes light up and faces become animated, speaking of the importance of preserving these concrete structures still spaced across the landscape, often hidden in back gardens or buried under 60 years of unchecked vegetation. Much of the interest must come from the national consciousness of 1940 as a defining moment in British history, the time when we stood alone against German military power, defiant, and resolute.

Winston Churchill's famous speech, 'We shall defend our Island, whatever the cost may be, we shall fight on the beaches, we shall fight on the landing grounds, we shall fight in the fields and in the streets, we shall fight in the hills; we shall never surrender …' itself seems to encapsulate the subject. There is a great nostalgia, I believe, for the oneness and purpose of those days, in particular when contrasted with the state of the nation today, when the very concept of our sovereign independence is under threat. So, rightly or wrongly, people look back at the dark days of 1940 as a time of great meaning which defined values and purpose, and they see in the surviving structures a physical representation of that time, something that needs to be protected and preserved.

In some ways, this is strange, and an abrupt turn-about from previous attitudes since 1945. Even before the end of the war, many of the anti-invasion defences had been removed; roadblocks were dismantled and anti-tank ditches filled in. The first priority was to get rid of military works that interfered with ordinary life and affected the economy of the nation, in particular agriculture. The process of removal continued throughout the 1940s and into the 1950s, the work being organised by the Ministry of Works (ironically the predecessor, in one of its functions, of English Heritage). Much more would have been done, but for post-war shortages of resources, including labour, that were often more extreme than those encountered during the war.

By the 1970s, people were beginning to look anew at the wartime structures that survived across the landscape, and one or two local surveys were carried out by private individuals to record what remained. One of the problems with the 1940 defences was a perceived lack of documentation about what had been built and where. The subject was already descending into myth, and we shall be encountering some of those myths as we go along. Because a neat record of the anti-invasion defences, complete with comprehensive maps, could not be found at the Public Record Office (now The National Archives), it was said that few records had been kept. The view was that the British Army had been too busy in those desperate days for record-keeping! The truth was exactly the opposite. Later research established that records, in fact, were numerous and highly detailed (see Chapter 3). The principal problem, as ever with written records, is what has been retained and what thrown away.

The man who began the process of pulling the subject together, and who tried to bring together the available strands of information and create a national record of what survived, was Henry Wills, a journalist and photographer, whose seminal book, *Pillboxes: A Study of UK Defences 1940* was published in 1985. In this he presented a gazetteer of sites, plotted onto maps, that was the fruit of the work of volunteers who had sent him records of sites throughout the country. Henry Wills was planning a second edition of his book, with a greatly updated gazetteer, when sadly he died. A collection of his papers, which include his revised gazetteer and some original documents and maps, is held by the National Monuments Record at Swindon.

Various individuals, inspired by Wills, now sought to take his work forward, and a proposal for a national survey of all twentieth-century military works throughout the United Kingdom was made. The genesis of this idea eventually resolved itself into the Defence of Britain Project, administered by the Council for British Archaeology, which ran from 1995-2001, and won the prestigious Silver Trowel Award at the British Archaeological Awards in 2002. This project used the work of over 600 amateur recorders, reporting in some counties to professional archaeologists, to create a database of some 20,000 sites, of which approximately 14,000 related to the 1940-1 anti-invasion defences. You can access the database today on-line through the Archaeology Data Service – http://ads. ahds.ac.uk/catalogue/specColl/dob/.

I worked on this project from 1998 until its conclusion, being based at the project offices at Duxford Airfield (part of the Imperial War Museum near Cambridge). English Heritage, who had been active from the early 1990s in a programme of work to evaluate twentieth-century military sites, were interested in the database as a record of surviving anti-invasion structures of differing types and condition that might be considered for statutory protection.

One day, John Schofield, who was to become head of English Heritage's Military and Naval Evaluation Programmes, came to see me at Duxford where I was working with the Defence of Britain Project. Surrounded as you are at Duxford by the buildings of the wartime airfield, and by the many artefacts of warfare stored there, the 60 or so years since the Second World War can slip easily away. Our project officers were within a former sergeants' mess, and were said to be haunted by the ghost of an airman who had died in a flying accident. On certain winter evenings, when a misty darkness had descended over the buildings around the former parade ground, I have to say I was glad when the time came to go home. Sometimes I sensed an oppressive atmosphere. There would be the sound of feet on the stairs, but no one came. The computers would load up programmes on their own. Whether the latter was due to viruses or ghosts it is hard to say; my incomprehension of both is about equal.

John Schofield does not look particularly like a military man. He would be the last person, I think, to want such an epithet to be applied to him. He did tell me, however, that as a small boy he remembered standing proudly at RAF Tangmere on the day when his father, the station commander, had presented Prince Charles with his 'wings'. Today, 30 years later, John considers it was his Tangmere experience that first directed his career towards an appreciation of the relics of pillboxes, control towers, Nissen huts, and gun batteries that make up our recent military heritage. As an archaeologist, however, he gives the same attention to recording the remains of the women's peace camp at Greenham Common as he does to the material remains of the Second World War. He is anxious to ensure the survival and preservation of a representative sample of all these things into the new millennium.

What English Heritage required, he told me, was a survey of particular areas of England where anti-invasion defences survived well in landscapes that had changed little since the Second World War, and to which there was also good public access. In that way, we would be able to evaluate the different types of defence works and how they related to each other within the topography of the defended landscape. Differing defence requirements and strategies could also be assessed. It would be necessary to do documentary research as well as field survey, in particular using records at The National Archives and air photographs at the National Monuments Record, to try and establish what had originally been built and since destroyed. Would I be interested in doing this work? And, if so, could I draw him up a provisional list of areas that met the English Heritage criteria, and which we could boil down to some 80 or so throughout England?

Was I interested?! With the Defence of Britain Project coming to an end, and wondering where my next paycheck would be coming from, I most certainly was. But there was more to it than that, far more. This would be a super job ('the one they all wanted') involving original research in what was still largely a new archaeological subject, and one which urgently demanded more publication. And it would be given reasonably generous resources to cover all the travel and accommodation that would be needed, both for the field survey and for the visits that would be needed to various archives for the documentary research.

The first list that I drew up of possible areas, which we termed 'defence areas' (the project was to be known as the Defence Areas Project) ran to some 300. A large number of these were in Southern England where the anti-invasion defences had not only been most concentrated but where survival was also best. However, we needed a good regional spread, so many otherwise good areas in the South had to be discarded so that a fair distribution of areas in the North could be included.

In this way, using the Defence of Britain Project database, a list of 78 areas was decided upon. Later, the direct experience of documentary assessment and fieldwork led to the discarding of 11 of these, so the final figure was 67. This book will take you through many of those lying in the South and East of England. These defence areas were prepared battlefields that came very close to becoming real battlefields – hence 'the battlefields that nearly were'.

The project started in April 2002 and finished in June 2004. I won't take you in laborious detail through how the documentary assessment and the fieldwork were done. Points will come out, and we will consider them, as we move from area to area. It is the sites on the ground that I most want to describe to you, and the various landscapes of England in which they are set. We will look at the different types of defence works in detail as we come upon them, as well as the different strategies of defence and how the topography was used to assist the needs of defence. We shall also visit the various archives, so those of you not familiar with how these work may gain more insight into their systems and the type of documents they contain. And we shall look at the opposing armies, and learn how they fought and what weapons they were armed with.

So we return now to the spring morning when I began the fieldwork in Kent, and was seated in my car finishing my late breakfast, reflecting on how it was I came to be here doing this work. My job was now to record what I saw on the ground. I was armed not with rifle or Bren gun, but with camera, GPS receiver, notebook, and binoculars. I carried clippers not against barbed wire but to cut back, if needed, the dense vegetation that covered many structures: sometimes the thorns and brambles were just as effective as coils of razor wire! I was booted and coated against the terrain and the weather. I was going to find out the hard way how tough a field survey could be.

2

FARTHINGLOE, NEAR DOVER TO SARRE, EAST KENT

I drove along the A20 towards Dover, leaving the main road to approach the western suburbs of the town by the B2011 which runs at the base of a valley between parallel ridges of high downland. During the war, Dover had been an army garrison town and an important naval port. The Army occupied the famous castle that rises to the east of the town (a garrison remained there until the late 1950s), as well as the Western Heights on the other side of the harbour front. Here is a maze of Napoleonic Wars and Victorian-period engineering, including the Citadel fort, from the 1950s a borstal and more recently an immigration removal centre. The area had been known as 'hell-fire corner' during the war, subject to heavy air attack as well as the shelling of German long-range guns situated on the French coast.

A defence perimeter had surrounded Dover. The defence area I was now seeking out was part of those defences on the western side of the town, at a point considered most vulnerable to attack had a German column advanced to capture the port from a landing point on Romney Marsh. I was heading for Farthingloe where the defence perimeter had crossed the valley between the heights of Long Hill to the south and Coney Hill to the north. There had been a roadblock here outside Little Farthingloe Farm, part of a defended locality manned in 1940-1 by the 7th Bn Hampshire Regiment, and later in 1941 by the 11th Bn East Surrey Regiment. My search of the War Diaries of these units at The National Archives had borne fruit. I had a list of their defence positions complete with a map.

A defended locality (often known as a forward defended locality or FDL) was the system by which infantry troops manned their defences. A defended locality was usually sited at an important point, such as a road crossing of a defence line

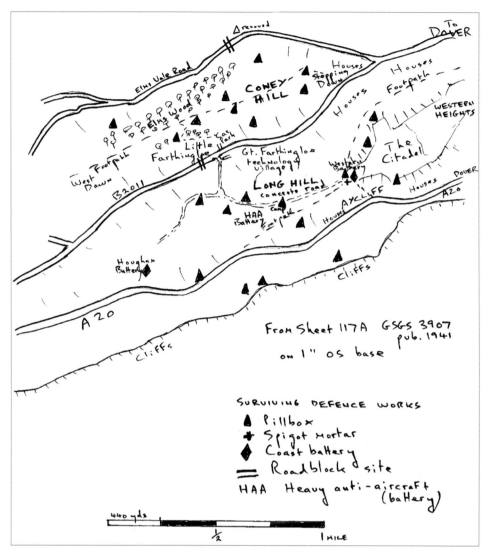

6 Sketch map (scale reduced) showing the defences at Farthingloe, Dover

or an exit route from a beach, and consisted of a number of defence positions, including pillboxes and slit trenches, as well as an observation and command post, the whole locality being set behind an all-round perimeter of barbed wire. Additionally, sometimes it was protected by minefields. Medium and light machine guns and mortars were positioned within an FDL, and, at the coast, sometimes beach defence guns were also within the perimeter. There would be a series of such FDLs along a sector of a defence line or at a beachfront, each interlinking with its neighbours with the aim of covering the entire front by interlocking fire.

My map made by the 7th Hampshires in February 1941 showed the defended locality at Farthingloe, with the roadblock and two pillboxes, and an anti-tank gun position, south of the road. A command post was established at Little Farthingloe Farm. Coils of barbed wire ran across the downland above this farm, and also around Great Farthingloe on the other side of the road (*colour plate 2*).

Little Farthingloe Farm has parking for visitors to its farm shops as well as to a small museum of the Women's Land Army, those girls in their corduroy breeches and green jerseys who did so much throughout the war, and afterwards, to grow more food to keep the nation from starving. In this corner of Kent during the Battle of Britain, they often worked under enemy fire. Unfortunately, it was too early in the year for the museum to be open.

An information board by the car park invites you to go for walks through the woods that cling to the sides of the downland above the farm. Entering these woods, I found various paths that twisted up the hillside: then I climbed higher through tangled vegetation, with brambles that seemed to be set deliberately at ankle height to trip me, until I reached the very crest of the down, which is followed by a public footpath. Here amongst a tangle of dumped rubbish and burnt-out cars (their presence explained by a track that leads here from the nearby suburbs of Dover) I began to find pillboxes – hexagonal Type 24s with most of their exterior brick-shuttering removed. A Type 24 is the most commonly found infantry pillbox, at least in the South of England, of hexagonal shape and similar in many respects to the smaller Type 22 we have met on the Royal Military Canal, although normally with thicker walls and roof. It is characterised by having two embrasures (normally small rifle ports) either side of the doorway in its rear face. The pillboxes I was seeing were survivors of the Dover perimeter defence line that led over Coney Hill, running across the grain of the country, on its way north to the next parallel valley at Elms Vale.

I pushed my way into a small copse on the summit of the hill as I thought I had caught a glimpse of something 'solid' amongst the undergrowth. Sure enough I came upon a low concrete structure with strangely angled brick pillars at the corners that only reached a couple of feet or so from the ground. This was almost certainly a defence work, but not one that I recognised or could interpret. I made a quick drawing of it in my notebook and tried taking a photograph. From experience I knew that the picture would not be very successful. Some 1940 sites are so overgrown that concrete merely peeps out in patches between branches and leaves, giving no idea of the structure's shape or size.

I returned down the hill through the woods to the car, and contemplated my next move. I needed to look next at sites on the downland to the south of the road, in the area of Long Hill. From here I should also be able to see as far as the edge of the white cliffs where the defence perimeter had begun, and look out upon the Straits of Dover across which the German invasion fleet so nearly came. The land of Great Farthingloe, once a farm, is now occupied by Farthingloe Technology Village, which a sign proclaims to be owned by Eurotunnel Developments Ltd (neither name meant much to me). It was all security fenced and I could see a couple of guards in the distance walking with a dog. There was no way through here to Long Down beyond. I would have to drive into Dover and hope to approach the area from the Western Heights: I was not sure if that was possible. If not, it would be a great pity as previous recorders had noted extensive Second World War remains on Long Down, including pillboxes of the 1940 defence perimeter and an anti-aircraft battery.

I parked in Dover in a car park beneath the Drop Redoubt – a vast nineteenth-century fortification on my left as I arrived breathless at the top of the steep slope on which it sat. I had to pass it with only the briefest look as my time had to be spent on Second World War remains only. Soon I had to descend again, crossed a narrow road, and took a footpath that made a shelving course across the lower slopes of the heights topped by the Citadel. To my right were the backs of houses, each with tiny gardens hacked out of the rising chalk hill. I smelt drifting wood smoke, and saw a column of smoke rising in the distance. Some people (both men and women) were clearing bushes and undergrowth, and burning the gathered scrub. They stood aside as I passed on the path, and bid me 'Good afternoon'. Now what were these people doing here? These were clearly respectable citizens of the town (volunteers, I would imagine) not council workers. A sign by the path a little further on gave me the answer, 'The White Cliffs Countryside Project. An excellent example of farming and conservation working together. New paths are being opened up'. I was in luck. It looked as if Dover Council was now providing public access to the land I was seeking to enter.

The path climbed a steep slope, and I came to a stile and hauled myself over, finding I was standing on a concrete road that stretched away as straight as an arrow to my right. I was on the spine of Long Hill at a point just to the west of the Citadel. A brief detour to my left and I came upon the Citadel's Western Battery. In the Second World War it had been armed with three 9.2in guns: the great concrete emplacements of the guns were still there. I climbed up above one, standing on the mass of dark-stained concrete that had protected it from incoming fire, and saw the waters of the Channel beyond the terraced houses of Aycliff below me (*colour plate 3*).

There is a pillbox beside the battery and a Spigot mortar pedestal as well. The latter is a new category of defence work to introduce, a weapon most commonly issued from the middle of 1941 to the Home Guard, Britain's emergency defence force formed from civilian volunteers, but which also had a limited deployment, as here, by the regular Field Army. We shall come across many other examples of these concrete pedestals, with their central stainless steel pintle (or pivot) upon which the weapon was mounted. It was primarily an anti-tank weapon, firing a 20lb armour-piercing projectile with a range of about 400yds. The mounting pedestal was often set in a circular concrete pit, with ammunition lockers around its inner walls, although sometimes the pits were simply a wood-revetted hole in the ground. At the end of the war many of these sunken emplacements were simply filled in, and so remain to be excavated today. In some cases, only the ever-bright steel pintle remains above the ground. (See also Chapter 4.)

I walked from the Citadel Battery along the concrete road running to the west, which was bordered by thick bushes so I could not see I was on the narrow ridge of the hill with steep slopes falling away on either side. This was a purpose-built military road. There was something about its directness, and its concrete surface covered in mud and dead leaves, that brought visions of the Roman Army to me. Had not their roads looked like this, carving through the forested expanses of the Weald? But, instead of glittering standards against the sky and the colour of red cloaks and gleaming bronze, I had to think of mid-twentieth-century troops marching here, in threes with great hobnail boots crashing on the concrete, and a bull-necked sergeant bellowing at them, 'Left, right, left, right … Get them up, get them up!', or of the three-ton trucks grinding along with the grinning troops cat-calling from the back.

This had been a heavily militarised area. Not only did the Dover garrison perimeter defence line pass through it, but there had been a heavy anti-aircraft battery here as well: a heavy battery was one with the 'heaviest', or most powerful, 3.7in guns generally positioned in concrete emplacements, as opposed to a light battery which was more mobile and had smaller calibre guns (usually the Bofors) positioned within earthworks.

I was approaching the site of the heavy battery. Because it was intended to be manned on a permanent basis, it had an attendant camp. I had viewed this on wartime air photographs, and seen the accommodation huts set here in regular lines. I took a path to the left and found myself walking on the concrete bases of the camp buildings. Two circular earthworks close by looked like they had been positions for anti-aircraft machine guns. Further on I came to the anti-aircraft battery site itself. Its four emplacements for the 3.7in guns, with their ammunition lockers, and circular connecting road, survived in good condition. This battery was operational throughout the war in one of the most intensely fought sectors of the air battles. In 1944-5, it was also involved in the Anti-Diver operations to shoot down the in-coming V1 flying bombs (or doodlebugs).

The crest of Long Hill, from which I could not only see the green downland ending abruptly at the cliff edge above the grey-blue sea beyond, but also Dover Castle standing square on its hill to the east, is the area of all my travels that is most redolent of the desperate days of 1940-1. Here there had been constant warfare – German aircraft attacking merchant ships out to sea, air fights overhead, the crash of the anti-aircraft guns, in-coming German shells seeking targets in Dover. Close by as well to the south-west was the coast battery at Hougham, and other coast batteries were also positioned on the heights above Dover. To the east, the masts of the Chain Home Radar Station at Swingate would have been etched against the sky.

I looked now for the perimeter line of pillboxes that had crossed Long Hill heading for Farthingloe which I could see in the valley below. I knew from the 1940 map and other documents that these defence posts had been given names, such as 'Knobbly No.1', 'Hedgerow No.4', and 'Lane No.2', and were joined by continuous lengths of barbed-wire entanglements. It was the last of these posts that I was seeking. Sure enough, here was the concrete-surfaced lane shown on the map winding down the hill towards Farthingloe. And here was 'Lane No.2', one of the pillboxes distinctive to the area, known unofficially as the 'Dover-type'. It was square, with wide embrasures in all faces, and had a distinctive overhanging roof slab. The western face of this particular example took advantage of the slope of the hill and was unique in having two levels of embrasures. Dover-type pillboxes do not look particularly strong, compared, for example, with some of the thick-walled Type 24s we shall meet later on our travels. The wide embrasures would have been very vulnerable to in-coming fire, and the overhanging roof slab looks as if one good blow would snap it off. As I examined it further, I saw that the brick pillars at the corners supporting the roof were turned at an angle to the main structure. I remembered that this was the same construction as the foundations I had found earlier in the wooded undergrowth on Coney Hill. That structure, therefore, had been a Dover-type pillbox as well, either demolished or, more likely, never completed. I wondered how these pillboxes were camouflaged as the large roof area made them prominent from the air. Camouflage was always a prime concern of the Royal Engineers building the defence works.

Another Dover-type pillbox lies to the west, above a concrete road carved into the side of the hill that is used today by the farmer as a hard-standing for his cattle. I passed a forest of nodding, chewing heads, and climbed to the hillside above them, aware of the inquisitive eyes following me, perhaps wondering what this strange forked figure bearing a green hump on its back was up to. This pillbox ('Knobbly No.1'), dug into the hillside, seemed to make a rather stronger defence position than the tall example I had just seen. At the top of the slope to the east, I found another, now so dug in that only its roof and the upper part of its walls were clear of the earth. I arrived back on the summit of Long Hill, at a point where it has been opened into large arable fields stretching away to the south-west. This has involved the clearance of some the defence works and I could see across the field in the distance two large piles of concrete and bricks that might have been until recently other Dover-type pillboxes.

7 'Dover Square' pillbox on Long Hill

8 Inside a 'Dover Square'

The only area I needed to search now was the southern slope of Long Hill below the camp site that I had walked through earlier. Here, my records showed, should be two more pillboxes. With some difficulty, I found one amongst thick bushes on the hillside – again, a Dover-type, almost entirely buried so that I was able to sit on its roof and write up my notes. But the other I could not find, although I exhausted myself in trailing up and down the hillside as far as the suburbs of Aycliff. Another easier approach to Long Hill, I now realised, would be from Aycliff, but I nevertheless recommend the walk from the Western Heights to allow you a full overview of the military landscape to the west of Dover Town.

As I retraced my steps up Long Hill to begin the long trek back to my car, I came upon two beautiful slit trenches on the slopes below the camp, one sharply-angled and scarcely overgrown at all, and the other, thick with nettles, appearing to form a T-shape. I say 'beautiful' because I have a special fondness for earthworks, in particular those which have been dug by muscle-power alone. The slit trenches would have been hand dug by the soldiers in the field. Many other earthworks, such as those for gun positions, would also have been raised manually. Even anti-aircraft landing trenches that divided up fields and other open areas to stop enemy aircraft and gliders landing were sometimes dug by hand because of the shortage of machinery. There are records, for example, of schoolboys being pressed into service by their masters to dig trenches across school playing fields. Although anti-tank ditches were usually machine dug, using the dragline excavators of the time, there are several recorded examples of sections being manually dug as well. I recall reading a document on the construction of anti-tank ditches by the British Expeditionary Force in Belgium during the winter of 1939/40, which stated that parties of 50 men could dig at a pace equivalent to a mechanical excavator. I wonder if that is still true in the day of the JCB.

When we look at the vast constructions made in previous ages, most notably during the prehistoric, do we really have any concept of how this was done? Guidebooks can talk blithely of antler picks and shoulder-bone shovels, but can you imagine using these for real? I often think that more experimental archaeology should be carried out on the subject of earthworks to see just how long it took to raise or excavate them, and how many people were involved; from a Bronze Age field boundary ditch, to an Iron Age rampart, from a Norman motte to an early Victorian railway cutting. We might add a section of anti-tank ditch to that list as well.

It is unusual to find unfilled sections of defensive ditches from the Second World War. Most that survive are on rough grazing land or heath, or amongst woodland, where their infilling was not considered as necessary as if they had been on agricultural land or in public places such as parks. Infantry trenches of the type I had found on Long Hill generally survive from training exercises. Here, however, they appeared to relate to the other defences on the hill, and it is reasonable to assume they had been dug in 1940-1, which makes them much rarer and doubly-interesting.

I eventually arrived back at my car somewhat weary. It had been a very long day. My notebook was full, and my film used up. High time for some food and perhaps a drink or two. I took the A256 road north towards the Isle of Thanet. Ahead lay the salvation of bed and breakfast. Tomorrow, my explorations would continue at the village of Sarre.

The bed and breakfast place had not been the best. The bed had been hard and the egg soft, rather than the other way around which I preferred. As I stood talking to the landlady of the King's Head at Sarre, I was thinking it might have been better if I'd stayed here instead. The landlady was Judy Olivier: she had only recently taken over the inn. It all looked very smart, and the place was full of the history of the Second World War as she had just been telling me. If I'd been here last night, I might have been able to pick up more information from the locals in the bar.

Sarre stands on what was once a promontory of the Isle of Thanet sticking out into the waters of the Wantsum Channel. There are remains of a harbour wall there, said to be Saxon. In the Roman period, the channel had been a strait of the sea cutting off Thanet from the mainland. The Romans had built two forts, one at each end – Reculver and Richborough. Slowly the channel had silted up, although it was still navigable from south to north in the seventeenth century. Barges came up the River Stour to Canterbury's port at Fordwich as late as the beginning of the last century.

Sarre had for centuries been an important communications point where the road from Canterbury crossed the drained bed of the former Wantsum Channel by an embankment known as Sarre Wall: earlier there had been a ferry there. At Sarre, the road divided, one branch heading for Margate and the other, Ramsgate. In addition to the King's Head, the town has another famous coaching inn, The Crown, with Dickensian associations.

In June 1940, Sarre had been designated as a Category 'A' nodal point. Nodal points were important centres of communications (usually, but not necessarily, towns and villages) that received all-round defence, including pillboxes, Spigot mortar emplacements (from 1941), roadblocks, fire trenches, and barbed-wire perimeters. They were categorised 'A', 'B', and 'C' in terms of their importance: a Category 'A' nodal point was required to hold out for seven days before being relieved. Its defence was usually the responsibility of the local unit of the Home

Guard. A further nodal point lay a short distance to the north of Sarre at St Nicholas at Wade.

The beaches between Margate and Dover were considered very vulnerable to a German landing. This was the area where Julius Caesar had come ashore in 55 and 54 BC, and probably (it is disputed) where the main Roman invasion of AD 43 had taken place. Thanet was intensively defended, the front-edge coast defence being carried inland by a series of nodal points. A stop line for XII Corps defending the South-East was constructed between Dover and Whitstable, and this acted as a back line to prevent the invading German forces, should they get ashore, from breaking out into the heartland of Kent on an advance towards London. We shall be looking at stop lines in detail later, but a stop line was essentially a prepared defence position with a continuous anti-tank obstacle, either natural (for example, a river) or artificial (a machine-dug ditch or lines of concrete obstacles), with the crossing points of the line by roads and railways defended by concrete emplacements for machine guns and anti-tank guns.

Between July to August 1940, Sarre was fortified by the 1st Canadian Pioneer Battalion as a demonstration, the unit's War Diary states, of what might be done elsewhere. A particular emphasis was placed on the defence of houses and other buildings, which probably received strengthened walls and ceilings and were pierced with loopholes. Extensive use of Canadian pipe mines (or McNaughton tubes, named after the Canadian engineer officer who invented them) was made: these were bored pipes packed with explosives, positioned at bridges, crossroads, and other strategic points, to be blown as the enemy approached.

A map of the defence positions at Sarre survives with the War Diary of the 1st Canadian Pioneers. Centres of the defence (defended localities) were at Sarre Bridge, the area around Bolingbroke Farm, the road junction at the town centre, and the mill just outside the town to the east. The mill also served as an observation post. A large house (Sarre Court) on the south side of the road junction became the headquarters of the 131st Infantry Brigade, which had replaced the 1st (London) Infantry Brigade here. Their underground battle headquarters (which we will be looking at shortly) was situated in an old chalk pit off the Margate road to the north.

A German air photograph of August 1940 survives showing the nodal point defences of St Nicholas at Wade to the north. In this an extensive system of defensive trenches and barbed-wire perimeters around the village can be seen, and by analogy we can assume the same thing at Sarre. It is probable that units of the regular Field Army manned many of these defences in the critical invasion danger period of 1940, acting in conjunction with the local Home Guard unit – the 6th Kent (Thanet) Battalion.

9 Pillbox commanding a ridge near Sarre Wall

I had parked my car in a side street that morning and braved the thundering traffic to walk down the A28 road to Sarre Bridge: it crossed the River Wantsum, a muddy remnant of the once open sea channel here. The bridge had been prepared with explosives for demolition in 1940-1, and there had been a roadblock here with pipe mines buried beside it. Another mined bridge crossed by a track lay a short distance to the north. I knew from Defence of Britain Project records that there were two pillboxes close by, and I found the first in a field close to the bridge – a Type 22 standing high in a prominent position on a low ridge. A sign said, 'No access. Field in crop', so I contented myself with viewing and photographing it from a distance, then moved on to locate the other pillbox. It lay across a further water channel from a footpath close to the second bridge; again a Type 22 on a low mound, and somewhat overgrown.

I walked back along the track towards Sarre, and came to Bolingbroke Farm, which, with other adjacent buildings, had been one of the most defended sectors of the Sarre defences. The farmhouse itself, with various white clapperboard outbuildings, still stands, but other adjacent buildings have been torn down and replaced by an expensive-looking housing development. I wondered if evidence of the 1940 defence had been lost at that time.

10 Bolingbroke Farm, Sarre – heavily defended in 1940

And so I came to the centre of the village, and stood outside the King's Head Inn trying to get my bearings. Externally, this building looks much the same as it did in photographs taken at the end of the nineteenth century (*colour plate 4*). A door opened and a woman called out, 'Can I help you?' It was the landlady, Judy Olivier. She had spotted me looking lost and had been curious as to what I was doing. This is a small town. Strangers who stand on street corners peering at maps are relatively rare. I already knew the King's Head had had a role in the defence of the town, so I followed her inside, pleased at the chance of acquiring some local information.

I had already acquired some details of the King's Head from Defence of Britain Project records. There were said to be tunnels leading off from its cellars, sealed by the military at the end of the war. What their purpose had been was unknown. Judy confirmed the existence of the tunnels, which, she said, were still bricked up. She also told me that there was a sign painted on the outside of the inn that seemed to have something to do with the Army and probably dated from the war. I went to have a look. The sign was on the side wall overlooking the passage leading to the courtyard at the rear. It was hard to read. The word 'Office' was clear, but the word in front might have been 'Duty' or 'Pay', or indeed something else; only the 'Y' was certain. An arrow pointing towards the courtyard was also painted underneath.

Possibly the inn was used as a headquarters, for an infantry battalion perhaps. Brigade headquarters were not far away at Sarre Court. Various letters from soldiers had been found when the bar was being refurbished; one is now displayed in a frame on the wall. The Canadian Pioneers' map did not show the inn as one of the defended buildings, but next door, Sarre House, at a key point commanding the road junction, most definitely had been: four firing points on two sides of this building were indicated on the map. Judy told me that when this house was being altered recently, wall paintings of Canadian flags had been uncovered. She also told me that, when Sarre Bridge (which I had just been looking at) was being replaced in recent years, explosives had been found still in place and in a highly unstable condition.

I whistled at this, and wondered, not for the first time, at what other explosives from the anti-invasion defences might still be lying about. Hundreds (possibly thousands) of bridges the length and breadth of the country had been prepared for demolition in 1940. Pipe mines and other depth charges had also been laid in profusion, together with thousands of anti-tank and anti-personnel mines, both at the coast and inland on the stop lines. I had found worrying references in contemporary documents to the inadequacy of the recording of minefields. The chance of other explosives having been left in place elsewhere seems to me to be very high, but I don't think it is something you need to have too much on your mind the next time you go to the beach! Yet the whole subject of the clearance of ordnance from defence sites and training grounds in Britain, together with that of the many unexploded German bombs which still turn up periodically, is an aspect of the Second World War that should perhaps receive more attention than it does.

Judy Olivier had been most helpful. I had come out of a pub, perhaps for the first time, knowing much more than when I went in and without even having had a drink! Strangely, however, what Judy hadn't known about was the most important surviving Second World War structure in Sarre − the tunnels of the underground battle headquarters bored into the side of an old chalk quarry. I wandered off in search of it.

These underground army headquarters are a feature of the anti-invasion defence system. They were all constructed from early in 1941, with the purpose of providing secure bomb-proof locations from which to fight the battles to defeat the invading German forces. In the South-East of England, the battle headquarters of South-East Command was within the Category 'A' nodal point of Reigate in Surrey, in tunnels drilled under Reigate Hill. The battle headquarters of XII Corps was in tunnels under Broadwater Down, south-west of Tunbridge Wells. Another underground headquarters is known in Canterbury, and others might reasonably be suspected for the brigades defending other sectors of East Kent: likely locations are at Ashford, Dover, Folkestone, and Sandwich. Elsewhere in the country, underground battle headquarters are known at Goring in Sussex and in Chester, for example, and there were undoubtedly many more: each Army Command, for example, would have required one. Several of these underground structures are known locally as 'Montgomery's Headquarters', although he is said, when interviewed on this subject, to have denied all knowledge of the buried XII Corps headquarters at Tunbridge Wells, the only one likely to have been associated with him. It seems Montgomery's name has become attached to military sites, whose purpose is inexactly understood today, in the same way as 'Julius Caesar' was attributed to a number of earthworks across the South of England by Victorian antiquaries.

The buried battle headquarters were constructed by the tunnelling companies of the Royal Engineers, who were working flat out as well to provide many other underground structures, including deep shelters under coast batteries, of which there are several examples in East Kent. The whole subject of the underground military structures of Britain (including sites such as the Royal Navy's headquarters of HMS Forward at South Heighton in East Sussex or the wartime tunnels under Dover Castle) is one of great fascination, and it is one that has been explored by the organisation Subterranea Britannica, which has an excellent Internet site and much on-line information.* None of the army battle headquarters is open to the public, but this is a category of site which lends itself readily to public display and would provide an excellent location for a museum of the anti-invasion defence of 1940-1. All that is needed is the site, some vision and energy, and perhaps a grant from the Heritage Lottery Fund. A good example of a museum laid out in wartime tunnels is the German Underground Hospital on the island of Jersey, while in England there are the wartime tunnels under Dover Castle, now open to the public, and, of course, Churchill's underground war rooms in London (see pp.60-1).

Army battle headquarters were established by all front-line units from commands down to companies, or so the surviving documentation indicates. Many appear to have been established within buildings, possibly in their cellars, which is why it is likely that the tunnels under the King's Head were such a headquarters. Others (for the higher-echelon units) were purpose-built underground, their rooms and tunnels being shored with wood and corrugated iron or faced with concrete. Home Guard units also had battle headquarters, and these are often listed as the local public house or inn. But here again, we must presume the use of a cellar rather than the comfort of the tap room!

The tunnel entrances to the underground brigade battle headquarters at Sarre are in the far wall of a disused quarry, when viewed from the A28 road, on the north side of the village. This grassed-over quarry is interesting by itself as there are a number

---

* www.subbrit.org.uk

of decaying, overgrown Nissen huts within it (a relatively rare survival) probably from a later army camp. There is no entry to the quarry as this is private land. However, a footpath takes you behind the quarry so you can at least stand close to the battle headquarters site, the tunnels of which extend underneath you. Its tunnels were explored in 1998 by Subterranea Britannica, and a plan and photographs can be found on their web site. There were three tunnel entrances from the quarry face, connecting with cross tunnels, lined with brick, forming rooms from which the anti-invasion operations would have been run. We must imagine tables, desks, filing cabinets, wall maps, and much communications equipment filling these rooms.

Not far from the quarry, amongst bushes on the other side of the road, I found the overgrown remains of an unusual pillbox, rectangular in shape with a central open section to allow for fire from a machine gun firing in an anti-aircraft role. This type of pillbox is rare in South-East England, most commonly being found in Lincolnshire where it is known as the 'Lincolnshire three-bay type'. I thought the pillbox could be freed of its overgrowth and displayed as a memorial to Sarre's wartime role. Few other locations had such a significant and well-documented place in the 1940-1 defence of the country as here at Sarre.

I climbed the path that leads to the mill, used during the war as an observation post. Until recently, I had been told, there was another rectangular pillbox here, probably of the type I had just inspected, but now removed. The mill is open to the public, and in its car park I found a board telling me that Sarre is on the 'St Augustine Trail', and detailing the Saxon history of the area. I find such boards very useful. It would be good if in some places information could be added on the Second World War legacy as well.

I returned to my car, and set off on the long journey home to Cambridgeshire. Next week would bring further explorations through the surviving anti-invasion defences of the South-East. For the moment I had to absorb what I had learnt, and get my records up to date. So, I said farewell for the moment to Sarre, which I had come to like with its solid red-brick houses with their facings of white clapperboard. There was a great deal more that could be done here. The tunnels should be explored fully and recorded, and the various houses within which defence posts had been inserted inspected to see if any internal evidence of their fortification survives. It would make a good project for a local history group. That sort of work takes time and involves getting numerous permissions.

As I drove out across Sarre Bridge, thinking of the explosives that had remained in place here for 65 years or so, unbeknown to the thousands of vehicles that pass every day, I reflected that I had less than two years in which to cover nearly 70 areas of England, regrettably not nearly enough time to undertake any of this detailed local work that was so necessary. But at least I would be able to point the way towards what might be done by others in the future.

3

DOCUMENTARY RESOURCES

I was walking from King's Cross Station into the Euston Road through such a maelstrom of noise and movement that it was with some relief that I reached the sanctuary of the British Library.

The reason I have digressed from my travels across the 1940 prepared battlefields to come to London is that I thought it might be useful for the reader, perhaps not familiar with the workings of the various archives that I have consulted for this project, to be introduced to them one by one, and to have a brief description of the types of documentary resources they contain which are useful to our subject, showing how these can be accessed.

I carried out all the documentary research for a region before setting out on the fieldwork, so that I completed the total work for each region from documents to fieldwork, concluding with the writing up of my findings with my recommendations and conclusions, before starting on the next region. The work was so complex and detailed that I could not attempt to do it in any other way. If I had tried, for example, to do the air photographic assessment for all my defence areas for the whole country before moving on, say, to documents at The National Archives, I would soon have got into a terrible muddle. By the time I came to starting the fieldwork, I would probably have forgotten much of what I had learnt, such is the mass of detail that accumulates of sites surviving, sites destroyed, defence strategies, tactical dispositions, army units defending, construction companies building, and so on, and so on.

So I proceeded in careful stages, and an early port of call was to the Map Library of the British Library at St Pancras, to which I have just brought you out of the mad rush of the Euston Road. I made use of this Map Library because the British Library is the principal copyright holder of the Ordnance Survey: if the Ordnance Survey has published it, the Map Library should have it. This was particularly useful for the large-scale plans I needed to consult, principally at the 1:2500 scale (about 25in to the mile). The surveys at this scale published after the war, in particular during the 1950s–70s, often show individual defence works, drawn onto the plan by the surveyor. Very often development has led to the subsequent destruction of these structures, so the map serves as a very important record. Hexagonal pillboxes are easy to make out, but you have to be careful with square and rectangular shapes as these may well be other sorts of buildings than defence works. A bit of practice normally gets your eye in, and you gain a feel for what to include and what to discard from your list for later field checking. Lines of anti-tank blocks are sometimes shown and labelled as 'Stones'.

The Map Library also holds the German defence mapping at 1:100,000 and 1:50,000 for parts of Kent, Surrey, Sussex, and Hampshire, and at 1:25,000 for certain Kent coastal areas. The Imperial War Museum in Lambeth has some of these map sheets as well as has the Bodleian Library in Oxford, but the British Library's holdings are more complete, although even here three sheets which the Germans are known to have issued are missing. The only source that I know of for the latter is the German military archive in Freiburg. The Royal Air Force Museum at Hendon also has a superb set of German 1:50,000 maps of the defences of the English coast from Thanet to Selsey Bill. All these German maps are produced from Ordnance Survey coloured base maps, which the Germans have reprinted at their own metric scales, adding by a series of coloured symbols, details of defence works obtained by aerial reconnaissance. Sometimes the detail is very good indeed, enabling many gaps in the British records to be filled. In other places, however, the German reconnaissance has clearly been very patchy, or not at all, because very little detail is given. Tree cover and camouflage, of course, played an important part in the Luftwaffe's ability to obtain air photographs showing defence detail.

The maps at the 1:50,000 scale (Befestigungskarte – Fortifications Maps) produced from the Ordnance Survey one inch series perhaps provide the most vivid representation of the defended landscapes, with a purple triangle indicating pillboxes, two parallel lines a roadblock, and lengths of three parallel purple lines sections of anti-tank ditch. The maps at the 1:100,000 and 1:25,000 scales also show by cross-hatching areas of the countryside where fields and other open spaces have been blocked against aircraft landing: why this information is not also given on the 1:50,000 sheets is a mystery to me.

The new building of the British Library, moved from the British Museum where the famous circular reading room is now preserved as a visitor attraction, is an impressive structure of red brick, an oasis of protective calm amongst the flying, chaotic world around, but nonetheless busy and bustling itself, once you are through the plate-glass doors of its entrance. You will need to obtain a reader's ticket to use the reading rooms. For this you have to make a prior application and have a short interview: you will need to be recommended by someone who can state the value of the research you are doing, and why you have to consult the holdings of the British Library rather than elsewhere.

Ordnance Survey large-scale plans are usually available in local record offices and libraries, so, if you are researching one particular area of a county, it may well be most convenient to use these local resources. But you may need (as I did) to look at plans across whole regions of the country, and the British Library is the only place that holds all these under one roof. I also wanted to consult the German defence mapping that I have described, and, as I have said, the most complete sets of these important maps are held here, so this will be a strong factor to state in your application for a reader's ticket.

The British Library's Map Library is tucked away on the third floor of the building. Whenever I was present, it was seldom busy. It is best to ask a staff member how to order the post-war 1:2500 plans, as this can be a fairly complicated procedure on the computer before you get used to it. The only draw back to the excellent service I received was the fact that there is a limit of 15 maps produced to any one reader in a day. I would generally race through these in a couple of hours, and had to plan other work in London so as not to waste the rest of the day.

You could go to the Imperial War Museum at Lambeth, for instance. Here you will be able not only to absorb yourself in the period through the museum's excellent exhibits, but you could also consult documents, books, and photographs, and possibly sound recordings and moving film. If you wish to carry out research here, I would recommend that first you begin by using the Imperial War Museum's excellent web pages, which include an on-line search facility of many of the museum's archival holdings. The Photographic Collection has still to be systematically trawled for photos of defence works: I am constantly surprised by publications which include outstanding pictures cited to the Imperial War Museum of which I was totally unaware. Similarly, moving film, including that concerned with Home Guard training, and infantry training and weapons training in general, are a little-used resource that requires greater evaluation. You will be well served with published works from the excellent and extensive Library, which will also produce for you the German defence mapping already mentioned.

To have access to any of the Imperial War Museum's collections, other, of course, than for the general museum displays, you will need to make an appointment by phone. When coming to the museum by public transport, in my opinion it is best to approach it from Lambeth North tube station, from where it is clearly signposted. If you go to the Elephant & Castle station, it is quite easy to get lost (I have done so more than once, finding myself in endless streets of tearing traffic that seem to go on forever without ever reaching a junction or signpost). You will know you have reached the museum (its buildings, perhaps appropriately, formerly housed the Bethlem Royal Hospital – the original 'Bedlam') by the Tibetan peace gardens in its grounds close to a bedaubed section of the Berlin Wall, and by the enormous 15in naval guns that command its entrance. If you have an appointment to consult books or documents (including the maps), you will need to report to the reception desk off the entrance hall. You will then be escorted up to the reading room which is situated beneath the dome you will have seen rising above the entrance portico. The Photographic Collection is housed in a building adjacent to the museum – All Saints Annexe in Austral Street.

You may also wish to visit the Imperial War Museum's outstation at Duxford, south of Cambridge. This former RAF airfield makes an interesting visit in its own right. It was established in the First World War, developed between the wars, and in 1940 during the Battle of Britain was the home of the legendary Douglas Bader's 'Duxford Wing'. From April 1943 it was occupied by the United States 8th Air Force. For anyone interested in the history of military aviation, this is an essential place to visit. Of outstanding interest, in my opinion, is the American Air Museum, housed in an amazing, futuristic building that serves as well as a memorial to the 30,000 American air crew who died flying from Britain during the war. There are also exhibits at Duxford to do with land warfare, and in Chapter 4 we shall be looking at some of these.

Duxford also holds various archival resources, including German documents that were captured at the end of the war. Amongst these are papers and maps concerned with the planning of Operation Sealion. Some individual documents have been translated and these translations are available side-by-side with their originals. The maps form a series entitled, 'Operations Maps: England' and they show the dispositions of the German forces in France and Belgium that were to be committed to Sealion, as well as their assault objectives in Kent and Sussex (IWM ref. MI14/558/12). Other documents concern the military government of Britain that the Germans would have imposed, and set out such matters as the penalty for further resistance (death) and the code of behaviour expected of the occupying forces.

Tucked away in one of these documents (MI14/823(a)) as a clause in a draft directive for the military government of England is an astonishing statement that quite frankly shook me when I first read it – 'The able-bodied male population between the ages of 17 and 45 will, unless the local situation calls for an exceptional ruling, be interned and dispatched to the continent with the minimum of delay'. Was this really to be carried out? The entire active male population of the country sent overseas for slave labour in the Nazi empire? What would happen to all their jobs in Britain – the doctors, the lawyers, the miners, the farmers, the factory workers, the office workers? The husbands and the fathers? The mind boggles. Surely the clause cannot mean exactly what it says? But there it is in black and white, as translated, and it looks pretty unequivocal to me. Perhaps reality after the conquest of Britain would have led to a modified policy (the 'exceptional ruling' based on the 'local situation') but one thing is pretty certain and that is that tens of thousands of British men would have disappeared into the Nazi system never to return again. This is something of an eye-opener for those people who think that the Germans would have treated the conquered British differently from the other races of the Nazi empire, and that we wouldn't have suffered the fate, for instance, of the Slavonic peoples of the East. The document serves a purpose in reminding us of what exactly we were fighting for (over and above, that is, the straightforward defence of our land and our homes), and the terrible consequences that would have followed defeat.

There is a library as well at Duxford, and within it are several contemporary German publications concerned with the British defences of 1940-1, including a superb volume entitled *Taktisches Luftbildbuch* ('Tactical air photograph book' – Ref: AL 2902). Within its covers, numbers of German air reconnaissance photographs have been set out, arranged broadly by type of defence work, as an aid to the recognition of these defences from the air. They show the extent, and the quality, of the German air reconnaissance of Britain in the critical invasion danger period, the results of which were used to produce the defence maps already described. Several of the photographs are beyond the areas which the Germans are known to have mapped; some, for instance, are from Norfolk, Suffolk, Essex, and the outskirts of London. They proved immensely useful for the study of several of the defence areas, as the defences noted by the German interpreter are drawn in on the photographs using the same system of symbols as are used on the maps. Indeed, the availability of these photographs was a strong factor in the selection of several of the defence areas.

A further manual on the British defences, dated 30 August 1940, is entitled *Einzelheiten und technische Angaben über die englischen Befestigungen* ('Details of the English defences with technical information' – Ref: AL 2901), and has a similar format to the volume above, with air reconnaissance photographs annotated to show different types of defence works, and accompanying pages illustrating these through close-up photographs, largely obtained, it would seem, from British newspapers and magazines. Unfortunately, the photographs are not of the same high quality of reproduction as in the other volume.

Also in the library are various manuals issued by the German High Command of economic and topographic intelligence on England acquired for the Sealion operation. One such series (*Militärgeographische Angaben über England* – 'Military geographical information about England') is bound in green paper covers and is divided into separate volumes for the South and East coasts. It includes pre-war photographs of seaside resorts and harbours as well as maps and coastal silhouettes, the latter showing the appearance of particular parts of the coast from the sea. A further series, this time bound in red, is entitled *Küsten-Beschreibung* ('Coastal description') and has air photographs of the coastline of Britain with information on specific points identified on the photographs. It too has separate volumes for the South, West, and East coasts. Yet another volume bound in red (*Die Küstenverteidigung Großbritanniens* – 'The coastal defence of Great Britain') contains details, with maps, of Britain's coastal forts and batteries.

If you wish to view any of the archival or library material at Duxford, you can do so by appointment. The curator is Stephen Walton, a fluent German linguist, and he has a small reading room in the building where these documents are stored: this is on the opposite side (the 'north side') of the busy A505 road from the rest of the museum. If you come here, you will have the extra interest of seeing the parade ground of the former air station, and the fine red-brick administration buildings surrounding it that were built in the RAF expansion period of the 1930s. Close by as well is the officers' mess, now used as a conference centre.

The volume *Taktisches Luftbildbuch* described above, with its high-quality reproductions of air reconnaissance photographs, brings us to the whole question of the main resource of German air photographs of occupied Europe in the possession of the United States National Archives at their repository at College Park, Maryland. These photographs were captured by American forces in the latter months of the war, and, after some examination by British historians in the 1940s, have been held in the United States ever since. The exact extent of the photographs included of Britain is hard to determine. I have written several letters to the National Archives in Maryland, but have been able to learn very little other than the record reference, Group No.373. The geographer, Oliver Rackham, referred to these Luftwaffe photographs in his work, *The History of the Countryside* published in 1986. He wrote:

Perhaps the most valuable of all historic photography is the great survey of much of Britain, especially the east and south, flown by the Germans in August and September 1940 when contemplating an invasion.[*]

---

[*] Racham, O. 1997 *The History of the Countryside*. London: Phoenix p22

If the main holding of these photographs is anything like the examples seen in *Taktisches Luftbildbuch*, then this will be an invaluable resource for a study of the anti-invasion landscapes. A project to assess exactly what the Americans have is very much needed.

The National Archives is situated at the end of a short road called Ruskin Avenue in Kew, once in Surrey but now a part of South-West London. You will probably come there by tube on the Richmond branch of the District Line; Kew Gardens station is one stop short of Richmond. Follow the signs from the station. Don't head towards Kew Gardens themselves as The National Archives have little to do with gardening. When I worked at The National Archives in the 1980s and 1990s (it was then called by its original name of the Public Record Office) we occasionally used to get a would-be researcher who had spent half a day looking for the archives amongst the glass houses!

The name change to The National Archives is only very recent, although the new name, of course, does state its function more clearly. With 'Public Record Office' there was always the prospect of confusion and we would receive the occasional enquiry about gramophone records. I well remember one lady who phoned and asked with breathless anticipation whether we had 'Wandrin' Star'! But the place had always been fondly known to both staff and researchers as the PRO (TNA does not have quite the same ring). It had been founded in the mid-nineteenth century as the official place of deposit for the growing number of documents of central government that were then accumulating on top of the long-held records of the kings and queens of England and the law courts. *Domesday Book* is one of the earliest and most famous records held by TNA/PRO.

For very many years you had to visit the original Victorian Gothic building in Chancery Lane constructed for the Public Record Office in the 1860s in order to consult the records. In the 1970s, however, space for the one mile of records (in terms of shelf space) that were added each year was running short, and a further building was constructed at Kew to hold what were termed the 'modern records' – in broad terms those from the mid-eighteenth century onwards. This building was extended most imaginatively and effectively in the mid-1990s, and the Chancery Lane office was closed down with all the records now centralised at Kew.

To the novice, The National Archives can seem a daunting place at first. However, it has one of the most friendly and helpful of staffs of any public organisation I know, and I am not just saying that because I used to work there! You will soon get the hang of the computerised document ordering system, so I shall not attempt to describe this here, but instead move on to the records concerned with the Second World War anti-invasion defences that you might hope to find.

You need to know that the records are not arranged by subject matter as such, but by the government departments who created them, and that they are divided into Record Classes according to the particular function or activity of a department. Most of the records to do with the Army have the designation WO, standing for the old War Office, although some (in the main the more recent ones) have DEFE, for the Ministry of Defence. Naval records are under ADM (for Admiralty) and Air Force records under AIR (*not* RAF). After the letters comes the number of the particular Record Class, e.g. WO 199 for British Army Home Forces Headquarters Papers and WO 166 for Home Forces Unit War Diaries. You will need to consult the Lists to these Classes in order to identify the particular documents you wish to consult. The Lists are held as hard copies in the Reference area of The National Archives, or you can view them on a computer terminal. You can also do a search of The National Archives' excellent on-line Catalogue of 9.5 million document descriptions using a keyword such as 'pillbox'. This will produce a document description and reference, for example 'Construction of concrete pillboxes (1940-1944)' – WO 199/36. The letters and numbers are the reference you require to order that document.

The two most important Classes of records you will wish to consult for the subject of Second World War anti-invasion defences are the two I have already cited (WO 199 and WO 166). The former is a miscellany, very far from complete, of papers from GHQ Home Forces, arranged by the various Home Commands – Southern Command, Eastern Command, Anti-Aircraft Command, and so on. The section for Southern Command is, in fact, one of the fullest. WO 199 contains a considerable number of documents concerned with the anti-invasion provisions of 1940-1, and is particularly useful for the higher command planning of the defences and for overall details of what was built and where. These records, however, have already been pretty well-trawled by researchers, although that does not mean, of course, that they will not be useful to you and enable you to gain new insights into the subject. There is always the chance of finding something significant amongst the listings of documents as not all have descriptions that are 100 per cent clear. To take an imaginary example, a document listed as 'Southern Command: provision of mechanical excavators' could possibly contain a plan of all the sections of anti-tank ditch dug in that Command. You won't know until you have ordered the document and had a look. I am sure many important discoveries remain to be made.

The Record Class, however, where you are most likely to make discoveries about the particular area you are researching is that of the Unit War Diaries (WO 166). Every unit in the British Army, from the Commands to the Corps, Divisions, and Brigades, and then down to individual infantry battalions, Royal Engineers field companies, Royal Artillery batteries, and so on, was required to keep a War Diary. This consists of a narrative description of the unit's activities, written day by day, usually typed but sometimes handwritten. Attached to the War Diaries as well are often many appendices – these can consist of orders, memoranda, intelligence reports, operation instructions, defence schemes, location lists, and maps. The last four categories of appendices that I have listed are those which can be most fruitful for anti-invasion studies.

Taking these categories in order, Operation Instructions are the formal requirements given to and by a unit relating to its operational deployment. For a unit serving in a defence role in 1940-1, they can provide the background to the strategy of the defence as well as the dispositions to be made by the unit, with details of particular defence posts and the lower-echelon unit manning them (e.g. battalion, company, platoon, section). Locations are given in six-figure, sometimes eight-figure, military grid references, known otherwise as 'Cassini references' after the particular map grid system used by the Army at this time. The best way to translate a Cassini reference to that of the National Grid is simply to have both maps in front of you and plot one from the other. There is a piece of computer software available that will do a conversion, but it is far from being 100 per cent reliable and does not have the exact accuracy you will require. You sometimes find the Second World War series of military (Cassini) maps (produced by the Geographical Section, General Staff, or GSGS) at boot fairs and in second-hand bookshops. I found 10 sheets just the other week at the Oxfam Bookshop in Saffron Walden. But, failing such a discovery, The National Archives holds a complete set in the Record Class, ZOS 3.

A Defence Scheme is potentially the most important appendix to a War Diary you will find. These are sometimes immensely detailed and may contain a complete geographical overview of the area being defended together with lists of particular types of defence works within the area, for example, pillboxes, roadblocks, defended houses, minefields, and flame fougasses. Details of Home Guard units and of civilian organisations may also be included; everything from police, coastguard, and petrol stations to the churches where the bells were to be rung in the event of an invasion.

Each unit (for example, a division, a battalion, or even a platoon section) drew up a Defence Scheme for the specific defence role it was allocated. Those that survive in War Diaries, however, are normally at battalion level upwards. A War Diary for a battalion might also contain the Defence Scheme for the brigade to which it was attached, or for the sector or other military area in which it was positioned. This reminds me to tell you that WO 166 also contains War Diaries for military areas (the system by which the country was divided for military administration) and these can prove to be particularly fruitful for details of inland areas crossed by stop lines and for information on the Home Guard.

Location Lists are most usefully found amongst the War Diaries of corps, divisions, and brigades for they detail all the units with their locations (often the address is given as well as the Cassini grid reference) making up the higher echelon unit or stationed within a particular military area: they will give, for example, the headquarters locations of units or the sites of camps. What is most valuable about this information is that it will enable you to obtain the titles of all the units serving in a particular area so that you can search the War Diaries of each in turn; for example, a Royal Artillery battery, a Pioneer Corps company, an infantry battalion, a Royal Engineers field company, and so on. By extending your search in this way, you stand a far greater chance of obtaining the details you are looking for, and may uncover a treasure such as an even more detailed Defence Scheme or a map.

Maps are often folded into a War Diary. They can be on paper or on tracing paper, the latter usually now in a fragile condition. Many have the detail clearly shown on their face using symbols that are normally explained by an accompanying legend while some (on tracing paper) are meant to be viewed with the appropriate GSGS paper sheet beneath them. The maps can be extraordinarily detailed. Some may be printed sheets with manuscript additions while others are entirely hand drawn.

There will be no indication in the List to Record Class WO 166 whether a map is present or not as the List only gives the names of the units whose War Diaries make up the Class. So it can be a journey of discovery to see what might be included with a War Diary. A map can suddenly emerge within the pages of the War Diary, and can add a whole new dimension to the area you are researching for it will provide a visual representation of its defences. I remember the excitement I felt when I found the Royal Ulster Rifles' map of their positions on the Royal Military Canal (described in Chapter 1). Here the degree of draughtsmanship to show all the defence detail was remarkable with some symbols on the map cross-referencing with further information available within the body of the War Diary. Some maps even show the fields of fire from particular gun positions. An example is the map of Sarre made by the Canadians and referred to in Chapter 2.

The National Archives is an excellent place in which to work. Not only do you have a friendly, helpful staff and systems that are quick and efficient (well, most of the time) but you have good facilities such as a restaurant and shop, surrounding gardens, ponds and fountains, and power for your laptop. There are also free on-line search facilities, not only of The National Archives' catalogue, but those of other archives as well. Indeed, access to the records at The National Archives is totally free: you will only have to pay if you require copies to be made of documents. However, there has been talk of charging for access, so I should hurry along there now before things change!

Next, we need to look at a further most important source for the study of the 1940 anti-invasion defences of England – that of air photographs. The prime repository of the aerial photographic record of England is the National Monuments Record Centre at Swindon, originally part of the former Royal Commission on the Historic Monuments of England, now merged with English Heritage.

I don't usually like to take swipes at parts of the country where other people live, and have a pride in their local environment and its history, but Swindon is a town that I long to get out of as soon as I arrive, which is a pity because my bouts of work at the National Monuments Record Centre usually lasted for several days. Swindon was once a market town (the Old Town) which was developed from the mid-nineteenth century as a major railway town on the Great Western Railway, with extensive works for building and repairing engines and carriages. In recent years it has again greatly expanded, with endless suburbs spreading their twisting tentacles across the shrinking countryside around, and with a labyrinth of roads connected by the biggest, most impenetrable system of mini roundabouts I have found anywhere. Modern Swindon to me is soulless. It has an ugly, concrete central shopping area, with its once busy streets fossilised into equally ugly and characterless outdoor pedestrian malls, peopled with aggressive beggars, skate boarders, and some of the worst burger bar rubbish chucking, foul-mouthed youngsters I have ever come across. And this was once the town of the nature writers, Richard Jefferies and Alfred Williams, and the poet, Edward Thomas: what would they think if they came back today? Do their spirits remain free on the high downland above the town, from which you can see the sprawl of Swindon like a vast ever-spreading canker over the landscape?

Having got that off my chest, it remains to say that Swindon retains a great pride in its railway past, and there is a museum of the Great Western railway termed simply, in the modern manner, 'Steam'. The granite facades to the former railway works have been carefully preserved, and within them can be found, not far from the Steam museum and a designer outlet mall with a good fish and chip restaurant, the buildings of the National Monuments Record Centre.

The NMR (as it's widely known) holds photographic prints of the various air surveys of England from the 1920s to the present day. Amongst these are the surveys carried out by the Royal Air Force, principally from after the war, but also including many vertical and oblique shots taken during the war, known as the 'military series'. 'Verticals' are where the ground is seen vertically (i.e. at a 90° angle to the surface) and 'obliques' where the camera has pointed at a lesser angle to the ground, usually at a lower height, often enabling the facades of buildings to be seen. 'Vertically', the ground is seen in plan, in much the same way as on a map. 'Obliquely', flesh can be added to the bones of the landscape seen in the vertical view.

You can only have access to air photographs at the NMR by prior arrangement and appointment. You should write to them[*] stating the area you are interested in and providing National Grid References for its bottom left and upper right corners, e.g. TQ 665439 x TQ 679450. They will then, for a fee, carry out a search for you of all available air photographs for that area, sending you a list of the results. You may have to request specifically the military series as this is not yet generally produced to the public: check on this when you write or phone. You will then make an appointment to view the photographs, and all that will remain is for you to wend your way to Swindon. If you come by train, the National Monuments Record Centre is within easy walking distance of the station. For car-borne visitors, there is a large car park. If it's your first visit, however, it's wise to obtain a detailed map as it's easy to get lost in the roads around with their myriad roundabouts.

Your air photographs will be delivered to you in transparent, acid-free archival envelopes. You should bring a magnifying glass with you, or ask the staff at the desk for a viewer. Certain series of prints can be viewed stereoscopically: again you will need to ask the staff for this equipment. I have to confess I did not use it, but preferred viewing the prints singly using a powerful jeweller's glass which provided both x 8 and x 15 magnification. Make sure you have a good seat with plenty of light coming through the windows. I used to ask for the blinds to be raised. Spotlights are also available, but best is direct sunlight if you're fortunate with the weather on the day you call.

Bring maps of your area with you as your first task will be orientating the photograph to find out what you are seeing. This can be a little confusing until you get your eye in. Check the courses of obvious features such as rivers or roads, or look for the shapes of housing estates or the pattern of streets. You will soon gain the knack of zeroing yourself in on the air view you have it front of you.

Once you know where you are, you can begin the work of trying to identify defence works. The most obvious will be linear features, such as anti-tank ditches or other earthworks. You can look at an air photograph for some time before you suddenly realise that staring at you is an anti-tank ditch, either open if it's a wartime or immediately post-war photograph, or perhaps newly filled-in so that it shows as a smudged soil mark. An anti-tank ditch will normally cross the landscape in a series of angled lengths, so its route is unmistakable. If it is yet to be

---

[*] National Monuments Record Centre, Kemble Drive, Swindon SN2 2GZ
(Tel: 01793-414600)

infilled (this had normally been carried out by 1946 or 1947) then you should be able to make out its width and the side where the spoil was placed. Look as well at any connecting natural waterways because sometimes you can see evidence of how these were 'improved' by straightening the banks or dredging them; the spoil from this can often be seen spread on the ground around. When viewing air photographs of coastal defences, always check to see if there is not evidence of an anti-tank ditch running to the rear. Sometimes these were formed as well from pre-existing drains and ditches, and the Second World War improvements can usually be identified through sharper definition, and by rounded, and sometimes in-turned, terminals.

Slit trenches, and other fire and communication trenches, also show up well on air photographs, usually at the coast but also alongside some inland stop lines or as part of the all-round defences of an urban nodal point. They were often constructed in short, angled lengths, and occasionally you will find one that has been dug in the manner of a First World War front-line trench, as a regular series of right-angled firing bays so that it looks from the air like the castellations of a castle wall. Some trenches, however, take a much more sinuous course, following the contours of the land. The air landing trenches dug to prevent enemy aircraft landing are usually easy to see because of the grid pattern in which they were excavated. Sometimes they were dug in broken lengths, like a dashed line, with the spoil thrown up in mounds alongside the trench. The poles and other obstacles set up across a blocked field can also sometimes be made out as a series of dark blobs: the best indicator is to find a regular pattern to the blobs as that is how the obstacles were usually arranged.

Other linear constructions such as anti-tank scaffolding or barbed-wire perimeters show up well on air photographs. On vertical views, these may appear as smudgy dark lines, but on oblique views you can sometimes see more detail including the criss-cross structure of the scaffolding and the individual posts of a fence.

When you look for pillboxes or other concrete defence works, obviously the lower the height at which the photograph was taken then the greater the clarity of the image and the more chance you have of identifying them. The hexagonal, or other multi-sided, pillboxes are the easiest to see, as their shape is unmistakable. Sometimes you will spot barbed wire around them or slit trenches. Rectangular or square structures can be more problematic because you may not be certain if what you are looking at is a defence work or simply a shed or other innocuous structure. The flat roofs of pillboxes and anti-tank gun emplacements, and the large size of the latter, are the usual give-aways, together with the harshness of the shadows they form. You need to remember, however, that often at the end of the war, and even into the 1950s, the original camouflage might still be in place, and that will break up the outline of a pillbox or even suggest another type of structure entirely: hexagonal pillboxes, for instance, were often turned into rectangular buildings and given pitched roofs. You will be experiencing the same problems as the Luftwaffe's air reconnaissance interpreters! I found on many occasions that air photographs taken in the late 1950s and 1960s would reveal a pillbox which just refused to show on wartime, or immediately post-war, views: clearly it took as long as this for the camouflage cladding to decay and eventually be removed.

A category of sites that can sometimes be revealed on air photos is that of roadblocks. These can show as small, white squares beside the road or close to a bridge (the concrete supports to take the horizontal rails) or as several rows of white dots (pimples or 'dragon's teeth'). Sometimes, where there is no other evidence of a roadblock, a darker line on the road surface can be made out, indicating perhaps a row of sockets to take vertical beams or showing where the road has been repaired consequent upon the removal of the block. When you are using photographs from the immediate post-war period, you should bear in mind that defence works, in particular in urban locations, were actively being removed in their hundreds and thousands at that time, and that it might be possible to see evidence of that removal, for example of disturbed ground where a pillbox had stood.

At their very best, air photographs, in particular the military obliques, can be superb, and can bring the wartime defended landscape to life. I recall one from Weybourne on the Norfolk coast (we shall be visiting there later) which showed in great clarity pillboxes at the head of the beach with scaffolding running in front of them, and, behind on the top of low cliffs, slit trenches, a deep defensive ditch, more pillboxes including an Allan Williams Turret (a metal cupola over a sunken cylindrical chamber – see Chapter 4), and, in the background, the butts of a rifle range. The amount of evidence supplied by this photograph of one section of the coastal defences was enormous.

The least helpful photographs will be verticals taken from a considerable height (2000ft plus) where there is no obvious linear feature such as an anti-tank ditch, and where most of the defence works are hidden by a wooded landscape. Woods, in fact, were a great form of camouflage, and many defence works, and other military constructions such as camps and ammunition dumps, were placed for this purpose under tree cover. This was particularly true during the build up of men, equipment, and ammunition for the D-Day landings, and a series of air photographs survives at The National Archives that were taken to test the camouflage. It was so effective that often all that can be seen in the photographs is the tree cover: you have to imagine that underneath are men, tents, stores, and vehicles.

While you are examining the air photographs produced to you at the National Monuments Record Centre you will want, of course, to make detailed notes. I found it best to do this by taking a modern map sheet (at 1:25,000 or preferably 1:10,000) and marking it in pencil with what I had observed. In that way, you will be able to calculate later the National Grid References of the defence works in question; either individual sites, or the various points of directional change along the course, for example, of an anti-tank ditch. You can also acquire, relatively inexpensively, laser copies of photographs at the NMR, and these might prove important later when you are checking the data recorded in your notes. I often found that a fresh viewing of a laser copy back home led me to modify my initial conclusions, and also, on more than one occasion, to see something obvious that for some reason or other I had totally missed before. If you think you will be publishing your work, then you may wish to order a copy photograph: this is not unduly expensive, and can be very worthwhile for the much greater clarity of the image.

4
THE CONTESTING ARMIES

Having looked at the various archival sources for the study of Second World War anti-invasion defences in the landscape, we now need to consider the troops that would have fought on these prepared battlefields and the weapons they would have used. We are all used to war films, either documentaries with archival footage of the fighting of 1940, or feature films with a Second World War setting. You will be familiar with the appearance of British soldiers at that time, the infantryman in his hairy brown battledress and bowl helmet, with ammunition pouches attached to webbing straps, water-bottle, small pack, belt with brasses, and gaiters, all to be blancoed to the approved shade of khaki. When I was in the school cadet force in the early 1960s, we were still wearing the same basic uniform, and applying blanco to webbing with scrubbing brushes, and polishing brasses, ready for the weekly drill day.

We also carried the Lee-Enfield rifle, albeit ours for drill purposes were of First World War date with white rings painted round the barrels to indicate they should not be fired. This .303 calibre rifle, in its Short Magazine Mk III version, was the standard British infantryman's weapon in the Second World War, with a magazine that held 10 rounds. It could only be fired a single shot at a time, but the British infantryman was famous for the rapidity with which he could operate the bolt and change magazines; 15 aimed shots a minute was easily attainable.

The British infantryman's weapon that features most in pillbox defence is the Bren light machine gun, with a distinctive curving upper magazine holding 30 rounds. The Bren gun came into service with the British Army shortly before the Second World War, and it was used for a long time afterwards: we were still training with it in the Territorial Army in the late 1960s. It was fired, normally in short bursts of three or four rounds, from a bipod stand towards the front of the barrel. This stand would have been set on the concrete shelves before the embrasures of an infantry pillbox such as the Type 22 or Type 24. It is the weapon that you can most readily imagine being fired from them.

Another light machine gun that would have been used in pillboxes was the Lewis gun, which had been superseded by the Bren before the war, but was brought out of store in the desperate days of 1940 and taken up again by both regular troops and the Home Guard. It was also fired from a bipod and had a distinctive circular drum magazine.

The Vickers machine gun was a much heavier belt-fed machine gun, although still termed 'medium'. It had been a mainstay of the British Army in the First World War, and fired from a tripod that would have been set on the concrete tables to be found within the emplacements designed for it. Vickers guns, up to six in number, were generally manned by a support platoon of an infantry battalion, although there were also a few machine-gun battalions who used it as their sole weapon.

The principal infantry platoon anti-tank weapon was the Boys anti-tank rifle, named after a Captain Boys who had been one of the development team. It had come into service shortly before the war, but unfortunately was ineffective against the thicker armour being introduced on German tanks. It gave a considerable jolt to the firer, and some of the embrasures of pillboxes were built with its firing in mind. Slots in the concrete were designed to take the monopod support on which the weapon stood with the butt against the firer's shoulder.

The main anti-tank gun used by the 1940 British Army was the 2pdr, which was mounted on a two-wheel carriage and had a protective shield for its crew. Its wheels were detachable and its trail legs could be splayed to create a stable base for firing. In some emplacements, slots in the concrete floors were intended to take these splayed legs to make the gun's firing position even more secure. Many of the anti-tank gun emplacements were intended for this weapon, but unfortunately owing to the enormous losses at Dunkirk (some 600) there were only 170 immediately available for the whole of Home Forces, and it is likely that the gun was never put in place in many emplacements.

To help make up for the shortage of 2pdr anti-tank guns, the War Office reconditioned some 400 6pdr Hotchkiss guns, which were static naval guns firing solid shot, originally part of the lesser armament of Britain's Dreadnoughts, but which had had an additional role in the First World War when fitted to tanks. Now they were to be used in an anti-tank role, and many emplacements were adapted to take them. If an emplacement received this gun, or was intended to receive it (as with the 2pdr it is doubtful if many of the guns were ever put in place) the indication is the presence of a 'holdfast' – a circular steel plate with nine bolts to which the gun was attached. The 6pdr was also placed in open gun pits, of which we shall see one example at Frilford in Oxfordshire.

The other anti-tank weapon (also an anti-personnel weapon) of which we shall find many material remains in our travels is the Spigot mortar (also given the medieval-sounding name of the Blacker Bombard after a Colonel Blacker who designed it). We have already met it at the Citadel Battery, west of Dover. Although usually intended to be fired from fixed concrete pedestals (which survive in surprisingly large numbers), it could also be used in a mobile role and fired from a four-legged mounting. From the middle of 1941, the weapon was issued to Home Guard units, and used, for example, in the defence of nodal points and the bridge crossings of stop lines, but it also had a role with the Field Army, principally in coastal defence.

Many other weapons were, of course, used by the Field Army and the Home Guard, but the above are the principal ones that affected the anti-invasion defence that survive today. Of the wide range of guns available to the Royal Artillery for field, coastal and anti-aircraft defence, the only one I will note here is the 25pdr field gun, which was a most dependable weapon and used throughout the war. Some 1000 field guns were lost at Dunkirk, but others had fortunately been left in Britain to serve in coastal defence. Field guns could also be employed in an anti-tank role, and there are a number of concrete emplacements, in particular in Surrey and Sussex, which may have been intended for the 25pdr (or possibly its predecessor, the 18pdr, which had been used at the end of the First World War).

Nearly 700 tanks were lost by the British Expeditionary Force during the fighting in France or were abandoned at Dunkirk. There were only two weakened armoured divisions left in Britain, equipped with a variety of light, cruiser, and infantry tanks (the latter so-called because they were designed to support infantry), which were generally inferior in armament and armour to their German equivalents. There were some 500 tanks in Britain in June 1940, but the great majority of these were outmoded. Of the battle-effective Matilda II infantry tank, which had done sterling service in France halting the German armour in an engagement at Arras that allowed time for the BEF to escape at Dunkirk, there were only a score or so. It should be pointed out as well that the British Army was equally deficient in all the supporting arms, including the transport that was necessary so that infantry could be deployed effectively in conjunction with armoured forces.

The basic appearance of the German soldier with his coal-scuttle helmet and jackboots, who might have come ashore on the English beaches or fallen from the sky amongst fields and woods inland, will also be known to most readers as there have been a thousand documentaries and feature films showing him. The field grey of the German uniform was, in fact, more of a grey/green colour. Tank crews wore a black uniform, and infantry units of the Waffen-SS (the armed wing of the Schutz-Staffel – the elite corps of the Nazis) wore camouflaged smocks in action. Airborne troops (the Fallschirmjäger – 'hunters from the sky') also wore a loose-fitting camouflaged jump smock, high boots, and a round, brimless helmet. Officers' uniforms are distinctive for the colour and embroidered detail of cuffs, badges, and epaulettes, and for their high-fronted caps.

The infantryman (or stormtrooper) of the Wehrmacht (German Army) carried a bolt-action Mauser rifle or a Schmeisser MP38 machine pistol (a sub-machine gun also favoured by the Fallschirmjäger) and his unit would have had a light machine gun, the belt-fed Mauser MG34. Another weapon associated with him is the stick grenade: many photographs of blitzkrieg (lightning war) fighting show German stormtroopers hurling these with arms raised against the sky, the released grenades arcing towards the enemy. Mortars (50mm and 81mm) were other weapons available to the German infantryman at this time.

A note on the blitzkrieg warfare referred to above – this was the new warfare unleashed by Germany when she invaded Poland at the beginning of the war, then employed again with devastating effect in the May attacks against the Low Countries and France. Lightning war was a war of movement, of armoured troops (Panzers) supported by air power, in particular the Stuka (JU87) dive-bomber with its 500lb bomb and shrieking siren, and of transport-borne infantry moving fast to consolidate the gains made by the Panzers. Glider-borne troops and parachutists, jumping from the JU52 transport aircraft, seized defences and communication points ahead of the advancing German forces. This was the type of warfare the British defences were designed to contain, and explains the emphasis on the anti-tank obstacle and the dividing up of the landscape into defended boxes so the German armour could not break out along roads and railways.

The mainstay of the German tanks was the Mark II with a crew of three which had a 20mm cannon and a machine gun, and operated alongside the lighter Mk I also with a 20mm cannon. Heavier tanks available to the Panzers at this time were the Mark III, with a crew of five and a 37mm or 50mm gun, and the new Mark IV with a 75mm gun. Armoured cars and self-propelled guns accompanied the Panzer columns, and infantry following in the wake of the tanks might be carried in steel-sided personnel carriers. However, although the leading units of the Wehrmacht were highly mechanised, much use was still made of horse transport to bring up artillery and supplies.

The fighting in France had shown that the German troops could attack and overcome pillboxes by firing at their embrasures with tanks and field guns. Stormtroopers were also adept at attacking pillboxes with explosive charges and grenades. The 88mm anti-aircraft gun was also used against concrete emplacements; this had a very high muzzle velocity and was also successfully deployed as an anti-tank weapon. The fire from this gun could penetrate the concrete of all but the thickest 'shell-proof' walls.

To gain more knowledge of the weapons referred to above, you should visit military museums. Most county towns have a regimental museum where you will almost certainly be able to find infantry weapons displayed such as rifles and machine guns, as well as uniforms and other equipment of the period. Additionally, there is often a display concerned with the Home Guard.

In addition to seeing exhibits relating to the 1940 defences at the Imperial War Museum in London, you should also visit its Duxford site, where at the far side of the airfield from the entrance and missed by many visitors, who either do not know it's there or do not have sufficient time or energy left to view it, is the Land Warfare Hall, with displays depicting ground warfare since the First World War. Here are many of the tanks, vehicles, and weapons that were used by the Germans and the British in the 1940 period. As with most museums, what is on display is only a fraction of the collections behind the scenes. By appointment, you can ask to see items from the museum's weapons collection, including the Spigot mortar and two other Home Guard weapons, the Northover Projector and the Smith Gun. Prior application should be made to the Department of Exhibits and Firearms.

In Hangar 4 at Duxford at the time of writing (2005) is also displayed an Allan Williams Turret (a type of pillbox that consisted of a rotating steel dome with sliding shutters that was set above a cylindrical shaft holding a two-man crew), which was brought to the museum from a site at Nazeing in Essex. Beside it is a Pickett Hamilton Fort (a hydraulically operated pillbox used for airfield defence which could rise from a position flush with the ground to a height of some 3ft in order to engage the enemy).

The other Imperial War Museum run site you should visit is that of the Cabinet War Rooms in London, the underground command bunker in Whitehall from which Britain's war effort was largely directed. Apart from the various rooms with the tableaux illustrating their functions, there is also a museum dedicated to the life of Winston Churchill. Amongst the displays look out for the small office of GHQ (General Headquarters, Home Command), and in an adjacent room (Churchill's bedroom) the splendid wall map entitled 'Home Defence Map'. I obtained special permission to have a close look at this one morning before the War Rooms opened to the public, and found it an invaluable and fascinating document that I think has been little studied. It is at the scale of a quarter of an inch to the mile, and is displayed in two parts. I remember I kept on having to move bits and pieces of Churchill's furniture standing in front of it to see parts of it more clearly.

It shows by a series of colour coding the degree of vulnerability to a German landing of the coastline, and gives the positions of all the coast batteries, with the calibres of their guns, and the locations of block ships and booms. Defended localities inland and airfields are also ringed on the map. The information shown appears to be relatively early in date (probably between June and July 1940), and does not seem to have been updated later. Therefore, it is remarkable that the map has survived as it would have had little practical value after 1941. It seems to have been present when the Imperial War Museum took over the Cabinet War Rooms from the Government in 1983. Perhaps Churchill simply liked looking at it.

I would also recommend that the next time you're in Dorset you visit the Tank Museum at Bovington, for here, amongst the many hundreds of tanks and other armoured vehicles of all countries and periods, you will find a display devoted to the German armoured fighting vehicles used in the 1939-40 blitzkriegs. You will also be able to see a 6pdr Hotchkiss gun, which stands amongst the First World War displays.

Other essential museums to visit as well are those of the Royal Artillery at Woolwich (called 'Firepower', located within the former Royal Arsenal) and of the Royal Engineers at Gillingham, with the more prosaic title of the Museum of Military Engineering. Both provide excellent days out, and you will be able to find much information, and see exhibits of equipment and weaponry concerned with these two highly-professional corps of the Army at the time of the defence of Britain in 1940.

5

PEVENSEY CASTLE, EAST SUSSEX

It was a damp morning. There were spots of rain on the breeze, but it didn't rain properly, nor did the grey skies clear. I dislike days like that. You can't relax, knowing what the day will do. What to wear? Waterproof or no waterproof? Cover my notes with plastic or let the spits of rain fall on them? In the end, I cast rain gear to one side and went out as if the day was dry. I had not imagined, however, how long and wet the grass of Pevensey Castle would be. And I had not put on my boots. Within a few minutes my shoes were soaked as if they were made of cardboard, and I could feel the water running in my socks. If the area had been in the open country, I would have dressed properly. But here at Pevensey I had set out as if I was in a town and would be walking on firm pavements. A big mistake. As I squelched along I hoped the day would get better.

I was back in the South-East, the front-line area that had been most vulnerable to German invasion. Under the Operation Sealion plans, the German 34th Division would have come ashore in Pevensey Bay, following in the wake, nearly 900 years later, of William the Conqueror's Army – the last successful invasion of England. William had landed on a beach which was then close to the walls of Pevensey Castle. He had stumbled and fallen as he stepped onto the shifting shingle, but had had the presence of mind to treat this as a good omen, not a bad one, for the benefit of his watching troops. He was embracing the soil of England, he had said, soon to be his kingdom.

The shoreline is now a mile away. Pevensey village and its castle stand on what was once a low peninsula jutting out into open water that slowly silted up over the centuries and was reclaimed by drainage. The former area of sea, marsh, and

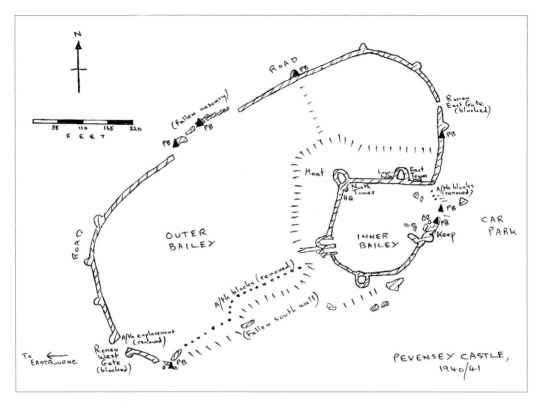

11 Sketch map of Pevensey Castle showing the positions of the 1940 defences

lagoon stretches away to the north as the Pevensey Levels, criss-crossed by many drainage channels.

Pevensey is a small village that now merges with Westham to its west. The busy B2191 road curves around the walls of the castle that dominates the village. The oval enclosure formed by these walls is the fort built here in the third century by the Romans, one of the chain of forts known as the Saxon Shore Forts as it is presumed their purpose was to protect the South and East coasts against sea-borne bands of marauding Saxons. In 1066 when William the Conqueror's Army arrived here, he used the Roman fortifications as his base camp, raising his own motte (a prefabricated wooden tower on an earth mound) at the south-east corner. Between the twelfth and the fourteenth centuries this was developed as a great medieval castle, with the area of the Roman enclosure serving as its outer bailey. The whole castle complex is today in the care of English Heritage. You have to pay for admission to the medieval castle, but there is public access to the Roman wall circuit; indeed, a public footpath runs between the east and west gates.

It is doubtful if a German commander slipping on the beach of Pevensey Bay would have delivered a speech about claiming the soil of England for Hitler, but he might well have kept close to the ground as the bay was ringed with defence posts. Inland, Pevensey and Westham were turned into a defended nodal point, termed here by 45th Division, responsible for the defence of this part of the Sussex coast in 1940, as a 'fortress'. The motto of 45th Division was 'Be Bloody, Bold, and Resolute', and preparations were in hand from June 1940 to make this key area as difficult as possible for the Germans to capture. Pevensey formed a defence sub-sector, the headquarters of which were established within the castle, which also served as the keep of the fortress – medieval defence terminology was clearly alive and well in the mid-twentieth century!

From July to August 1940, the infantry regiment based at Pevensey Castle was the 4th Bn Duke of Cornwall's Light Infantry. Their commanding officer was a Lt Col Harrowing (a marvellous name for an army officer: you'd never invent such a name if you needed one for a novel!), and it appears to be he who organised the defence of the castle itself, the evidence for which is still so clear today. In conjunction with the local Royal Engineers commander, he may also have planned the perimeter defences of the fortress. To the east of the castle, at the point where the road crosses the Salt Haven River, there was a roadblock and a concentration of anti-tank blocks. Further south-east at Pevensey Halt Station was a pillbox as well as road and rail blocks. To the west, at the crossroads in Westham and by the railway a short way to the south, there were several pillboxes and a further concentration of anti-tank blocks. Along the south side of the castle, on the line of the fallen Roman wall, a row of 48 anti-tank cubes was built, and this line may have been continued east from the south-east corner of the castle to join with the A259 road (although the evidence for this is not certain).

I had left my car in the car park for the castle near the east gate. The ground surface here is made up of laid bricks, and I realised I was treading the floor of the cattle market that had stood on this site until after the war. As I approached the castle, the medieval walls loomed above me. At their highest point, I made out a wide, narrow slot in the masonry, and realised I was looking at one of the embrasures of a machine-gun emplacement that had been built within the ruins of the medieval keep. This type of wide embrasure, of which we will see several examples around the castle, is fairly rare in England. There are some similar ones, probably built by the same contractor or designed by the same Royal Engineers officer, built into machine-gun pillboxes on Camber sands to the east. Looking at the embrasure, I could see how the defence post was disguised within the medieval masonry: the concrete structure was partly built within the masonry and partly added to it, but camouflaged with a flint and stone facing.

12 The vanished south wall of Roman Pevensey Castle defended in 1940 by a line of anti-tank blocks

In front of me, as I peered over a fence, I could see several embrasures of another rectangular machine-gun emplacement set amongst tumbled masonry. On top of the wall further to the right, close to a Roman bastion and just south of the east gate, I spotted another embrasure (*colour plate 5*). I passed through the Roman gate into the castle enclosure and inspected the other side of the wall at this point: a solid, cast iron Ministry of Works sign affixed to the stonework stated '1939-1945'.

After the war, there seems to have been (if I may say so) a highly intelligent decision made by someone at the Ministry of Works to keep many of the Second World War defences in place as part of the continuing history of the fortification of the castle. So many defence structures were removed soon after the war as unwanted 'eye-sores' that it's refreshing to find that here from early on they were recognised as part of our heritage, important reminders of one of the most critical periods in our nation's recent history. Indeed, at the time the defence works were being added to historic structures and sites, despite the danger of the period and the need for speed, there was considerable self-conscious realisation by curators and Ministry of Works inspectors that what was taking place was a process of re-fortification that had happened many times already in the course of England's history. Efforts were made to minimise any damage to the historic structures.

At Pevensey Castle, for instance, as the 48 concrete blocks were being laid along the line of the south wall, the curator was inspecting the holes dug for them to see that nothing vital was being cut through or significant artefacts thrown up. Similarly, at the Saxon Shore Fort of Richborough Castle in East Kent, when an anti-aircraft gun was being positioned within the castle enclosure, a careful watch was kept on the earthworks that had to be dug. There are other examples where army commanders did not act quite so responsibly; some times the attitude, 'Don't you know there's a war on?' prevailed. The military had the power under the Defence Regulations to do more or less as they wished, without too many questions being asked, and it was down to the responsibility of individuals to avoid unnecessary damage.

I left the path that leads into the interior of the Roman enclosure from the east gate and walked across the sopping grass at the edge of the moat of the medieval castle. Beyond the moat, rose the north wall of the castle with its two towers, the East and North Towers. Both these were occupied by the Army in 1940, and strengthened with inserted concrete walls and ceilings. The North Tower was the headquarters of the Pevensey Sub-Sector as well as that of the defending infantry battalion – the 4th Bn Duke of Cornwall's Light Infantry, which was replaced in October 1940 by the 11th Bn East Surrey Regiment. Looking at the East Tower, which also probably served as part of the headquarters, I could see to one side of it another loophole in the medieval wall (the terms 'embrasure' and 'loophole', by the way, are generally inter-changeable for the firing slot of a defence post: I tend to use 'embrasure' when it has been purpose-made and 'loophole' when it has been cut through existing masonry).

I crossed the bridge over the moat and passed through the gatehouse, spying the English Heritage booth where I had to pay. Here I met Allison Muir, the curator, in her cosy little hut, and told her of my Second World War pursuits. It was a chilly morning, and, with my soaking feet, I was glad to squeeze in amongst the postcards, videos, and guidebooks for the cup of coffee which Allison kindly offered. I was the only visitor. With the grey clouds and spitting rain, I thought it must be lonely here manning this castle by yourself, but Allison seemed as prepared and undaunted as any of her military predecessors. She told me there was a great deal of interest from visitors about the Second World War history of the castle. Clearly, eyes quickly picked out the gun emplacements with their

Ministry of Works plaques. I thought it was a pity there was not more on-site information about this recent period of the castle's history, although later, when I had had a chance to read the guide book, I found that a useful section on the Second World War was included.

Allison showed me a book she kept which noted comments made by visitors. One man had served here during the war: he had given his regiment as the East Surreys and described how he had done sentry duty at the gatehouse. There were comments from Canadian and American visitors as well. Between 1942-3, the Canadian Seaforth Highlanders were in occupation of the castle. They had carried out cliff assault training by climbing over the walls. Later American troops were based here, including units of the US Army Air Corps.

One aspect of the castle's Second World War history that Allison had not heard about was that in May 1940 it had been proposed as a prisoner of war cage: I had found a reference to this in a Ministry of Works document at The National Archives. Eight thousand German prisoners were stated to have been on their way to Newhaven, and the castle was needed as a transit camp. But the record did not say whether they actually arrived at Pevensey. Where had these 8000 prisoners been coming from in May 1940 anyhow and why were they going to Newhaven? It was all a bit of a mystery. I sensed another great untold story of the Second World War – a plot to rival Jack Higgins' *The Eagle has Landed*!

There is no access now to the interior of any of the machine-gun emplacements. Allison told me that some years ago one was re-opened and it was found that the interior was contaminated in a way that could be potentially harmful to visitors. So it was hurriedly resealed. The aim is also to keep out birds and other creatures. With some of the emplacements, I have to say, it is hard to see where the entrances would have been. More work on that point is definitely needed, and possibly the whole subject of contamination might be re-examined at some stage. It would be good if there was public access to the inside of one at least of these defence posts.

A little warmer from the heat of the hut, I continued my journey of inspection around the castle. The machine-gun emplacement on top of the ruined keep dominates the inner bailey, with a second embrasure facing to the west. I walked around to the east side of the keep and was rewarded by a close-up view of the Second World War addition (duly labelled with a plaque) at its most impressive. The ground falling away in front of me here was protected by the rectangular emplacement with multiple embrasures that I had earlier seen from the car park. I was now able to inspect it more closely. Concrete anti-tank cubes, long since removed, blocked gaps in the defences at this point. A further pillbox once stood by a block of fallen masonry at the edge of the car park. It was demolished long ago as it was impeding access between the castle walls and what was then the cattle market.

I next turned back inside the inner bailey and inspected the East and North Towers, descending into the basement of the latter and seeing the added concrete walls and ceilings. From here the battle of Pevensey Bay would have been directed. Then I climbed to the top of the curtain wall, and, with a widespread view before me, imagined the terrible fighting that would undoubtedly have taken place around the Castle had the Germans landed. There had been one previous blood-bath at Pevensey, in the year 491, a slaughter of the inhabitants by a Saxon raiding party. In 1940 blood would have flowed again by these grey walls and death thundered all around. When we commemorate the air fighting of the Battle of Britain on 15 September each year, we would do well to reflect on our deliverance from the horrors that might have been.

I left the medieval castle behind me and followed the line of the fallen Roman south wall, against which the open sea had once washed. Only a few fragments have survived, and there was consequently a long gap in the defences which had to be blocked when the castle was re-fortified in 1940, hence the new wall of concrete anti-tank cubes that was positioned here. My feet became even wetter as I scrambled on the bank, checking to see there were no more machine-gun emplacements hidden amongst the chunks of masonry. Close to the Roman west gate is a detached block of fallen wall in which two clear embrasures stare out like narrowed eyes, so the effect is that of an ever-watchful giant. The masonry between the two embrasures is even raised so it resembles a nose. This is one site children would have fun finding, I thought – the Pevensey giant!

13 Disguised pillbox inserted in the ruined Roman north wall

14 Machine-gun emplacement built on top of a Roman bastion and medieval tower

The Roman gates themselves were blocked by concrete walls. The large and still powerful west gate where I was now standing had also had an anti-tank gun emplacement built beside it, or so the guide book told me: it had been removed immediately after the war. I have found no independent evidence of its position, but I imagine it stood to one side of the gate just inside the enclosure.

I followed the outside of the great Roman walls by walking on the grass beneath them (that grass again; the water seemed to cling to it this morning as if it was a great sponge) until I reached a part of the north wall that has collapsed. Here were two further machine-gun emplacements, built amongst the tumbled chunks of masonry. The second one I came to was clearly an inserted purpose-built pillbox. It was cleverly concealed. Brick and concrete could just be made out beneath a facing of ivy-covered flint. Another Ministry of Works metal plaque was fixed to it – 'Gun emplacement. 1939-1945'.

Beyond this fallen section of the north wall, I crossed the road and looked at the next Roman bastion I came to. The medieval castle builders had added one of their towers to it. It stood high above the level of the Roman wall, and at the top I picked out the by now familiar long embrasure of a machine-gun emplacement. I thought the position looked suitably dramatic against the grey, weeping sky behind.

That completed my tour of Second World War Pevensey. I would like to say that I then had a three-course lunch in the Priory Court Hotel opposite the castle, toasting my wet feet in front of a blazing log fire. But, unfortunately, no: that would be a bit grand for English Heritage's funding. I had an egg and cress sandwich in my car, and read about Mr Blair's war in Iraq in the newspaper. Fortunately, I found some dry socks. Then I drove north-east towards the town of Battle.

6

CRIPP'S CORNER, EAST SUSSEX

Battle, as most people will know, is named after the Battle of Hastings that took place here in the year that everyone remembers – 1066. Nine hundred years later Battle formed another Second World War fortress of the type that we have seen at Pevensey, but here with perimeter defences formed of massive concrete blocks. Almost all of these have long since been swept away, but at a further fortress 5 miles to the north, a small village called Cripp's Corner, they survive largely complete.

This is heavy Wealden countryside, with thick tracts of wood, narrow roads and twisting sunken tracks, steep-sided hills, and small fields enclosed by thick hedges. It would have been difficult country for the Germans to fight across, in particular if their armoured columns were denied access to the few roads. The conditions would have been very similar to the Normandy bocage that the Allied forces encountered after D-Day.

Cripp's Corner is only a small settlement, but it is at the junction of three roads and is an important centre of communications, which is why it was made a fortress. The west–east B2089 road, in fact, is carried over the north–south B2244 by a viaduct, and, if on your first visit you were to be dropped down in the centre of the village, the roads that go off in all directions are so confusing that it would take you a while to work out in which direction you were facing. There is a public house (the White Hart) and a garage, and some houses, but little else. Parking is difficult. I would recommend to you a lay-by I found on the B2089 on the east side of the village, but, unless you are a dedicated walker and wish to risk life and limb at the side of these busy, narrow roads to see the various groups of defence works, you will probably need to move your car as I will describe to you.

Cripp's Corner lay between two west–east stop lines – a Corps Line (XII Corps) following the River Rother to the north and a Division Line (45th Division) running through Battle to the south. The whole of the Weald, in fact, was divided by a series of grid 'fences' that were defended at their crossing points, and which joined with the stop lines. The aim was to turn the countryside into a series of boxes, using the natural topography, in order to make a German advance very difficult indeed. Under the Operation Sealion plans, it would have been the 1st Mountain Division of the German 16th Army that attacked here, with the objective of forming a bridgehead perimeter that ran parallel with the coast to the north of Cripp's Corner.

As I arrived in the village, a light rain was falling. The view looked dreary and bleak – dark, dripping woods, and wet roads on which car tyres hissed, and a sense of all-encompassing greyness emanating from the rain-laden air. I pulled on my wet-weather gear and my boots: I was certainly going to need them here. I got my notes and maps together on a clipboard, trying to cover them with plastic sheets against the rain, and stepped out into this fortress of 65 years ago. I was not going to be downhearted by the weather! As ever on this job, I was self-conscious of my appearance. With my official looking red clipboard, and its attached paperwork, and my brisk, determined manner, and my clumping big boots, what did the locals, even now peering out behind the net curtains of those well-maintained bungalows over there, think I was about? At two other defence areas, widely-separated, that I shall be coming to, I was mistaken as the man who had come about the drains – hardly flattering! It was my conceit that I looked rather more military, efficient, and organised, as befitted the job, than a sanitary man. Would he weigh up his lengths of pipe regardless of wind and rain as I now calculated my tactical dispositions? Then a car swept by and soaked my legs, and a slide of rain-spattered paper began beneath the clip of my smart red board, and this general had to retire to his car to recover and start again.

My first job was to get my bearings. I knew that there were lines of anti-tank blocks, of an exceptionally large size, running at different parts of the landscape around Cripp's Corner. There was also at least one pillbox to the south of the village. Now, how on earth to work it all out? Standing outside the White Hart, and wondering if I shouldn't go inside and ask for advice – the parallel with the King's Head at Sarre came back to me – I worked out at last which road was the north-running B2244, and started walking along it. After a short distance I was relieved to come to the bridge carrying the B2089 overhead, which confirmed my direction was right.

The information I had gathered from the Defence of Britain Project, together with some evidence from a German defence map, told me the anti-tank blocks

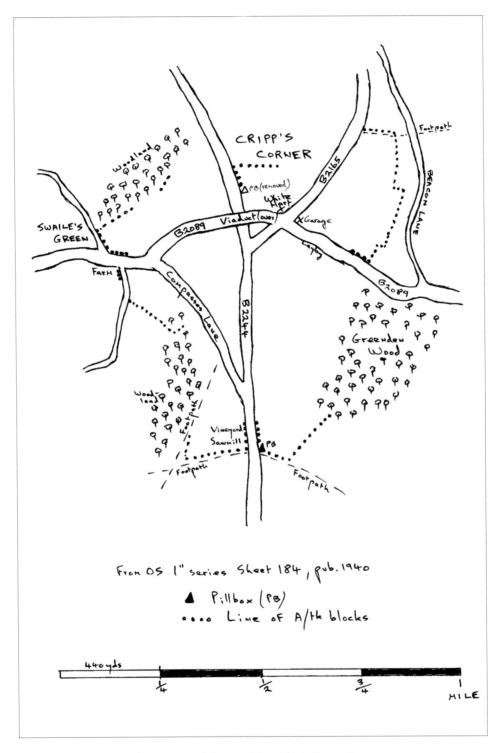

CRIPP'S
CORNER

SWAILE'S
GREEN

Woodland

B2165

BEACON LANE

Footpath

PB (removed)

White Hart

B2089 Viaduct (over)

Garage

Farm

Compasses Lane

B2244

B2089

Greenden
Wood

Wood land

Vineyard
Sawmill

PB

Footpath

Footpath

From OS 1" series Sheet 184, pub. 1940

▲ Pillbox (PB)
•••• Line of A/tk blocks

440 yds

¼   ½   ¾   1
                            MILE

15 Sketch map showing the perimeter defences of the Cripp's Corner Fortress

should be running at the edge of the road on my right. And suddenly there they were. And they *were* immense. To find Second World War structures like this, abruptly appearing through the gloom and the undergrowth, running wet and festooned with creepers, is an exciting sensation, as thrilling in its own way as the discovery by an intrepid explorer of a Mayan temple in the Guatemalan jungle.

Running at the edge of the field to my right was a line of rectangular concrete pillars, standing over 5ft high and nearly 4ft broad. They had a distinctive shape, with the upper edges of two of the faces chamfered, so that the remaining faces had an appearance something like a tombstone. I followed them on the other side of the hedge along the road until I came to the driveway of a house. Here the line turned and ran away from me at right angles to the road. One or two blocks were clear at the side of the drive, but I could not get right up to them without trespassing.

I retraced my steps, reflecting on these obstacles designed to stop, or at least hold up, armoured fighting vehicles. Concrete anti-tank blocks came in all sorts of shapes; some were pure cubes, some, cubes with pyramidal tops added, others, cylinders formed from concrete-filled drainage pipes, and yet others the dragon's teeth (or tetrahedron-shaped 'pimples') that I described on the Royal Military Canal. The shape I was seeing at Cripp's Corner was new to me: it seemed it was unique to this part of East Sussex.

I had come across documents at The National Archives describing tests of concrete obstacles carried out in 1940. The conclusions were that they could deter a tank for a while, and force it to go somewhere else, but they couldn't keep it out forever. They could be destroyed, for example, by shells fired by the tank. Their main purpose was to serve as a check, giving time for fire from the defenders to be directed at a temporarily exposed tank. But where had the emplacements been for the anti-tank guns? My records told me there were none at Cripp's Corner. Were there then anti-tank guns in earthwork positions within the perimeter of concrete blocks? I didn't know. The records didn't say. Given the shortage of such weapons after the Dunkirk defeat, I thought this was unlikely.

My records told me that the point where I should be able to see other lines of blocks was at Swaile's Green which lies on the B2089 a few hundred yards to the west of Cripp's Corner. I found a parking place at the head of Compasses Lane leading off to the left, and crossed the road to look over the fields that fell away before me. In amongst the tangle of undergrowth that formed the hedge by the road were blocks of the same 'tombstone shape' that I had already seen. I traced them to my left, and they turned to run beside a side lane, and then turned again to follow the far hedge of the field. An opening to the field, awash with mud, had been made between the blocks. I followed them with my eye into the distance until they reached a wood and I could see them no more.

16 Tombstone-shaped anti-tank block at Cripp's Corner

17 Blocks running at the edge of a field at Swaile's Green

I did not have permission to walk here so I retraced my steps to the main road, passing as I did so a single concrete cylinder by the side of the lane, probably from a roadblock at this point. On the other side of the B2089 at the side of Swailes Green Farm was a narrow lane running between steep banks. Near its top on the right-hand bank was a short line of five blocks, exposed on their forward face by the eroded bank to their full height of almost 7ft: it was clear that some 2ft of each block was intended to be set in the ground. Each block by itself was a massive work of concrete, formed around an internal framework of metal reinforcing bars.

I walked down the lane. There were no more blocks here: the deep hollow of the lane itself had probably served as the anti-tank obstacle on this section of the defended perimeter. But further down the lane, I saw the blocks again by a house heading away to the south-east. I had expected them here for I had seen them on post-war air photographs at this point running towards a belt of woodland.

As I could not follow the lines of blocks any further from this location, I returned to my car and drove down Compasses Lane to its junction with the B2244 running south from Cripp's Corner. Just south of this junction were a group of houses, a saw mill, and a vineyard. Opposite these buildings on the east

18 Massive blocks forming part of the perimeter defence at Swaile's Green

side of the road was a field opening, and there were the blocks again striding away magnificently at the top of a bank between the fields. This part of the southern defence perimeter of Cripp's Corner is about half a mile from the village centre.

I couldn't park here, but found a muddy lay-by a couple of hundred yards further to the south, and walked back through the drizzling rain. As I faced the on-coming traffic, dodging the occasional spray of water from the cars that swept by me, I saw ahead of me the line of dark blocks like so many soldiers in file marching along the low ridge (*colour plate 6*). At last I reached the field opening. There is a footpath here so you are not trespassing; not to begin with anyhow.

In a wooded spot between the road and the end of the blocks, I found a red-brick pillbox, built to fit its site here so that it was almost triangular in shape. The embrasure in the east face was set at a slant so that a light machine gun or rifle could fire north *into* the interior of the enclosure formed by the blocks. It was all rather strange. Here was further evidence of an anti-tank barrier that defended nothing but an open field, and with only one light pillbox to defend it. Its fire would have bounced off German tanks like pebbles. Where were the anti-tank gun emplacements to blast away at the German armour as it was halted by the blocks? They had apparently never been built.

19 Angled embrasure of the only surviving pillbox at Cripp's Corner

I scrambled away from the pillbox and followed the lines of blocks which ran on three sides of the field. There were over 130 here: only a few had evidently been removed to make gaps into the field. This was the best place to see the blocks for I could walk beside them, and measure my height against them. They stood almost as high as me, and I am 6ft tall: as we have seen, a further 1ft or more was set into the ground. There was less than 3ft between each block.

I marvelled at the work needed to erect these lines of blocks. Each would require a hole dug for it, probably by hand, and then the concrete would need to be cast in situ to a set template. I could not imagine the blocks being constructed elsewhere and brought here by lorry. The weight would have been tremendous, and their loading and off-loading, and shifting into position, would have required immense labour and heavy machinery. But, even with the blocks being made where they stood, it must have been an enormous construction programme. How many men had been involved in it and how long had it taken? I had no information on the first question, but probably only a couple of months would be the answer to the second. Perhaps it was my over-active imagination, but, as I stood before the line of concrete blocks, seeing them stretch away to right and left, I thought they had certain affinities with the megaliths of the Neolithic and Bronze Ages. Without records, what future ages would ever guess the purpose of the Cripp's Corner 'stones'? Perhaps they would think the place had once been a great sanctuary like Avebury!

I followed the blocks around the third side of the field, admittedly away from the footpath, but there seemed little harm in walking here and no one was about, until I found they finished abruptly at the edge of a wood. How was the anti-tank barrier continued through the wood, I wondered? Had an anti-tank ditch been dug here? If so, there was no surviving evidence, and I had found no air photographic or documentary evidence for this. There must have been a continuation of the anti-tank perimeter as the presence of a wood alone would not have been considered a sufficient barrier. Possibly trees had been cut down, and their trunks wired together to make a continuous obstacle, a bit like the timber breastworks of an Iron Age rampart – or so my imagination told me as I trod back to the road over the wet, grey field.

On the opposite side of the road, the footpath continued between the vineyard and the saw mill, and I found more blocks here running by the path as far as another wood. I was realising that the lines of blocks that I had seen now at four locations did not stand in isolation, but had once formed a continuous defence perimeter around Cripp's Corner, linking up roads, tracks, and woods. But what had been the other defences of this small village, and why had so much land around the village been incorporated into the defence? My notes told me that, other than for the pillbox I had just seen, there was only one other pillbox known anywhere in the area, and that was now demolished, its base being used as a garden shed. It had stood by the first line of blocks that I had viewed north of the viaduct. Clearly, these massive perimeter defences had been designed to deny the area to German tanks just by their very presence. The enclosure, or series of enclosures, that were formed by them made up the fortress, which had the principal purpose of preventing the German armour from reaching the road junctions at Cripp's Corner, forcing it to strike across difficult, enclosed countryside. That was one reason why the southern perimeter was so far out from the centre of the village: it made the distance the Germans would have to travel before they could get back on the road system even further.

As at Pevensey, however, the fortress must have had a central keep, and that had probably been formed amongst the houses of Cripp's Corner village itself. We have seen how Sarre was defended largely by fortified buildings. The same thing must have happened here. Had the pub, for example, been prepared for defence, with added concrete walls and loopholed exterior walls? I had one note from a War Diariy that told me the construction programme at Cripp's Corner had been carried out by the 205th Field Company Royal Engineers, with the assistance of several civilian contractors. Amongst a reference to pillboxes and roadblocks being built, there was a note that 'various houses and other buildings were placed in a state of defence'. Strangely, however, there was no mention of the anti-tank blocks.

If I had had more time, I should have gone into the pub and asked a few questions, but the day was drawing on, and dusk was beginning to creep in to darken further the drizzling greyness of the air. I still had another part of the perimeter defence to investigate – the north-east quadrant. I drove back to the lay-by where I had first parked, and walked along the B2089 heading east away from the village. The records I had of anti-tank blocks here were rather disjointed. I was not sure what I would find. But I soon located the familiar concrete shapes running by gardens on the left side of the road, and then they abruptly disappeared.

I walked on and came to a road maintenance yard run by East Sussex Council. Here amongst a variety of construction materials, I suddenly spotted some concrete cylinders lined up just inside the fence. These had come almost certainly from the site of a roadblock. But which one? I knew there had been roadblocks on all the routes out of Cripp's Corner, close to the points where the lines of anti-tank blocks reached the roads. So presumably these cylinders had been uprooted (fairly recently it seemed) from a roadblock reasonably adjacent to the position of the council yard. My records told me there had been three roadblocks, in fact, in this area – two on the main road and one on Beacon Lane to the left, which I was about to turn into.

I walked on into the fading light. At least the rain had stopped, but a chill dampness clung to me. A few hundred yards along Beacon Lane I came to the driveway of a house on my left. I walked along it. If the blocks continued here covering the north-eastern section of the Cripp's Corner perimeter, would they have crossed this drive? And there indeed they were – a magnificent sight – crossing from left to right, running in a straight line along a fence. I returned to the lane and walked on further, knowing from my map that there was a public footpath that might also cross the line of blocks. In fact, the path passed between two of the blocks, which then turned to run parallel with it, the concrete pillars so embedded in the hedge on the right that they could scarcely be seen. But I knew they were there, and I followed them triumphantly until we at last we both reached the B2165 road north of the village. And, there, I had to leave them, and trudge with aching legs back to my car. There were no more sections of the lines of blocks of which I had records, although there were several gaps in the perimeter and other lengths might indeed survive.

I sat in the car and I did a calculation from the notes I had made that afternoon. The anti-tank perimeter of Cripp's Corner had been formed of a minimum of 850 individual concrete blocks, each of them to the same pattern, some 7ft tall, with a width and depth of 4ft, each one only some 3ft from its neighbour. The holes they had been set in must have had a minimum depth of some 18in, which meant the blocks had stood originally to a height of almost 6ft above the ground surface. It was an enormous construction achievement, and makes Cripp's Corner today one of the finest and most interesting anti-invasion sites to see in England. I vowed to return when the weather was better and perhaps find out more, but for the moment other defence areas in the South-East demanded my attention.

7

CUCKMERE HAVEN, EAST SUSSEX

Cuckmere Haven is a place I have known well for some time, so my visit to describe the anti-invasion defence works here is from an earlier period before the English Heritage project began, when I came here on a fine summer's day with a friend, Elizabeth, and a Jack Russell called Spot.

Elizabeth has a practical, and literally down to earth, farming background and was an unlikely candidate to become enthused by the subject of Second World War defence works. When I first became attached to the Defence of Britain Project, and was learning the ropes, there was something of a chill on car journeys when I suddenly began jamming on the brakes, and swinging onto the grass verge in a cloud of dust, in order to take a better look at a pillbox I had just spotted.

However, rather to my surprise, she soon threw off her earlier antagonism with its dark mutterings about anoraks and middle-aged men pretending they were once soldiers, and began to join in the game of spotting pillboxes. She developed a consummate skill (far better than mine) at making out the outline of pillboxes, even while at some speed on green-leafed country roads. Her sudden excited cry of 'Pillbox!' usually meant I would have to stop and turn round, and go back, peering uncertainly into the landscape, to find out she had been quite right and identified a Type 22 pillbox, with an attached blast wall, in a distant hedgerow while we were passing at 65 miles per hour.

I have to admit that I even began to grow a little depressed, when, having thought I had recorded every defence site that there was on the borders of North Cambridgeshire and Norfolk, I would regularly receive reports from her of new discoveries she had made in the course of her travels – an anti-tank gun emplacement on the bank of a dyke near Upwell, a pillbox behind a hedge near Manea, a Spigot mortar pedestal by a house outside Downham Market, a possible length of open anti-tank ditch at Littleport, and, further east, a major triumph, a pillbox on the golf course at Bungay, hitherto entirely unrecorded. Her greatest achievement was to spot a small circular pillbox, sunken to the level of its embrasures, to one side of the driveway to Docking Hall. For this one, I had to return later, treading diffidently up the gravelled drive to record it.

So Elizabeth's presence on the Cuckmere Haven visit was going to be an asset. Of course really we were taking Spot for a walk and seeing the sea, and showing Elizabeth a part of the country she was not familiar with – that wide land south of London that ended in the chalk cliffs above the English Channel. But I knew there were anti-invasion works here, and this was the perfect setting for them, with the famous white cliffs of England, and the green downland, and Churchill's words and Vera Lynn's singing all mingling together with the restless surge of the English sea – that first and foremost anti-tank ditch against Hitler's Panzers in 1940. This had been another landing target under the Operation Sealion plans, to be attacked by elements of the 6th Division of the German 9th Army.

South of the A259 road running from Seaford to Eastbourne, the Cuckmere River follows a winding course through a valley between high chalk-downland rising on either side. It meets the sea at Cuckmere Haven, a broad shingle beach overlooked by a row of cottages on the heights to the west (a much photographed view) and by the famous Seven Sisters white cliffs to the east (*colour plate 7*). It is best to approach this valley from the Seven Sisters Country Park at Exceat where you can park your car.

We came here on a hot summer's day, picked our way through the Visitor Centre, and took the path running south on the east bank of the river. There used to be a light railway following the course of this path, built to carry shingle from the beach, but it was dismantled in the early 1960s. It must have been used by the Army during the war, I thought. Spot pulled ahead on his lead, eager for some excitement after the long, hot car journey. I think he had thoughts of rabbits, and I could see their burrows on the steep chalk slope to my left. Jack Russells are devoted dogs to their owners, but they are liable to attack anything moving on sight – cars, tractors, postmen, political candidates, newspaper boys, rabbits …. Unchecked, they tend to create a trail of devastation in their wake, so a lead is a sensible precaution.

By keeping my eye on the evidence of rabbits to my left I found the first pillbox (of course, Elizabeth spotted it first, a fraction ahead of me), a lovely Type 25 – a small circular pillbox made with corrugated-iron shuttering so that the exterior concrete is all ribbed. The type is also known as the 'Armco', the name given to it by the company which made it. Several commercial companies, in fact, sold pillbox designs to the War Office (as the government department controlling the Army was known at that time). We have already met one (the Allan Williams Turret) and we shall come across some others later in our travels. To reach this Type 25 involved a good scramble up the chalk slope from the path. I gave Spot his head, and he went up like a rocket towing me behind. The base of the pillbox is becoming undermined by erosion and rabbit burrowing (hence Spot's enthusiasm) and there has been talk of its removal to a museum at Shoreham. So I suggest you see it now while you can and look through its small embrasures at the view across the Cuckmere Valley.

Further south, by following a path to the left across the shoulder of the rising chalk hill, we came to another Type 25 pillbox, with a rectangular pillbox close by. A short distance further on, we found two more pillboxes dug into the lower slope of the hill, one an unusual type with a wide embrasure for a medium machine gun and the other, a square, brick-shuttered Type 23 with an attached, unroofed area at the rear where an anti-aircraft machine gun was mounted. At the very base of the slope between these two sets of pillboxes was yet another, almost completely buried by hill wash and by vegetation. Spot found it and immediately tried to attack it. I had to drag him off.

20 Pillboxes dug into the eastern slopes overlooking Cuckmere Haven

21 Anti-tank blocks, half-buried, at Cuckmere Haven

These pillboxes make an impressive group, set against the green grass of the rising chalk hills, and facing across the shingle expanse of the beach fringed by the long rolling lines of the pounding surf. But there were originally many more defences here that show clearly on both Luftwaffe and RAF air photographs taken in 1940 and 1941. Firstly, there was an anti-tank ditch that ran parallel with the shoreline behind a sea bank, following a line from the foot of the cliffs to a point near the river: from here, the obstacle was continued by a row of anti-tank cubes, many of which can still be seen. Part of the ditch survives, although heavily silted, ending today at the edge of an area of open water that has been formed since the war.

In front of the anti-tank ditch at the head of the beach itself was a continuous run of anti-tank scaffolding erected in the spring of 1941. This scaffolding, known as 'Z1 scaffolding' was placed either at the high-water mark as a defence against boats landing, or at the top of the beach to prevent enemy armoured vehicles getting ashore. Contemporary tests by the Army proved that of all the anti-tank obstacles scaffolding was the most effective. It was an endless fiddly job to erect it, usually carried out by Royal Engineers troops rather than private contractors, often working under demanding conditions, washed by the incoming tide and in danger of air attack. Many lengths, away from the popular bathing beaches, were left in place for several years after the war. It was as time consuming to remove as it had been to erect. Often the bottom sections were simply chopped off leaving the base in place covered by sand and shingle. Scouring tides over the years can often cause long lengths of rusting, weed-draped metal to reappear, although I don't know if that has ever happened at Cuckmere Haven.

German photographs show long lines of barbed wire forming a series of boxes behind the beach. These were almost certainly marking the perimeters of minefields, which were extensive here running for several hundred yards inland beneath the cliffs. There were also several other pillboxes between the sea bank and the sea, long since removed.

We walked along the top of the shingle banks where the scaffolding would have run, with the waves crashing on the steeply shelving beach below us. Other people were walking here as well, and this is where Spot attracted an audience for he spied a piece of timber bobbing in the surf, and, released from the lead, he immediately dashed into the water, wildly barking, to attack it. Both Spot and the timber balk fought the waves for a while, getting dragged back by the retreating surf and then swept in again. There were murmurs of concern from the gathering crowd. Eventually, Elizabeth and I, by wading into the water, were able to get hold of his collar as he was swept in for the third time, still attached to his great log as if he was a surfer trying to mount his board. There was an audible sigh of relief from the holiday crowd, who dispersed happily as if all this had been thrown in as part of their day's entertainment. The rest of the day was spent with wet lower limbs, and Spot was hauled off in disgrace back to the car.

Elizabeth and Spot had had enough of anti-invasion defences for that day, but I still had to inspect the west bank of the Cuckmere River. When I had first come to Cuckmere Haven, I had thought rather foolishly through inadequate map reading that there would be a bridge at some point in the valley to cross the river. Unfortunately, that bridge is Exceat Bridge way back close to the Seven Sisters Country Park. Exceat Bridge, in fact, had been a defended locality in 1940, with the bridge mined for demolition and with roadblocks and pillboxes. One of the latter had stood alongside the Golden Galleon public house which I was now passing to take the footpath from here back to Cuckmere Haven.

This is National Trust land. The footpath, part of the Vanguard Way, runs at the base of the rising downland leaving the flat marshy valley of the Cuckmere River, intersected by drainage ditches and winding river tributaries, to the left. It would have been difficult country for the Germans to advance over. In 1940, it had been defended by the 45th Division, and was part of the Seaford Sub-Sector of 'C' Sub-Area. Cuckmere Haven beach front was classified as 'C26'. Troops of different infantry brigades occupied the two sides of the river, with an infantry company on the west bank, where I was walking, that was known officially as the Cuckmere Garrison. They had medium machine guns, two 7pdr guns, and were supported by an anti-tank battery of the Royal Artillery.

I came to the sea front, and looked across the river to where I had just walked with Elizabeth and Spot. They were now on a happy shopping journey into Eastbourne, leaving me to worry about the anti-invasion defences and the German threat of 65 years ago. At the point where the path I had followed joined with other tracks was a square, brick-shuttered pillbox dug into a bank, overgrown and looking rather forlorn. To its left was a strip of water, once an anti-tank ditch formed from a pre-existing waterway. Forward of that was a sea bank, on the far side of which was a magnificent line of anti-tank blocks with concrete slabs between them so they looked like the great crenellations of a castle parapet. The area where they stood was wet and marshy, washed by the sea in stormy weather. There are plans, I understand, to allow parts of Cuckmere Haven to flood to create an expanse of salt marsh, in which case this will probably be one of the areas that will be lost. It will be a great pity as these are some of the best examples of concrete anti-tank defences from 1940 that I have seen.

I scrambled down the bank and examined them at close quarters. They were massive, over 6ft wide by 5ft high, and had been formed with corrugated-iron shuttering. At a point nearer the river, they became a continuous anti-tank wall where there were once two pillboxes set into the bank above the water. They show clearly in a photograph I had found at The National Archives of Cuckmere Haven in 1950.

I retraced my steps and climbed back up the bank, coming to a low ruined building which was once the cable house built in 1917 for a submarine telegraph link to Le Havre. It had been guarded by a machine-gun emplacement erected at the same time as the cable house, and was probably occupied as well during the last war. Certainly cables ran from here to France after D-Day. This reminds me to tell you of the other military uses to which Cuckmere Haven and Valley were put during the war. The valley was the site of a decoy set out with lights to make German bombers think they were attacking Newhaven harbour and the Ouse Valley rather than Cuckmere. It was also a practice artillery range, and the shoreline was used for assault training for D-Day: much of the anti-tank scaffolding was removed at that time. So this area, now so peaceful, with its parties of visitors and school children (some of the latter perhaps not peaceful at all!), has seen an enormous military presence within the lifetime of surviving veterans. Unlike our modern army, seen today at a distance on TV newsreels in far flung places, such a deployment in the home landscape (and a landscape as well so redolent of England) such a short time ago seems extraordinary, and almost impossible to imagine today, however immersed in the subject you are.

Thinking of England and the famous white cliffs over which the blue birds soared, I climbed the green slopes of the downland, passing the well-known white-painted coastguard cottages beside which further defence works were once situated. They had been occupied by the defending troops who had their battle headquarters within them. Below them on the shingle shore lay fallen anti-tank blocks from a long line of blocks which once reached the sea here. Now they were covered with weed, and eroded into rounded shapes, and one day will be reduced to the size of the shingle.

High on the hill, I had a magnificent view over Cuckmere Haven. I could see the white cliffs stretching away to the east, and to the north was the river, with its twisting side channels, flowing towards the sea from the bridge at Exceat. Further up the slopes behind me, the chalk had been deeply trenched to stop German aircraft and gliders landing on these open spaces. I sat on the grass, and took off my still damp shoes and socks, feeling the sun on my back and smelling the good, clean sea air. Beneath me was the warm solidity of the English earth, with its short-cropped turf all about me, and in the distance were longer grasses bending to the breeze against the blue rim of the sky. I thought these are the simple things that men fight for; not for great abstractions, however noble sounding, like freedom and democracy, but for their own land, and the things they love and which are familiar to them, the soil from which they come and to which one day they will return.

8

BARCOMBE MILLS TO OLD LODGE WARREN, EAST SUSSEX

I need now to mention for the first time the GHQ Line – the most important of the stop lines. GHQ is the abbreviation for General Headquarters, and this was the stop line that defined the overall strategy in June to September 1940 of defending London and the industrial Midlands from possible German landings on the South or East coasts. Other stop lines were built in front of it, but the GHQ Line represented the ultimate defence, behind which the mobile reserves were placed to counter-attack, had the Germans broken through from the coast.

The GHQ Line has been called 'Ironside's Line' after General Sir Edmund Ironside, who was Commander in Chief of Home Forces in June 1940 and instructed by the government to prepare the country for ground defence against invasion. Ironside has been much criticised as 'one of the old school' of commanders who thought in First World War terms of static lines of defence. Much of this is part of the mythology that surrounds so many aspects of 1940. I saw Ironside portrayed recently (July 2004) in an absurd television programme as a confused, red-faced blimp whose only strategy was to 'prepare a line of pillboxes'. This is not only grotesquely unfair to him, but is plain wrong.

Ironside, in fact, had had a distinguished military career, and had been one of the few Allied commanders who had anticipated the new blitzkrieg warfare that Hitler was to unleash on France, attacking with armoured columns supported by air power. He had also foreseen the danger of the Germans attacking through the Ardennes around the end of the Maginot Line. But in June 1940 there was little he could do with the limited resources he had for home defence (the defeated British Expeditionary Force had left most of its equipment, vehicles, and weapons in France) other than to defend the coast of England and prepare defence lines in the interior.

The creation of defence lines was standard practice by all mid-twentieth century armies operating in defence of territory: the Germans built them later in the war, both in Italy and in defence of their own homeland. Of course, the best way to defeat an enemy seeking to invade Britain was to prevent him getting ashore at all, but, if he did so, then to meet him with powerful mobile forces that would sweep him back into the sea, not to wait for his advance against prepared positions. But in June 1940 we did not have the strength to do this. All Ironside could plan for was the establishment of a defence system that would give the British Army the chance of holding up a German attack and prevent it scything through the British hinterland as had happened in France. With such a blocking of the German advance there might then be the chance to build up strength to counter-attack, while attacking the German forces with an undefeated RAF and cutting off their reinforcements by the power of the Royal Navy.

Later, in July 1940, Ironside was replaced by General Alan Brooke, because Churchill wished a commander who exuded a more aggressive spirit and was not tainted with the earlier defeats. As Britain began to recover from Dunkirk, Brooke was able to put into place a defence plan that relied more on mobility and less on stop lines and pillboxes. But in June, Ironside could not have done this. The defences he had prepared were nevertheless a massive achievement, and many were built into Brooke's later strategy. Warfare is a fast-changing business. Ironside had been unfortunate: he had been in the right place but at the wrong time. We owe him a great debt. It was he who responded to the first and immediate threat of invasion when our defences were at their weakest, and it was he who organised most of the surviving defence works that we see today. For many today, these evoke 1940 and our nation's resistance to Nazism.

There had been GHQ Lines on the battlefronts of the First World War. These represented prepared, strategic positions to which troops would advance (or retreat) as the battles developed. In its Second World War home landscape context, however, as with the other stop lines, the GHQ Line was primarily a continuous anti-tank obstacle, fortified along its length by machine-gun pillboxes and anti-tank gun emplacements, with defended localities at particular strategic points such as road and rail crossings that were also obstructed with blocks. These defended localities had all-round perimeters of fire trenches fronted by barbed wire, in places supported by minefields. The GHQ Line was additionally a demolition belt inasmuch as bridges and other communication structures along its length and for a broad distance in front of it, such as viaducts and canal locks, were prepared for destruction in the event of invasion. The defence of the Line also merged with a system of defence in depth based on nodal points, anti-tank islands, and centres of resistance, each with all-round defences, both in front and to the rear of the Line.

The GHQ Line was built in a few short weeks from June to August 1940, and represented an enormous construction programme, planned and organised by the Royal Engineers, but largely built by civilian contractors. It had two principal branches, with additional switch and back lines which we shall come to later in our travels. The first ran broadly west to east across the South of England from the North Somerset coast, passing to the south of London, where it joined with the second, a south to north line from the East Sussex coast, crossing the Thames east of London, and following a coarse parallel with the east coast as far as Richmond in North Yorkshire. From here it was later connected by a further series of stop lines into Scotland. It is the second of these branches of the GHQ Line, running north across East Sussex from the coast at Newhaven, that concerns us next.

I came to Barcombe Mills in the valley of the River Ouse north of Lewes as the mothers were taking their children to school in the nearby village of Barcombe Cross. The twisting lane from the A26 was full of fast-moving Japanese 4-wheel drive vehicles, each with its regulation blonde-haired mum and crop of giggling 'gals'. I was looking for my turning, and for pillboxes in the fields around, and grew tired of the shiny bumpers three inches from my rear-view mirror. I passed through Barcombe Mills without seeing anything, and turned abruptly left into a lane where I slid thankfully into a small dirt pull-off. I walked back.

Rather than braving the road, I followed a convenient footpath across a field, and came straightaway to a brick-shuttered Type 24 pillbox in a corner of the field at a sharp bend in the road. I poked my head through the open doorway. On the anti-ricochet wall was stencilled in white paint the reference 'A254'. All pillboxes, and other defence works, were once numbered in this way. In the Barcombe area, most of these references survive, so it is possible to work out that none is missing from the sequence.

We have already come upon the Type 24 pillbox near Dover, although the examples there were in poor condition, and it is worth repeating here, now that we are face to face with the type in quantity and quality, that it is the most commonly found pillbox in the South of England. It is hexagonal, very often shuttered, as here, with brick, with a longer rear face in which was set a central doorway with a small embrasure (more of a rifle port) on either side. Each of the five other faces had an embrasure at its centre for the fire of a light machine gun – the Bren gun. As we have already seen in Chapter 1, these Brens were often set up on fixed lines using special mountings (Turnbull mounts) so that they could be fired under battle conditions in smoke or in darkness to cover the important points the pillbox was defending without the need for further sighting and aiming. The arcs of fire of the fixed lines were marked up on boards within the pillboxes, and very occasionally these survive. As you walk around a pillbox, you should reflect that all the ground around was measured and marked in this way, distances taken, landscape features noted, all fields of fire recorded in the most detailed manner.

A Type 24 pillbox was manned by an infantry section of some six men – the numbers given in documentation that I have seen vary from four to nine. It would have been camouflaged, possibly painted in swirling bands of browns and greens, perhaps by netting with earth and grass affixed thrown over its roof, or very likely with a wood frame built against it to simulate some other structure in the landscape such as a farm outbuilding. Great pains were taken with the camouflage and some remarkable schemes were developed so that pillboxes looked like cottages complete with chimneys and surrounding gardens, or haystacks, or even just piles of rubbish. As I have said, pillboxes should not be viewed as fixed small forts, but as temporary field shelters for weapons and their crews. They were often defended themselves by surrounding slit trenches and by barbed-wire perimeters.

The stop lines were planned to be manned by the Field Army as the battles against the advancing Germans developed, but it seems unlikely that very many positions were ever occupied in this way by regular troops. As the defence strategy altered, many pillboxes and other defence works were handed to the Home Guard to be maintained and built into their own local systems of area defence where this was desirable. Often supplies of food, water, and ammunition were kept in pillboxes, and a minority of pillboxes were equipped with wooden, or perhaps steel, doors for their greater security.

The pillbox I was standing by at the corner of the field was one on the southern (Wealden) branch of the GHQ Line as it ran north of Lewes following the course of the River Ouse. Until fairly recently, there had been a pub close by used by local fishermen, known appropriately as the Angler's Rest, but it had now closed. The adjacent railway line had also been abandoned: it was one of those shut down by Dr Beeching. I came to the old station buildings, now converted into a house, from which to the south I could see another pillbox standing by the low embankment of the former railway.

I walked along the road. It was much quieter now. School had begun: good people were at their work, as indeed was I, recording these defence works from some 65 years ago. I crossed the Ouse by the road bridge, and could see that to my left the river divided into several streams forming a virtual island. On this island there were what looked like two pillboxes, but I could not work out how to get to them. I came to a narrow lane, and was pleased to see from a sign that this part of Barcombe Mills, with its network of waterways, was run by the Environment Agency, and that visitors were encouraged to come and walk here. A car park for them stood a little further along the main road.

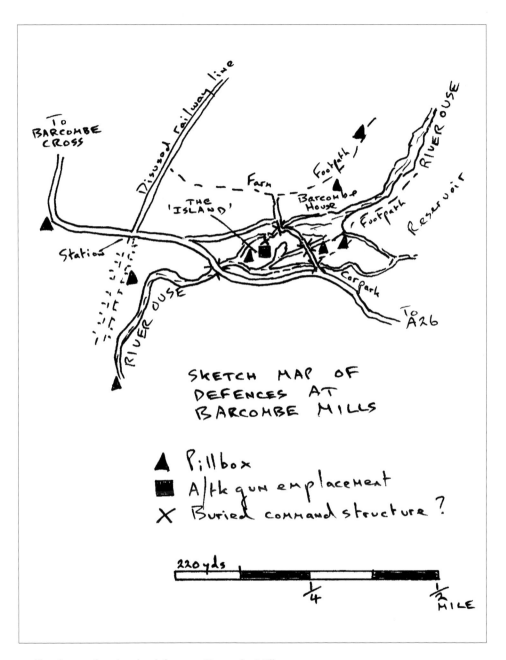

22 Sketch map showing the defences at Barcombe Mills

I needed no second bidding. I followed the lane which crossed one of the channels of the Ouse by a hump-backed bridge. A sign told me that this had once been a toll bridge, clearly on the original line of the road, the oldest toll-collection point in Sussex. Another sign told me that the last of the mills the water channels had served, whose function had been to make buttons, had burnt down in 1939. It was a secret, hidden place here, with a farm and Barcombe House standing just to the north, secluded and detached from the busier world around. What a discovery, I thought; what a place for a picnic on a fine summer's day.

I walked onto the 'island' that I had noticed earlier: it was not quite an island but was surrounded on three sides by water. I could see that one of the two pillboxes I had noted was, in fact, an anti-tank gun emplacement. Its doorway and main embrasure were blocked up, and a wreath in the design of the cross of St George was leaning against it. I read the attached card. It was in memory of L/Cpl H.L. Spicer who had recently died. This is the first and only time I have ever seen a defence work in the English landscape used as a place of commemoration in this way. I wondered if L/Cpl Spicer had perhaps served here in 1940 or 1941, or possibly he had simply lived locally and this was considered an appropriate and peaceful place in which to remember him.

Anti-tank gun emplacements are one of the categories of defence works that we shall be looking at in more detail later. They were designed to take either the 2pdr anti-tank gun operated by the Royal Artillery, a wheeled weapon that could be dragged into the emplacement and set up on splayed legs, or the 6pdr Hotchkiss gun, which was fixed into place by a circle of nine bolts on a concrete base – a 'holdfast'. Often these bolts survive and show that it was the 6pdr that was planned for the emplacement, although for the reasons mentioned in Chapter 4 it seems unlikely that many guns were actually put into place.

Because there was no access to the interior of this emplacement, it was impossible to tell in this case which type of anti-tank gun it had contained firing south-west towards the road bridge. Close to it was a Type 24 pillbox also facing south-west. On the north edge of the 'island' I came upon another concrete structure, roughly square and apparently deeply buried. I wondered if this had been a sunken command post: it was hard to tell. Barcombe Mills had clearly been an important defended locality on the GHQ Line, at a point where it was also crossed by a west–east Division stop line. Advantage had been taken of the complex of waterways here to create a strongpoint that had perhaps included the buildings to the north and which would have probably been surrounded by perimeter defences of slit trenches and barbed wire. Barcombe House, and adjacent farm buildings, might well have been fortified as part of the defence. To the east of the 'island' I found two further Type 24 pillboxes, each with its reference number clearly stencilled inside. They were also set amongst waterways in front and behind, and confirmed the natural strength of the defence position.

23 Type 24 pillbox at Barcombe Mills

24 A pillbox's reference number stencilled on its central wall at Barcombe Mills

From Barcombe Mills it is possible to follow the line of Type 24 pillboxes on the west bank of the Ouse (five of them in fact) all the way to The Anchor Inn at the next bridge to the north. The pillboxes lie either on or close to a public footpath, and this makes an excellent walk through the green meadows with one canalised channel of the river flowing for much of the distance to the right. By The Anchor Inn, which stands in a remote position at the end of a narrow lane, a further pillbox can be seen dug into the side of the railway embankment, and a little further north, stranded amongst the water meadows, is another brick-shuttered anti-tank gun emplacement. You can return to Barcombe Mills along the line of the disused railway.

It was a fine, sunny spring day. I felt invigorated by my discoveries that morning at Barcombe Mills, and by the walk I had just made, with a pillbox appearing to order every few hundred yards. Back at my car, I consulted my maps to work out the route to my next planned defence area, again on this Wealden branch of the GHQ Line, but some 15 miles to the north as the crow flies.

I drove along the busy, twisting A26 road until its course suddenly straightened and we came like an arrow into Crowborough, a town that has vastly expanded in recent years. This is part of the Wealden uplands, the high land of Ashdown Forest, with sandy open heath interspersed with areas of thick woodland. In the First World War there were army camps here, and Ashdown Forest was used for training, as indeed it was in the Second World War.

The GHQ Line had switched from the River Ouse to follow the River Uck as its main front-edge anti-tank obstacle, past Uckfield and through the dense Wealden scenery of hill, wood, and steep-sided valley to Jarvis Brook, just east of Crowborough. For the last part of its course, it had been necessary to excavate an artificial anti-tank ditch. North of Jarvis Brook, this machine-dug barrier ended and the anti-tank line was continued by the natural obstacle of a stream running in a deep gully through woodland with a railway line behind it. In 1940-1, the woodland had been much more open heathland than it is now. In the First World War, in fact, the area had been used for army training, and air photographs show a large number of earthworks scattered across it, evidently from that period, with a rifle range on the west side of the railway line. The central part of the area is known as Old Lodge Warren, now managed by the Woodland Trust, and it was here that I was headed.

Bounding the recently built north-eastern suburbs of Crowborough is a lane called Palesgate Road. Coming from Jarvis Brook, I splashed through a ford, and found a dirt pull-off on the right. I left my car there, and walked up the lane until, just before the bridge over the railway, I took a footpath leading over a tricky, rocking stile to my right. The anti-tank ditch crossed the field on the

1 Type 22 pillbox at Ruckinge on the Royal Military Canal

2 Little Farthingloe Farm from Long Hill, west of Dover

3 9.2in gun emplacement of the Western Battery at the Citadel, Dover

4 The King's Head Inn, Sarre

Monthly
Village Market
Saturday 13 December

Pevensey Bay
St Wilfrid's Hall
9.00 - 11.45 a.m.

The Food and Health
Partnership will be cooking
local produce for tasting
Local goods by local people

5 Machine-gun emplacement close to the Roman East Gate of Pevensey Castle

6 'Like soldiers on the march' – part of the southern perimeter of the Cripp's Corner Fortress

7 Cuckmere Haven seen from the downland slopes to the west

8 Looking through the doorway of the anti-tank gun emplacement at Long Bridge, Penshurst, showing the holdfast for the 6pdr Hotchkiss gun

9 Opposite: Looking over the roof of the Box Hill Anti-tank gun emplacement showing the hollow of the infilled anti-tank ditch crossing the meadow on the far side of the River Mole

10 Massive anti-tank cube on the former towpath of the River Medway north of Maidstone

11 Anti-tank blocks by the busy A240 road at the Drift Bridge, Epsom

12 Octagonal Type 27 pillbox standing amongst the parched summer grass west of Cheshunt Park

13 Shell-proof Type 24 pillbox near to Hartford End

14 Pillbox with the Wakes Colne (or Chappel) Viaduct in the background

15 Pillbox and cows in Sudbury Meadows

16 Type 27 pillbox by the River Stour south of Sudbury

17 Spigot mortar pintle with name incised in the wet concrete of the pedestal, close to Jude's Ferry Bridge on the River Lark

18 Anti-tank defences lining the beach north of Bawdsey Quay

19 Anti-tank blocks on the beachfront at Walberswick

20 The pillbox addition to the Manor House in the centre of Acle

21 Pillbox still defying the sea at Weybourne

22 Defensive trench on the cliff edge east of Weybourne Hope

23 Wide doorway to an emplacement to take the 2pdr anti-tank gun, at Oaklands Farm in the Sulham Valley

24 'I could see the line of the infilled anti-tank ditch as a darker strip in the parched summer grass' – Hancock's Farm near Chequers Bridge

25 The remarkable loopholed enclosure at Waverleymill Bridge, near to the ruins of Waverley Abbey

right, ending at a point marked by a Type 24 pillbox, once brick-shuttered but now with most of the brick robbed away, that you soon come to. This pillbox stands in a private field, and you should not approach it without permission, particularly as there is another close by beyond the gate that you come to next.

However, we now meet the main problem of this area – so different from Barcombe Mills – which is the fact that most of the pillboxes here are immensely overgrown and very difficult to find. So this will be a challenge for you (as it was for me) to hunt for the pillboxes and to persist despite tearing yourself and your clothes to pieces. Perhaps this is not the greatest fun for an afternoon's walk, but it's certainly rewarding as a test of your navigational skills and endurance, depending, of course, upon the degree of your fanaticism about pillboxes!

There was a very good article published in 1993 in the journal, Fortress, of the Fortress Study Group (an organisation dedicated to the study of military fortification worldwide) by one I.D. Greeves, who in 1940 had been a civil engineer for the company, Mowlem, which had been contracted to build this branch of the GHQ Line. He describes how he had his headquarters in Jarvis Brook, and how bricks from the Crowborough Brickworks were used for the shuttering of the pillboxes. It is these bricks which you will see built into the Old Lodge Warren pillboxes. There are 11 pillboxes from Palesgate Road to the sewage works at the north edge of Hornshurst Wood, all of them basically Type 24s, but with some interesting variations, bar one strange pillbox (the northernmost) which we will consider separately.

Some of the pillboxes are easy to discover; others, standing at the edge of the steep-sided stream bed, much less so. I will leave you to find them. I must confess I had to use my GPS receiver (Geographical Positioning System linked to American satellites, surprisingly cheap and essential for all serious outdoors work) to navigate myself to the right grid references that I had earlier obtained from the Ordnance Survey 1:2500 plan. One pillbox has been blown up at some time, perhaps as part of an exercise later in the war as there can have been no point in trying to remove it otherwise, and its reinforcing bars and shattered concrete interior are wildly overgrown with brambles and creepers.

If we concentrate on those pillboxes that are relatively easy to find, you will come first to one built into the railway embankment, standing tall on a 3ft-thick concrete base. Its entrance is on its north side, and there is a brick and concrete wall built at the rear to protect it against land slippage. Further on, past a series of dangerous-looking pools associated with the disused pumping station of a reservoir, a pillbox dominates a footbridge over the stream, standing high on the bank above it. Its base is slowly being eroded by the stream, and has become considerably undermined. It is to be hoped that work could be done to consolidate the structure before it topples forward into the water. The pillbox is in good clean condition inside, and you can enter it via a flight of steps on its north side, shuffling around the interior anti-ricochet wall and looking out through the small embrasures, splayed inside with grooves cut into the brickwork. The latter were to take the mounts on which the Bren guns were set on fixed lines.

Take the path running from behind the pillbox, and you will pass another overgrown Type 24, and then come to one constructed with a redder brick than the dark Crowborough stock bricks used elsewhere. This pillbox is in excellent condition, and you can enter its whitewashed interior by two steps down to the entrance, reflecting on the thickness of the walls (at least 3.5ft) revealed by the depth of the splayed embrasures.

And now we come to the runt amongst this line of Type 24 pillboxes. A couple of hundred yards further north, in the narrow gap between the railway and a bend in the stream, is a clump of vegetation, which, when examined closely, reveals itself as a small squarish pillbox set low in the ground. The shape, with protruding embrasures, is highly unusual, and there is no evident reason why the standard Type 24, built with variations to suit the ground, was abandoned here. Because of the vegetation, it is hard to make out the form of the structure completely, and it would be good to see it freed of its overgrowth. Certainly some work is needed here because there is an open hole in the ground close by leading to a buried chamber (purpose unknown) which constitutes a real danger. I could see our Jack Russell, Spot, heading straight into that and disappearing forever, or a crop of broken legs of horses and humans.

Just beyond this point, crossing the fields by the sewage works, is an open drain, and I imagine this was followed as the anti-tank ditch supplementing the barrier supplied by the twisting, rushing stream in front of it. Here I ended my explorations of this section of the Line. Another important area awaited me further to the north.

9
PENSHURST, KENT

I was coming to Penshurst in Kent, an attractive village lying a few miles to the west of Tunbridge Wells. Penshurst is famous for its great house (Penshurst Place) the home of the Sidney family from the mid-sixteenth century. I have never been able to find out what use the house was put to during the war. Almost all great homes, in particular those in the wartime 'frontline counties', were requisitioned for some war purpose or other, but the guidebook to the house says merely that it was in a rundown state at the end of the war. Certainly it was within a heavily militarised area. The author, Katharine Moore, wrote in her diary on 1 July 1940:

> Very hot … drove to Penshurst …. Many troops passing through and the beautiful meadow below Penshurst gardens cut up with dug outs, army lorries, etc.

The Army's interest in Penshurst was because it lay at the junction of the Rivers Eden and Medway, and the two branches of the GHQ Line, from the west and the south followed the river courses and met here. In addition, Penshurst village itself was a Category 'B' nodal point with its own all-round defences (it had a garrison of 57 men from the 21st Bn Kent Home Guard), and, to its north, was a small airfield which in 1940 was defended by a training company of the 8th Bn Royal West Kents.

The GHQ Line crossing the Weald from Newhaven had split into two branches south of Tunbridge Wells, one passing to the east of the town, and the other (known as the Ashurst Switch) to the west. The latter was the branch that made the junction at Penshurst with the Line following the River Eden from the west. Tunbridge Wells itself was a Category 'A' nodal point containing the headquarters of XII Corps, defending the South-East of England. Adjacent Tonbridge was a designated fortress, with its medieval castle re-fortified and serving as a keep, although, unlike Pevensey Castle, there are no signs of the Second World War occupation today.

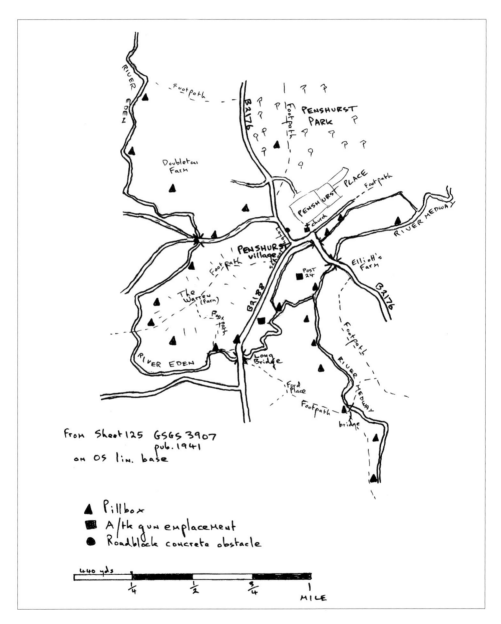

25 Sketch map showing the defences around Penshurst Village

There is a convenient lay-by in which to park at Penshurst, lying on the B2176 road just north of the central junction in the village. Having lived not far away for several years, and visited here frequently, I was familiar with the Penshurst landscape, and aware of the pillboxes scattered across it, so this was not going to be quite such a journey of discovery as in some of the other defence areas. But, even so, there were new things to be found, and one was just a few yards from the lay-by. The B2176 runs here beside the park of Penshurst Place, with a stone wall fronting a belt of dense undergrowth. I thought I would check this location for any surviving evidence of a roadblock (Penshurst must have been ringed by roadblocks, but unfortunately I had not been able to locate any documentary evidence to give me their precise positions), and to my delight saw two pimples (dragon's teeth) lurking in the bushes, providing an excellent example of what can survive, totally overlooked and almost forgotten, and a sudden, vivid reminder of the 1940 defended landscape.

Buoyed by this discovery, I walked on, and took the Fordcombe Road (B2188) until I came to the primary school where the children were being delivered by droves of brightly chattering mums, with cars and push chairs, the occasional harassed-looking dad mixed up amongst them. I threaded my way through, and took the footpath that runs by the school. Before long I came to some cottages and a farm at The Warren, which is a superb hill position commanding the valley of the River Eden flowing in a curve below. This is such an obvious defensive spot that I imagine that the farm buildings here would have been occupied by the Army. Surely there would have been at least an observation post at this point; but unfortunately once again the documentary evidence is missing.

I stood for a while looking at the glittering, sunlit landscape below me, the dark woods and bright green fields, with the twisting line of the river, all beneath the pale blue canopy of the sky, and I thought here is another landscape that seems to embody the spirit of England. It seemed incredible to think that only some 65 years ago this might have been a battlefield, with the quiet countryside ripped suddenly apart as if there had never been quiet order here, the silhouettes of German tanks on the hills, lines of camouflaged SS troops working from hedgerow to hedgerow across the valley.

I descended the slope to the river and started finding the red, brick-shuttered Type 24 infantry pillboxes that dot the Penshurst landscape. There was one just to the right of the path and two others amongst the meadows by the river. The pillboxes were on the east bank of the Eden, showing that the Line here was being defended against attacks from the south and the west. As we shall see, the pillboxes along the Medway to the south are on the west bank, indicating that attacks on this branch of the GHQ Line were expected from the east, although Tunbridge Wells and the other diverging branch of the Line also lay in that direction. It is hard to work out the exact thinking behind the strategy at this important junction of the GHQ Line. Probably the intention was to defend the entire Line from attacks in either direction, but in the event of an attack from the west some pillboxes at least would have been forward of the principal anti-tank obstacle of the Medway.

To the north, I could see the pillboxes continuing beside the Eden. A lane, running from a point just to the north of the lay-by where I had left the car, crosses the river here. There is a pillbox by this lane, protecting a roadblock at the river bridge close by. A concrete block from this roadblock survives on the west side of the bridge, and it is worth undertaking this little diversion to view the juxtaposition of pillbox and roadblock here.

First, however, I returned to the footpath and retraced my steps to the road at the school. Then I walked south towards Long Bridge, which was a crossing of the River Eden that was mined for demolition and formed a small defended locality. There was also a roadblock there that was overlooked by two infantry pillboxes and by an anti-tank gun emplacement.

The Fordcombe Road is a dangerous one to walk beside once the Penshurst pavements have finished, and before I reached Long Bridge I had to seek refuge from a passing HGV in a field opening that fortuitously presented itself. By a happy chance, I found that an anti-tank gun emplacement on the ridge above Long Bridge, and firing south towards it, also stood at the edge of this field. The square emplacement had been built with brick-shuttering and was now badly overgrown. Its main embrasure and wide entrance, however, were clear of vegetation, and I was able to go inside and inspect the holdfast of nine bolts on which the 6pdr gun would have been positioned (*colour plate 8*).

Further along the Fordcombe Road, I found a pillbox amongst trees and bushes on the right at a bend in the road. You would miss it if I did not tell you it was there, so overgrown is it. Be careful looking for it, as the traffic whizzes round the corner here. Just before reaching Long Bridge, I took the lane to the right. Dug into the bank above the river on the left side of the lane was another very overgrown pillbox, recently fenced off. At the end of the lane I was able to look across a fence and see a pillbox in the fields in the distance. This was part of the line we viewed earlier from The Warren.

Next, having reached the narrow brick parapets of Long Bridge, I escaped the growing prospect of immolation by white van and dumper truck by taking the footpath leading from the bridge towards the east. I passed by Ford Place Farm and some cottages, then crossed a large open field where another Type 24 pillbox was clear to my left. As the field was in spring crop I did not attempt to approach it. (You should always follow these common sense rules: never do any damage at all to crops, and always get permission to enter land where you can.)

26 Type 24 pillbox near the River Eden, Penshurst

Another Type 24 was now ahead of me amongst bushes by a footbridge over the River Medway, and I was able to go inside this one and have a good look at it. The interior was clean with a concrete anti-ricochet wall and whitewashed embrasure surrounds. Unlike pillboxes at Old Lodge Warren, however, there were no slots cut in the brickwork to take weapon mountings.

I was now standing on the west bank of the River Medway, and I realised that I had moved across from the branch of the GHQ Line coming from the west to that approaching from the south (the branch we followed last at Old Lodge Warren before it joined the course of the infant Medway). The junction of the two rivers (the Eden and the Medway and therefore of the two branches of the GHQ Line) was about half a mile to the north, and I planned to walk in that direction next, back towards Penshurst village. However, you can follow the line of pillboxes by the Medway, all of which survive complete, for a long way south to the Saints Hill Waterworks and Colliersland Bridge, which is dominated by another anti-tank gun emplacement now standing in the rear garden of a house. It makes a good walk through river meadows with the pillboxes appearing every few hundred yards.

27 Interior of a Penshurst pillbox showing the concrete firing-shelf beneath an embrasure

As I trudged back towards Penshurst, I took a track running along a ridge from which I could see several pillboxes in the meadows below. A hundred yards or so from the junction of the track with the B2176 at Rogues Hill, with the tower of Penshurst church in view, I spied a brick-shuttered pillbox by the river, and beyond it a further red-brick shape by a hedgerow. This was another anti-tank gun emplacement for a 6pdr gun, one I knew a little more about because the War Diary of the 922nd Defence Battery Royal Artillery at The National Archives includes a plan that shows it, together with a light machine-gun position and slit trenches close by, forming their Post No.24. There is no public access to view the emplacement, however, unless you get permission from Elliott's Farm and approach it from the far side of the river.

As I descended Rogues Hill towards the village, I crossed two attractive stone bridges which would certainly have been prepared for demolition and been blocked against traffic. Penshurst Place was now before me, and I turned right into the estate through a stone gateway and followed a narrow road running below the southern wall of the gardens leading to the car park. Amongst the trees at the edge of the channel of the Medway to my right, I found two more overgrown infantry pillboxes. The meadows seen from here are probably those that Katharine Moore was referring to in her diary extract quoted earlier.

There is only one pillbox standing now in Penshurst Park itself (although it is likely that there were once others), and I made a small detour to visit it on the last lap of my journey back to the lay-by where I had left my car. The pillbox stands just to the left of the path beyond the cricket ground as you head away from the house. Its doorway is now half blocked, but it is worth a visit as it stands alone and does not relate to either of the branches of the GHQ Line. I think that what we have here is a lone surviving defence work of the northern perimeter of the nodal point. It is strange, however, that its main field of fire is to the east, rather than the north, and it's possible it had a role in defending whatever military occupation of Penshurst Place and its grounds may have taken place. A local resident will almost certainly know, and once again we are back to the importance of oral history while we can still hope to obtain this.

Penshurst is a wonderful centre for walks. If you are inspired to come here, you can also explore the high land to the north of Penshurst Place, where there are beautiful paths and only nature to occupy your thoughts. However, if you are really determined in your pursuit of the Second World War, you can push even further north and find the site of Penshurst Airfield at Chiddingstone Causeway where there are several pillboxes.

10

DORKING GAP TO SIDLOW BRIDGE, SURREY

Box Hill is well known to Londoners. For very many years it has been a popular place to come to at weekends, to scramble on its steep slopes and walk amongst the woods that crown its summit, including tangled groves of the box trees that give the hill its name. It forms part of the North Downs which are cut here by the River Mole flowing on a course from south to north to join eventually with the Thames. The broad valley that is thus formed through the chalk ridge, known as the Dorking Gap, is dominated to the east by Box Hill rising sheer from the river to a height of some 600ft. To the west of the valley are the heights of Ranmore, and to the south lies the town of Dorking.

The Dorking Gap's place in military thinking has long been established. In 1871 G.T. Chesney's *The Battle of Dorking* created something of a sensation with its fictional account of a German invasion that culminated here in a defeat for the defending British troops. The book did much to alert the Government of the day to deficiencies in the country's land defences. In the 1890s, when an entrenched defence line to protect London was planned, one of the Mobilisation Centres where arms and ammunition would be stored, and where troops would assemble, was built on the top of Box Hill. Known as Box Hill Fort, it stands close to the National Trust visitor centre – much of the Box Hill estate is owned by the National Trust.

A much earlier military role for Box Hill has been proposed recently. It has been put forward as the scene of the final battle of the Romans against the Boudican rebellion (Boadicea as she is more popularly known) of AD 60. The Roman historian describes the Romans occupying a narrow valley (perhaps the Dorking Gap itself) with a forest behind (the wooded expanse of the Weald).

Dorking was a Roman settlement on Stane Street (their road from London to Chichester) which probably was built as a military road.

Enough of theorising! Let us get to grips with the real and deadly threat of 1940 when the Dorking gap was defended as part of the GHQ Line. This sector of GHQ Line 'B' (running from Farnham to Penshurst) crossed the broad valley between Ranmore Common and Box Hill, the main front-edge anti-tank obstacle at this point being a machine-dug ditch. When it reached the Horsham to London railway line and the dual-carriageways of the A24, both these important communication routes running here side-by-side were protected by blocks, the roadblock being supported by a number of large concrete cubes either side of the road with several as well between the two carriageways. A further roadblock on the A24 lay to the north close to the track that leads to the car park at the stepping stones across the River Mole.

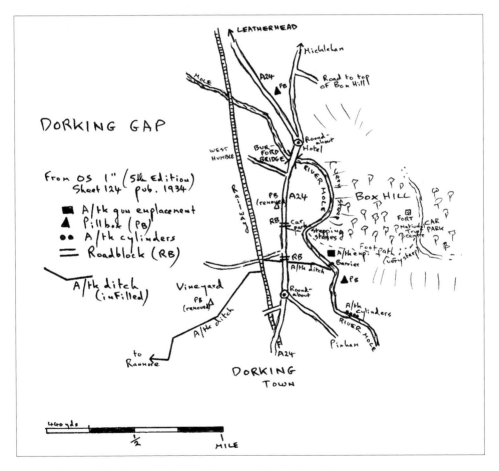

28 Sketch map of the Second World War defence of the Dorking Gap

It was here that I parked my car. The car park is easily missed as it demands a sudden sharp turn off the busy A24 south of the roundabout at Burford Bridge where the road crosses the Mole. If you walk south down the A24 you pass Bradley Lane on your right and some houses on your left. The southern roadblock was here, and the anti-tank ditch cut through the trees just beyond the houses on its course towards the Mole. If you cross the A24 (be very careful – the traffic here moves as if on a race track) and walk down Bradley Lane you come to the railway line at the point where concrete blocks and steel hairpins (the latter a bent steel rail affixed to a concrete base) once lined both sides of the track. The anti-tank ditch ran off at an angle to the south-west across land now occupied by a vineyard.

In view to the south are houses of the outer suburbs of Dorking which have spread here in the period since the war. Dorking was a Category 'A' nodal point in a vital position blocking the southern approaches to the vital pass (the Dorking Gap) through the North Downs. This would have been an important route for the German forces on their drive towards London, as had already been anticipated in the nineteenth century.

I retraced my steps along the roaring A24. You might like to keep on the road for a short distance beyond the track to the stepping stones. Where it begins a gradual bend to the right was the point on the northbound carriageway where the storage of vehicles, arms, and ammunition for the D-Day landings began, continuing for several hundred yards to the north. Temporary huts and other shelters were erected on the road surface. The road was still being used for this purpose in August 1944 as the evidence of air photographs of that date shows. Many other stretches of road in the South of England, in particular the dual carriageways around London built in the 1930s, were used in this way.

It was a gloomy, drizzling spring day when I came to the stepping stones across the Mole and found that the river, swollen by recent rains, was washing over them. This was an ancient route, now termed the Pilgrims' Way, although I doubt if any pilgrims ever used it: they would surely have kept to the principal roads (the old Roman roads) rather than slogging along these muddy trackways at the base of the North Downs. I have the feeling the Pilgrims' Way here is an invention of the Victorians.

Whoever had once used the Pilgrims' Way, however, must have been of sterner stuff than me for there was no way I was going to cross the stepping stones with the waters of the Mole gushing about my feet. I took a detour to the north and found a steel footbridge that got me across the river without risk to life or limb. I was now amongst thick trees at the foot of the steep slopes of Box Hill.

29 Anti-tank gun emplacement dug into the steep side of Box Hill

I was not sure of my route and tried several paths, each time in my earnest attempts to find the right one passing a couple in an amorous clinch by the river who must have become convinced I was intent on annoying them. I said nothing: 'Sorry' does not seem the right expression at such a time. To save you any comparable confusion, in order to find the anti-tank gun emplacement (which is what I was seeking) simply follow the bank of the Mole to the right from the footbridge until you come to the stepping stones, and then keep going along the river bank. It is a tricky overgrown path, not really a path at all, but after a few hundred yards you will be rewarded by the sight of a great square embrasure set in brickwork staring down at you from the chalk slope to your left.

I scrambled up this slope with some difficulty on the slippery chalk, supporting myself by grabbing at the branches of bushes on the hillside. At one point my feet slipped away beneath me, and I was left suspended on a bush desperately wrapping my free hand around my camera to keep it away from the dirt. At last I reached the front of the emplacement and peered inside the embrasure. There was the holdfast with its nine bolts for a 6pdr gun. Beyond was a blank brick wall daubed with spray-can graffiti. The tenacity of the vandal in seeking out remote places never ceases to amaze me. Such a quality should be put to worthier causes.

I pulled myself around the side of the emplacement, and found the entrance. What a job it would have been to haul the 6pdr gun into place here. Had this actually been carried out? I thought it probably had. This was a most important position, firing along the eastern length of the anti-tank ditch to the roadblock beneath. If the Germans had forced this pass through the Downs there was little to protect London other than for three rings of anti-tank lines. We shall be looking at the outer of these later.

Behind the pillbox, a brick and concrete revetment had been built to prevent earth and chalk rubble falling from the upper slopes onto the emplacement. So far it had done its job most effectively. But for how much longer, I wondered? Here is a most important structure, evocative of the desperate days of 1940, and complementing the other military building on Box Hill, the nineteenth-century fort. I feel it deserves some form of recognition and protection. There should be at least a mention of it in the National Trust's literature on the Box Hill estate instead of the current total omission.

I scrambled back down the slope to the path and continued my journey along the river bank. I was looking for concrete piles by the river that I knew were somewhere ahead of me. They had been recorded by one of the Defence of Britain Project's most indefatigable volunteers, a sprightly gentleman in his seventies. If he could find them, so could I – but I was beginning to wonder how. The path had disappeared, and I now found myself balanced on the steep slopes above the river, deep amongst prickly bushes, fighting my way through them, then losing my footing and sliding back down to the river on my backside. I arrived in a cascade of chalk pebbles, my trousers thick with mud, and with the passing thought: Why the hell am I doing this?!

And then suddenly what seemed pointless became worthwhile for close to me on the river bank, with the water gurgling almost up to them, was a strange cluster of cylindrical concrete posts sticking out of the mud. Looking across the river I could see there was another group on the far bank. Had they supported a bridge? I thought that was improbable. Much more likely was that cables had been stretched between them to form a barrier across the river. The purpose would have been to prevent the anti-tank ditch being outflanked in any attempt to advance along the river itself. The Germans had proved themselves the masters of river assault crossings during the fighting in France, using special rubber boats for the purpose. In this remote spot, it felt strange looking at these concrete posts and contemplating their role 65 years ago, the form and purpose of which is now all but forgotten. This is probably a unique site amongst the surviving anti-invasion defences of the Second World War.

The anti-tank ditch had crossed the broad green meadow that I could see stretching away on the other side of the river and reached the bank close by. The ditch would not have actually been cut into the river, but a small distance left between the two. Such a gap in the anti-tank line was usually blocked with concrete obstacles, but, if these had been erected here, they had all been cleared away.

I returned to the stepping stones, trying to scrape some of the mud from my knees and elbows on the way – and, yes, the courting couple were still there. They did not seem to have moved, but, as they were still standing up, I presumed they were alive. I did not linger to make sure, but took the path that led up the hill, a very steep route designed to test the fitness of middle-aged men such as myself who like to pretend they are still as active as in their youth. Soon I was blowing like a sea creature rising from the waves. I had a welcome breather at the point where the path passes above the anti-tank gun emplacement I had just visited. From the height here, I could clearly see the line of the anti-tank ditch as a slight hollow crossing the far meadow (*colour plate 9*).

I always find the sight of an infilled anti-tank ditch like this exciting. Here was a great defensive earthwork, built for one of the most critical purposes this country has ever known, and then abandoned almost as soon as it was completed, its line now revealed once more. I find the anti-tank ditches and other earthworks of the anti-invasion defences more compelling than the concrete structures. There seems something timeless about digging the earth for protection, in conformity with the long history of such earthworks over the many centuries. And here was the latest example, almost totally unknown to the modern generation. Talk of the defences of a Roman camp, or the ramparts of an Iron Age hillfort, or the linear banks of the Dark Ages, and you will get some knowing nods from a knowledgeable audience. Archaeologists will have studied them and written books about them. But talk of the hundreds of miles of anti-tank ditches that were dug in the Second World War (by far the greatest system of defensive earthworks the country has ever known) and you will be greeted with blank looks. I think it was in the 1960s that the archaeologist and recorder of Roman roads, I.D. Margary, when investigating the line of Stane Street in the Dorking Gap was confused for a long time by a dark, linear feature he discovered on air photographs: he thought it must be the course of the Roman road. Later he was told by 'someone who knew' that, in fact, it was the in-filled line of the anti-tank ditch crossing the valley floor. This story shows how knowledge is soon lost even in our own age of supposed detailed record.

I resumed my journey up the hill, where my torture was now accentuated by the presence of occasional sections of wood-revetted steps, admittedly of great assistance when descending, but a muscle-destroying series of obstacles when coming up. I reasoned through my gasps for breath that the hill had to end at some time as long as I kept moving upwards, and eventually I staggered my way to the top, emerging by the National Trust visitor centre and car park (you can drive here by a zigzag road from Burford Bridge if you don't wish to emulate my walk) and had a welcome cup of tea and a sticky bun at the adjacent cafe. Then I walked the short distance down the slope beyond the visitor centre to see Box Hill Fort, where there is now an excellent National Trust information board to tell you all about it.

There are three other anti-invasion sites to see around Box Hill, but all three are on private land and difficult to pick out at a distance. Firstly, on the east bank of the Mole a little further upstream from the concrete piles I had visited (but quite impossible to approach along the river unless you are in training for the SAS) is a Type 24 pillbox which is unusual inasmuch as it was made using corrugated iron for the exterior shuttering, and corrugated iron at that placed with the corrugations running vertically rather than the more usual horizontal. Now there's one for the aficionado! If you become hooked by this subject, it's only a matter of time before you too start dwelling with relish on such details.

A few hundred yards further on there is a row of some 12 enormous anti-tank cylinders on the east bank of the Mole, set into a massive concrete base, looking from a distance on a mist-shrouded day like a line of dark-cloaked soldiers passing across the margins of the field. Their purpose was to strengthen the bank of the river, evidently considered at this point not of sufficient height or steepness to serve as an effective anti-tank obstacle. It is a pity that there is no general public access to this site, as the cylinders are a fine example of their type.

The final Second World War structure that survives in the Dorking Gap lies further to the north – north of Burford Bridge, in fact, on the right-hand side of the A24 going towards Leatherhead. It is a brick-shuttered Type 24 pillbox, in a rather dilapidated state, now in an area of new plantation not far from the road. It probably once commanded a roadblock here. If you push up the wooded bank of the road and peer over the wire fence you can just about make it out. I have to confess I did a little bit of trespassing here in order to take some photographs and pinpoint the position of the pillbox with my GPS receiver. The landowner would probably have been gratified to see me trip on the fence on my return, sending me for another muddy slide down the bank towards the road. This day was beginning to tax me, and I still had another area to survey.

I was driving along the A25 road towards Reigate. In Reigate centre I turned onto the busy A217, and after a mile or so came to Sidlow and started looking for a place to park.

I came over a bridge and saw a garage on my right and a turning, which I swept around, and, wonder of wonder, there was a lay-by with a space vacant. I shot into it with a scrunch of gravel, and allowed the line of cars behind me, clearly irritated by my sudden manoeuvre, pass on their way. I let out a sigh of relief. I was parked at Sidlow Bridge. It didn't happen often. You should be aware of this if you come here during the working day. Parking is difficult: you may have to put your car at some distant point and walk back as I had done on a previous visit.

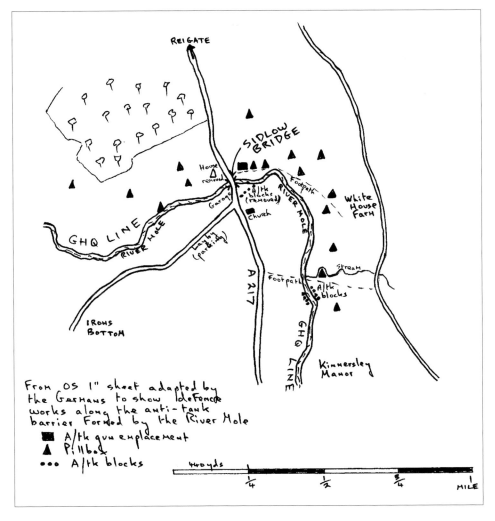

30 Sketch map showing the defences of the GHQ Line at Sidlow Bridge

But here I was, once more on GHQ Line 'B', some 8 miles (as the crow flies) from the Dorking Gap, but several more if following the winding course of the River Mole as the GHQ Line did. Sidlow Bridge was a defended crossing point of the Line, where the A217 road, running like an arrow towards Reigate, was blocked by a roadblock and a bridge that could be blown in an emergency. Anti-tank cubes on the south-east bank of the river further strengthened this defended locality. Pillboxes were set back from the north bank of the river, both to the west and the east of the road. To the west, in fact, there was a concentration of pillboxes, positioned in depth towards the outskirts of Reigate. To the east, they mainly followed the course of the river as it bent towards the south carrying the course of the defence line.

Reigate was an important military centre. Not only was it a Category 'A' nodal point, together with adjacent Redhill, controlling access to the North Downs ridge, beyond which lay the sprawling outer London suburbs, but from 1941 it contained the headquarters of the British Army's South-East Command in a battle headquarters beneath Reigate Hill, comparable with the buried headquarters at Sarre. I have not seen this site, but I understand the concrete tunnels are still there cut into the chalk of the hill. Reigate and Banstead Council might care to consider allowing public access to them as they form an important historic structure. The Council, in fact, has other tunnels in its care since an extensive network of medieval (and later) sand quarry tunnels runs under the town and its castle.

I walked past the garage and peered at the muddy Mole flowing under the road bridge. The river here is some 80ft from bank to bank, and would have formed a considerable obstacle to the German invading forces if the bridge had been destroyed. Fire could have been laid down on the bridge from pillboxes to the north-west (out of sight here with regrettably no access to the land) and also from the east, which we can visit. A footpath on the north-east side of the bridge leads into a field, and you will find here an anti-tank gun emplacement and two Type 24 infantry pillboxes on a slight ridge overlooking the river. The emplacement contains a holdfast for a 6pdr Hotchkiss gun, of the type we have already met at Penshurst and in the Dorking Gap. Cattle now use the emplacement as a shelter, and it is in a fairly unpleasant condition as a consequence. Also unpleasant are the two pillboxes close by which, when I was there, were also being used as shelters – this time by humans. Blankets and a foul-looking sleeping bag were draped around. I did not go in. I was feeling pretty dishevelled myself with the mud of the Dorking Gap still adhering to me, and thought if anyone came by they might think it was me who was squatting here!

The emplacement and the pillboxes had a great deal of their exterior brick-shuttering missing. Sometimes this falls away owing to the effects of frost, or other natural erosion, over the years. Here, however, it looked as if it had been deliberately removed, presumably for the value of the bricks for rebuilding or perhaps as hardcore.

31 Close-up of the pre-cast concrete embrasure of a Sidlow Bridge pillbox

You will find other Type 24 pillboxes, some very overgrown, by the path that leads to White Owl Farm. This farm has been built since the war, although the surrounding field pattern is the same as in 1940. One last thing remains to do at Sidlow, involving something of a trek, but worth it to see the type of defence we could not get to earlier below Box Hill – anti-tank blocks supporting a river bank.

If you walk south down the busy A217 passing the Victorian church on your left (it was damaged by bombing during the war), you come to a crossing of footpaths at the top of a slight rise. Take the left hand of these, and you will be on a path crossing broad pasture land. A pillbox is tucked away in a loop of a stream (a tributary of the Mole) on your left, but bear across the field to your right following the river and you will come to some 36 pyramid-topped anti-tank cubes, about 18 on each bank. This is a remarkable survival tucked away in this lonely spot. The river was clearly considered to be insufficient as an anti-tank obstacle at this point so the banks were strengthened with concrete blocks.

32 South of Sidlow Bridge, concrete blocks on both banks strengthen the anti-tank obstacle of the River Mole

One can see the contractors working here to construct these blocks, bearing their equipment from the road along the path you have followed, always mindful of the needs of camouflage so as not to make too obvious a trail, and casting the blocks in situ here beneath the trees by the river – a scene of busy, urgent work, the reason and purpose of which is now virtually forgotten. Indeed, much of the subject has already descended into myth, which popular TV programmes and magazine articles do much to perpetrate. Common is the idea that the anti-invasion defences were pretty useless, and would not have kept out a hay cart let alone a German tank. Other myths have it that pillboxes were badly sited and were often built carelessly around the wrong way, or that they were constructed more as a sop to keep civilian morale up rather than for any useful military purpose.

The way these myths have originated and spread, even perhaps before the war was over, is extraordinary. They have much to do with that facet of the British character that says that in military affairs we tend to make a mess of things before, by some miracle usually provided by the navy or the air force, whose professionalism is grudgingly admitted, we eventually muddle through. And yet such an argument does not hold up when confronted by reality. We may have had our early defeats in war, but we have beaten enemy after enemy over the last 200 years (the great powers: France, Russia and Germany) and on top of that there have been all the colonial wars we have fought in every quarter of the globe. Our armies had become vastly experienced and battle hardened. Our various technical corps, of which the Royal Engineers is one, responsible amongst many other duties for the construction of field fortifications, had – and still have – a particular world-wide reputation for their professionalism. There was absolutely no way when defending our homeland (still at the time the head of the greatest empire the world had ever seen) that we were going to go to the vast effort of constructing defence works that were virtually useless or built just to make the civilian population feel more secure.

The main problems in 1940 were shortage of weapons and building materials, given the fact that we had just suffered a massive defeat in France and were in the process of building up our war economy in order to combat the greatest threat to our survival that this country has ever faced. That it was all a perilously close-run thing is very true. That it was done by old men with pitchforks, or effete officers who didn't know which way round a pillbox should stand, is pure mythology, the stuff of popular TV programmes, but not of history.

11

RIVER MEDWAY AT MAIDSTONE TO HOO, NORTH KENT

In order to remain on the GHQ Line, we are next going to travel to North-West Kent, although this was not the exact order in which I undertook the survey. When I came to Maidstone, and then continued on to the Hoo peninsula by the estuary of the River Medway, it was high summer and very hot, not the grey, drizzling spring day I have just described at the Dorking Gap and Sidlow Bridge.

The months of October through to March are, in fact, the best times in which to do this type of field survey work. Many sites are so heavily overgrown that it is difficult enough finding them in winter. When they are covered by summer leaves, and surrounded by high, rank vegetation, they can be virtually impossible to locate or approach. Fields in winter are also usually fallow, or newly ploughed, and in this condition farmers will generally not mind a brief foray across them to inspect a pillbox. When newly planted, or with growing arable crops, however, the situation is quite different, and under no circumstances should you cross land in crop. As many pillboxes were built alongside hedgerows, there is usually little harm, however, in walking at the edge of a field if this can be done without causing any damage to the crop. Always ask, if you can – at a nearby farmhouse for instance: you will probably be directed to the right person if it is not their land. In remote locations, however, where no building, or no person, is in sight, I will normally approach a pillbox if it is no great distance from a road or footpath and I am clearly doing no harm. It is all about common sense, responsibility, and judgement. But, however careful you feel you are being, never forget it is not your land. You should not be there; there is no doubt of that. If you are caught unexpectedly (as has happened to me on a few occasions) then always make a point of apologising first. This usually disarms even an angry landowner. I have never met with any real unpleasantness, indeed just the opposite: most landowners are usually very interested in the subject, and may be keen to help.

As I say, it was a hot summer's day when I drove to Maidstone, the old county town of Kent standing on the River Medway, which has now widened enormously from the infant stream that we saw at Penshurst. The Medway is tidal, in fact, as far as Allington Lock, close to the northern outskirts of Maidstone. I was heading there, or hoped I was, having left the M20 and taken the old A20 road towards the city centre. By a stroke of good fortune I saw a road on my left called Castle Road, and swung left. I knew there was a castle at Allington: hopefully this would be the way towards it. I crossed the railway line, and on my right found a beautiful car park by a recreation ground, which was not signposted at all. All car parks seem beautiful when you are not sure where you are and are looking desperately for somewhere to leave your car.

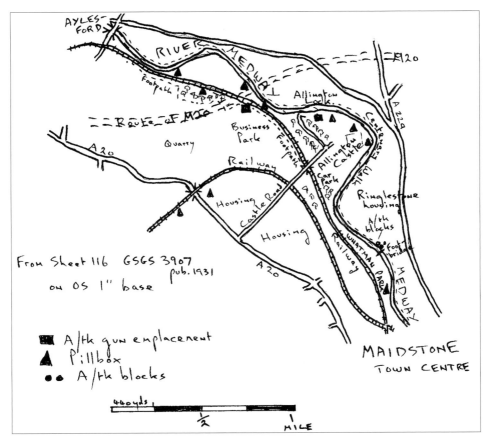

33 Sketch map showing the defences along the River Medway, north of Maidstone

I gathered my equipment together, put on my boots, consulted my map, and set forth. The heat hit me like a wall. This was going to be exhausting work. I wended my way along a path that ran beside the railway line sandwiched between it and an industrial estate to my left. I could hear the roar of traffic ahead of me, and emerged from trees to a sudden vista of a blazing white expanse of concrete studded with whirling, coloured steel chariots – the M20 as it crossed the Medway on a broad new bridge. To my left, tucked away amongst the trees and half buried by earth and rubble, was a 6pdr anti-tank gun emplacement. For this is the GHQ Line once more, the Newhaven to Cliffe branch that we have followed across the Weald at Barcombe and Old Lodge Warren, and saw approaching Penshurst from the south. The Medway had carried the Line all the way from Penshurst, the anti-tank obstacle provided by the river becoming ever broader. It passed through the centre of Maidstone, which in 1940-1 was a designated fortress with a garrison of 985 men, mostly from the Home Guard but with some detachments as well of regular troops. North of Maidstone, the GHQ Line continued from the perimeter defences of the fortress, still following the river, passed through Allington and wound its way west and then north by the Medway Valley through the North Downs. We shall pick its course up later at Hoo.

The anti-tank gun emplacement I was standing by was in poor condition, so deep in earth and accumulated rubbish that I had to bend double to get inside and inspect its 6pdr holdfast. As I walked further west following the river and the railway, I found Type 24 pillboxes, all terribly overgrown, so I could scarcely see them beneath the summer growth even when close up. I crossed the river by a new bridge at Aylesford, seeing its famous medieval bridge, happily now preserved from traffic, shimmering in a haze of heat some 200yds further to the west. I topped up with bottled water at a newsagent's shop, and took the towpath on the north bank, now heading back towards Allington and Maidstone. I passed decaying wharfs and half-sunken barges, sad remnants of the days, now long passed, when the river was a great commercial highway, and many businesses and warehouses lined its banks.

After what seemed a very long way, with the coolness of the slow moving, muddy waters to my right looking increasingly inviting, I came to Allington Lock. It's possible to cross the river here over the lock gates, and, as I did so, I spotted another anti-tank gun emplacement on the far bank, seeming to my heated imagination like a great, grey whale stranded beside the frothing waters of the lock. The emplacement is used as a store by the Environment Agency, who manage Allington Lock, with a wooden door now in place across the entrance, and the main embrasure and side light machine-gun embrasures blocked off.

I returned across the river to the towpath. From here towards Maidstone it is known as the Centenary Walk, part of a grandly titled, recently opened Millennium River Park. Certainly the surface of the towpath was now much improved as befitted its new status, for which I was grateful as I was becoming increasingly footsore in the heat. I passed a pub on the river bank, seeing customers lounging outside on wooden benches nursing their pints of frosted lager. I took a quick sip of water. Sometimes I did wonder about this job, blundering about the landscape looking for concrete defences while the rest of the world seemed to be reclining at its leisure. My turn would come later, I told myself!

My records showed that there were infantry pillboxes around the lock and the castle, which stood a little further upstream. Allington Castle was rebuilt in the Victorian period as a grand house, and is now occupied by an order of Carmelite friars: I did not have permission to enter the grounds. There are possibly pillboxes close to the river both to the north and south of the castle, but I could see nothing through the trees lining the river as I peered across from the opposite bank. Other pillboxes on the west bank of the river that I had located on air photographs seemed to have been removed, although I could not be totally sure looking from a distance.

I had not yet determined where I would set the southern boundary of this defence area, and I kept on walking as I had records of more pillboxes and some anti-tank blocks to the south. I was unsure what I would find, and it was a surprise when a bright blue, tubular steel footbridge spanning the river suddenly came into view, in the shade of which were some of the most massive anti-tank cubes I have ever seen, each about 6ft high and 6ft wide. Five cubes standing now almost underneath the bridge ran in two lines towards a new housing estate that looked out over the river, while three cubes in a single line lay a short distance further to the west. One of these, made with corrugated-iron shuttering, stood at the very edge of the towpath (*colour plate 10*). These blocks lie on what was the northern defence perimeter of Maidstone fortress, and were part of the anti-tank defences at the point where the perimeter met the river and the GHQ Line following its course. They make an impressive reminder of the strength of the Maidstone defences.

I climbed the high river bank by a zigzag path and crossed the footbridge, entering the recently created Whatman Park that occupies the site of former water meadows on the west bank of the Medway. This is a bright wonderland of paths, flights of steps, terraces, pavilions, and foaming white fountains, with a coloured tapestry of gardens stretching down to the river. Three pillboxes were built in this area between the river front and the railway line bordering the park. I asked a young lad weeding a flower bed if he knew where the pillboxes were, and he directed me without hesitation towards one. I found it carefully preserved in a shrubbery, with its entrance and embrasures blocked. The helpful lad ('It's my first day in this job', he told me) thought there was another pillbox somewhere, but I could not find it. A third I knew had been in an area now covered by a skateboard park, so I was left to assume it had either been destroyed or buried.

I wanted to linger in the shade, watching people with more energy than myself pass with children and dogs under the hot sun. However, time was pressing on and I had to bestir myself. It was a long way back to my car.

Later that day I came to Hoo on the North Kent coast. The village of Hoo, now more of a small town than a village, lies close to the west bank of the Medway estuary, north of the cathedral town of Rochester and the once great naval shipyards of Chatham. It is on a broad peninsula that ends in marshlands bordering the River Thames, which to the east becomes the Isle of Grain – a bleak flatland of petrochemical works and cooling towers, with many scattered relics of England's coast defences over the last 200 years. The road from Rochester to the Isle of Grain is the busy A228, which as it passes to the north-west of Hoo is called (for reasons unknown to me) the Ratcliffe Highway.

It was through this landscape that the GHQ Line, which we have followed at Barcombe Mills, Old Lodge Warren, and Maidstone, ran to meet the Thames. North of the river, the Line commenced again, crossing Essex and Cambridgeshire on its way to the North of England. The Hoo peninsula, however, was the point where it left the South-East of England, having protected the approaches to London from German forces advancing from the East Kent coast.

The Ratcliffe Highway was being widened. A strip of earth to one side of the road was being worked by machinery. Cones and tattered hazard strips littered the verge. I passed signs to the left for Chattenden Barracks and Lodge Hill Camp. The Royal School of Military Engineering is now based at the site occupied during the war by a Royal Naval Ammunition Depot. On the rise of a ridge, I came abruptly to a crossroads, and swung off to the right. The road works were at their busiest here. It looked like this dangerous junction was about to be replaced by something much safer, probably a roundabout. I knew one of the pillboxes I had come to see stood here, and I would be able to record it shortly before it was destroyed.

I drove down the side road to Hoo, passing a housing estate to my right which stood on the site of a former army camp (Kingshill Camp) closed down in the 1970s. In Hoo I found a small car park and consulted my maps. The GHQ Line had run from the bank of the Medway close to Hoo across the Isle of Grain peninsula, reaching the River Thames at Cliffe and Higham Marshes. For this

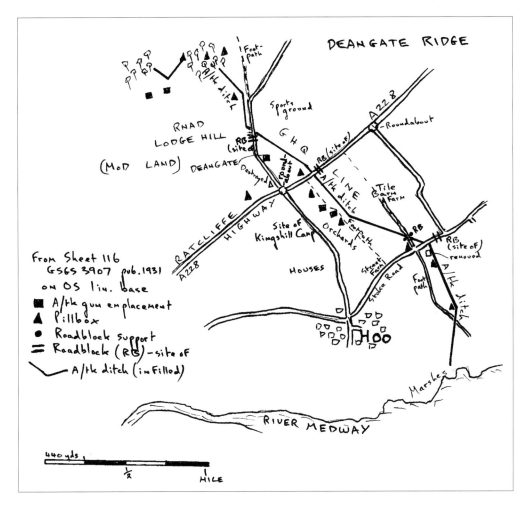

34 Sketch map showing the defences at the Deangate Ridge, north of Hoo

sector between the two rivers the main anti-tank obstacle had been a machine-dug ditch.

It seemed even hotter here than at Maidstone as I set out to find what survived of the 1940 defences. I walked along Stoke Road leading east from Hoo through a flat landscape of orchards and fields with the square shape of a power station, surrounded by chimneys and pylons, seen through the heated air in the distance. Beyond Street Farm, with its caravan park that my records said hid a pillbox, I came to a track leading off on the left. Here, beside an electricity sub-station, was a Type 24 pillbox of a design unique to this area where the brick-shuttering was not carried above the embrasures, leaving the concrete like a long grey scar in each face.

35 Supporting block for a horizontal rail roadblock east of Hoo

I walked further along the track and found the particular site I was seeking – concrete support blocks that had held the horizontal rails of a roadblock, a rare survival anywhere in the country. The blocks had evidently survived because they were at the side of a minor route and had not been considered an obstruction when they fell out of use. On busier roads these concrete supports for roadblocks generally impeded on the pavements and carriageway and were usually removed even before the war was over. The blocks here had a vertical groove in the face fronting the track. Into this, one or more steel rails (RSJs – rolled steel joists), would have been slotted in the event of an emergency. They were kept by the roadside for this purpose and were manhandled into position.

I was carrying a copy of a German map that marked the site of the roadblock and the course of the anti-tank ditch, all observed by the Luftwaffe in the summer of 1940. The ditch had crossed the track diagonally at the roadblock, and run to the north-west across the field I was now gazing at. A couple of horses returned my stare curiously. Yes, I could see the ditch! It had been infilled at the end of the war, but the soil had settled and I could make out its slight hollow crossing the field towards me as straight as an arrow.

It was unmistakable. As at the Dorking Gap, I found the sight exciting: it seemed to bring this defended landscape of 65 years ago vividly to life. The ditch would have been some 10ft deep and 15ft wide at the top, probably with the spoil from its construction piled as a rampart on its defended side, or just possibly on both sides. The whole excavated strip would have been some 50ft wide stretching for mile after mile across the countryside. Anti-tank ditches did untold damage to agriculture, dividing farms and cutting off livestock from their grazing fields. Sometimes temporary wooden bridges were erected by the Army to help the farmers. It has to be remembered that farming and food production was a state-directed operation during the war, as vital to the nation's survival as any other front-line activity.

There had been a roadblock on Stoke Road as well a few yards further to the south where it was crossed by the anti-tank ditch, but all evidence of this block had long since been cleared away. On the far side of the road, the anti-tank ditch ran just to the east of the track that runs from here to the banks of the Medway. Close to the house that stands at the corner of road and track was an anti-tank gun emplacement, destroyed in recent years.

I retraced my steps along Stoke Road until I reached Street Farm again, and took the right of way that passed the farm shop and a little further on became a path running at the edge of a field with an orchard on the left. The anti-tank ditch I had just followed as a hollow crossed the field diagonally from my right before turning to run parallel with the path I was on a few yards into the field. Through one of the gaps into the orchard I found a Type 24 pillbox, and a little beyond it a rectangular anti-tank gun emplacement, brick-shuttered, with its wide entrance now closed with a door. After 20yds or so, I came upon a further anti-tank gun emplacement buried in the hedge, and then another Type 24 pillbox: there was no access to either of these.

This concentration of defence works indicates the strategic importance of this section of the GHQ Line, defending against an attack from the east consequent upon a German landing on the Isle of Grain or on the marshes bordering the River Thames. With the Chatham naval dockyards to the south and the war production industry of the Medway Valley beyond, the area was vitally important. Nearly 300 years earlier the Dutch fleet had penetrated the English defences here and burnt the king's flagship at anchor. The disgrace had rocked the nation at the time. In 1940, every effort was made to see that something similar (or much worse) did not happen again.

In addition to the defences of the GHQ Line, Hoo itself was a 'defended village' with a garrison of some 60 men from the 14th Bn, Kent Home Guard. Kingshill Camp (the site of which we have already seen) was a designated defended locality manned by 100 regular troops. Another defended locality was around the village of High Halstow a short distance to the north, with a garrison of over 300 men of the Royal West Kents. The area was additionally protected to the west by the defences of the Royal Naval Ammunition Dump at Lodge Hill, which were manned by a further 300 men with 11 medium machine guns, a high number of this weapon given the shortages after Dunkirk. All in all, it was one of the most militarised areas that we shall come to in our travels.

I reached the Ratcliffe Highway with its thundering traffic, being almost swept off the road by the rush of air from the great HGVs as they passed. Another roadblock had stood where the anti-tank ditch crossed this road. On the far side of the road, earth moving machinery was busy at work. The roadworks were just beyond the line of the anti-tank ditch, otherwise it might very well have been revealed by the removal of the topsoil. It would have stood out as a strip of darker soil against the brown clay that I could see being thrown up all around me.

I walked for a short distance by the road, and then plunged off into a thicket on my right. There were two sites here – a Type 24 pillbox and, next to it, a buried Royal Observer Corps monitoring station from the days of the Cold War, its ventilation shafts and entrance hatch still visible. It was closed as recently as 1991. I braved the rest of the walk by the side of the road until I came to the crossroads that were to be converted into a roundabout. A Type 24 pillbox with the distinctive concrete cut outs above the embrasures stood here: this was the one doomed to destruction in the road widening. I took a photograph and bade it a solemn farewell: it had stood for a long time protecting these crossroads.

36 Type 24 pillbox on Deangate Ridge

I turned up the lane running to the north. The defence line was over to my right crossing the fields on its way to join the lane ahead of me. I knew there was an unusual anti-tank gun emplacement to see here, and I found it attached to Deangate Cottage beside the lane. A terrace neatly fringed by wooden fencing had been built on the emplacement's roof by the house owners, one of 101 modern uses Second World War defence works have been put to – sheds, summer houses, cricket sight-screens, cattle shelters, the bases for radio masts, booking offices, public latrines, and so on. The main embrasure of the emplacement still faced defiantly north, pointing towards yet another roadblock where the anti-tank ditch had crossed to run on the left side of the lane. Here I was close to the eastern boundary of the Lodge Hill training area. I could see its high steel fence like a sharp, black knife cutting through the trees.

Where the lane turned sharply to the right, I took a bridleway that ran up a low hill ahead. It was cooler here with a breeze that stirred the grasses by the track. I could see a pillbox to my left, standing high on a raised concrete base amongst a clump of trees. Other pillboxes were dotted around woodland ahead of me where the GHQ Line had made a bend to the west. There was no access to any of these sites, which lay close to the modern military fence that I could see slicing across the green fields. I was too tired to walk much further anyhow.

I looked out from the hill to the north where I could see the broad waters of the River Thames shimmering in the sun and beyond the flat shores of Essex where the GHQ Line continued its journey. We shall be going there in due course, but not today; certainly not today. All I wanted now was to get back to my car and find something to drink. I had foolishly left all my water in the car, back across the roaring hell-run of the Ratcliffe Highway. I did the return journey feeling like a traveller in the desert with the lure of water as an oasis on the horizon. Never has bottled Tesco's water tasted so good! Tomorrow I would be heading towards the outskirts of London itself, the focus of all these defences we have seen in the South-East – the capital of the British Empire at war with Nazi Germany, and in 1940 in danger of catastrophic defeat.

12

DRIFT BRIDGE (SURREY) TO CHESHUNT (HERTFORDSHIRE), OUTER LONDON

The prime objective of the invading German forces would have been the capture of London. The system of defence put in place from June 1940 recognised this fact, protecting London by a series of stop lines, including the GHQ Line, from attacks from landings on the South and East coasts. The stop lines were also designed to prevent encircling movements by the enemy forces to the north and west of the outer London suburbs.

London, the heart of nation and empire, was protected further by three concentric encircling anti-tank lines. The outer of these was known as Line 'A' and ran for some 121 miles around London on a route approximating in some places to that of the present M25. Approximately 5 miles further in ran the Centre Line (Line 'B'), and lastly there was the Inner Line (Line 'C') which protected the heart of the City and Whitehall and ran to the north of the Thames only, with the river itself as its south boundary.

The Outer London Line was developed as a continuous obstacle, making use of rivers, canals, and machine-dug ditches along its course, with a series of roadblocks covered by pillboxes and fortified houses. It was to one of the sections of this line that I was heading now – to the area of the Drift Bridge near Epsom where the suburbs meet the Surrey countryside on the southern fringes of London.

On a summer's day, which was the season when I came to the Drift Bridge, the London suburban traffic is very busy, the roads hot and congested, the people tired and ill-tempered, longing to turn south towards the countryside but condemned to drive these bitter, boiling roads forever. I know this area well. Years ago I had driven through the junction at the Drift Bridge every day on my way to work. But I had not known then that it had stood on the Outer London Anti-Tank

Line. Would I have cared about that anyhow in those halcyon, dreamlike days of the 1960s? Probably, for I had grown up very much aware of pillboxes and dragon's teeth. In the area of Surrey in which our family had lived they had been all about us. We had had picnics perched on concrete blocks by streams where fields of dragon's teeth lined the banks. As horrible, scrapping little boys we had fought battles in pillboxes, attacked them with Molotov cocktails – bottles filled with petrol like the Home Guard had prepared 15 years earlier. Where had we learnt about these things? Probably at school. They were the days when boys brought .303 rounds into the classroom, when we played war games in the playground, throwing stone grenades at each other. We knew all the movements, all the combat crawls in the infantry manual. It was part of the world around us. Our fathers who had served on the battlefields of the Second World War were only then in their mid-thirties. The war was still very immediate and very real.

I had passed the Drift Bridge in my white MG Midget all those years ago little thinking that I would return one day to record the lumps of concrete from the Second World War that remained there at the beginning of the twenty-first century. So, wondering a little at the strange quirks of life, I parked my car in a narrow space by a parade of busy shops in Ruden Way, and walked back to the A240 Reigate road. The area here is known as the Drift Bridge after a bridge which carries the railway line from Epsom Downs Station to central London on a high embankment over the A240. Various roads also converge close to the Drift Bridge, one leading off towards Epsom, only a mile and a half away at the foot of the chalk downs where the famous Derby is held. But why *Drift* Bridge? That, I'm afraid, I don't know, although I'm sure any number of local historians will be ready to supply an answer.

The Outer London Anti-Tank Line had followed the railway embankment at the Drift Bridge, protecting the approaches to the capital from the south. Even though the embankment is some 20ft high, it was still considered necessary to dig an anti-tank ditch at its base on its inner (northern) side. A roadblock stood on the south side of the bridge, and another blocked the Epsom road at its junction close by.

I passed a car showroom and walked under the bridge, the traffic thundering by alongside me. On the far side was what I was looking for – lines of anti-tank blocks (or cubes) which had continued the anti-tank ditch to the roadside. On the right-hand side of the road they ran through a wood, overgrown and disappearing beneath bushes and creeper, each block about 4ft high and 4ft wide, and only about 2ft from its neighbour (*colour plate 11*). What a sight this was in such a built-up landscape. Together with the pillboxes close by that we shall be looking at, they had only survived because north of the Drift Bridge there is still an area of woodland, fields, and market gardens which development has not yet removed. I can see this land being built upon at some future date, however. It must have a tremendous value sandwiched here at the edge of the London suburbs.

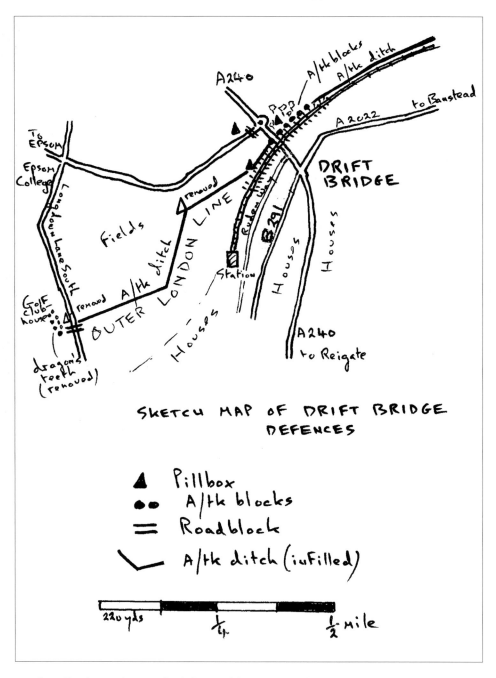

37 *Above:* Sketch map showing the defences of the Outer London Anti-tank Line at the Drift Bridge near Epsom

38 *Opposite:* The Drift Bridge railway bridge

I inspected the woodland more closely. Through the trees I could see a dark shape festooned with vegetation. Possibly that was a pillbox, almost entirely hidden by the overgrowth. Another pillbox, buried under a clump of bushes, stood in a field on the far side of the road to Epsom. My records told me there should be a further one in a field north of the main road that passed under the bridge, and I took my life in my hands and did an Olympics sprint in front of the wheels of the advancing traffic. A conveniently sagging strand of barbed wire allowed me access to the field, and I walked thankfully away from the road into a cooler area of grassland where a few ponies grazed. Perhaps I should have sought out permission, but I was not going to go very far or do any harm.

This field had been traversed by the anti-tank ditch which left the railway embankment and crossed it in a series of angled lengths. I could see its hollow running at the foot of the embankment. At the point where the ditch changed course towards the centre of the field stood the pillbox. It was overgrown, with rubbish piled against it, but it was unmistakably a Type 27.

39 Overgrown and half-buried Type 27 pillbox at the Drift Bridge

Although otherwise relatively rare in the grand gallery of pillboxes, Type 27s were constructed fairly widely on the Outer London Line. The type was a large pillbox normally with eight faces (but occasionally only six), each with an embrasure for ground defence, but with an open well additionally at the centre with a mount for a machine gun firing in an anti-aircraft role. It was usually entered through a covered porch which served as well as a blast wall, and entry to the central well was through steel doors opening from the pillbox interior. So the example I was standing before was an important structure despite its dilapidated condition, with rusting sheets of corrugated iron pressed against it and earth heaped around to the height of the embrasures. It would have had a crew of as many as 10 men, and, as with other pillboxes, would have been surrounded by slit trenches and barbed wire. Now it sat mouldering in this field, its moment of purpose virtually forgotten.

Next, I wanted to look at an area to the west of the Drift Bridge that I had studied on air photographs where I had seen a veritable forest of dragon's teeth arranged in rows. These had been at a point where the anti-tank ditch had crossed the B288 road leading to Epsom Downs. I returned to my car and drove through the Drift Bridge, turning onto the Epsom road, and then taking the first left by Epsom College. The defence line had crossed the playing fields of the school. I had read that the boys had helped dig anti-airlanding trenches across their sports fields, which must have introduced a few new rules into the games of rugby and cricket in the seasons of 1940 and 1941.

The road I was following began to rise and I came to the clubhouse of a golf course on the right. I had seen this tall, brick building on air photographs with lines of anti-tank pimples curving towards it. Where shiny, expensive cars were now parked, the dragon's teeth had stood in long rows. On the opposite side of the road, I could see the gap between the houses through which the anti-tank ditch had passed running up to a roadblock at this spot. Standing in the sun, with my camera and my recording gear, with golfers coming to their cars from the nineteenth hole, I found this place very atmospheric. I could see the great ditch slicing through the white chalk, the soldiers manning the barriers, the construction workers casting the rows of great concrete teeth. And all the noise and movement of a nation at war, the vapour trails in the sky, the crash of anti-aircraft guns on the Downs, the boys on their bikes looking upwards excitedly, the air-raid wardens in their steel helmets. Today it all seems an age away, yet there are many still alive who have lived through those days. What do they think now, I wonder, of the sacrifices of the war that have made modern Britain possible? There have been such changes in our society that the Britain of 1940 seems to have disappeared beyond comprehension. The concrete remains I was recording appeared to me to form a tangible link with the past, a positive certainty in a time of ever-growing unease.

It was in the summer of 2003 that I came to Cheshunt, on the hottest day ever recorded in Britain – over 100 degrees Fahrenheit in the shade. The heat was like a burning steel barrier set between the earth and the sky. Everything seemed to go into slow motion, except the traffic, that is, blasting along the A10.

The defence area north of Cheshunt was also on the Outer London Anti-Tank Line, but this time north of London in Hertfordshire. As the crow flies, it was almost diametrically opposite the Drift Bridge some 30 miles to the south, and yet I was on the same encircling defence line, such is the size of London and its suburbs. I left the A10 and entered a nightmare world I could not get out of – long suburban streets with little roundabouts with names to places I had never heard of and could not recall from my map; and nowhere to stop and get my bearings. This place I was in (wherever it was) did not seem to have any boundaries; it just went on forever, and all remembrance of time and place was becoming lost.

I switched up the air conditioning and got a grip on the situation. At last I found the road I was seeking (the B156) going the way I wanted (not to Waltham Abbey or Wormley or Nazeing, or any of those other places that have little meaning to those of us who grew up to the south of London), and after a while I found a side-road that was on my large-scale map, Park Lane. It was narrow, with at first more even smaller roundabouts, then it ran (rather surprisingly, I thought, after all the dense suburbs) through countryside that stretched away to the right. I knew I was close now to my defence area, but I could see nowhere to park in the narrow road. Every time I tried to halt in a roadside pull-off, I found it was a drive to a grand, sprawling bungalow, surrounded by manicured gardens, and with high gates and fences controlled by a security system that would not have been out of place in war-torn Baghdad.

In desperation I turned left, and at last came to a wide place on a corner where I could leave the car, right by a green footpath sign. I sat on a log in the shade and contemplated my maps. My journey had worked out well after all. All I had to do was to walk through Thunderfield Grove ahead of me and I would come to the landscape crossed by the anti-tank line. After the frantic drive, a welcome calm descended on me. This area, despite the heat, was going to be good and it was going to be easy. I had had enough for the time being of scrambling up hillsides and ferreting about on river banks. My premonition was to prove partly right and partly wrong. It certainly proved an excellent defence area, and it was flat, and access was relatively good, but the amount of walking I had to do on the hottest day in the history of time certainly made it memorable.

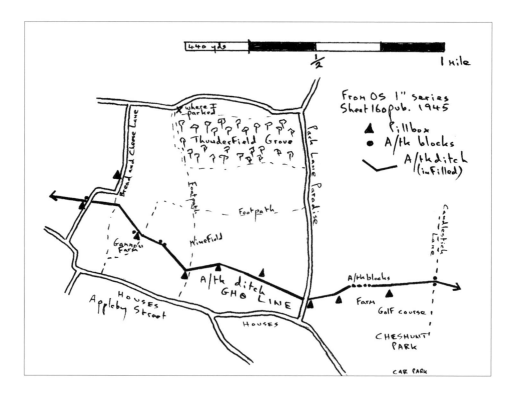

Thunderfield Wood is a nature reserve. I walked beneath the cooling trees, and came down a gentle slope to cross a stream by a plank bridge. Everything was still in the heat: even the birds had given up singing. I crossed a broad track. This had once been a lane leading to the delightfully, and possibly appropriately, named Gammon Farm. Ahead of me now was a long grassy slope. The anti-tank ditch, running at right angles from left to right, had crossed these fields in sharp-angled lengths, with a pillbox at each change of direction. I spied one in front of me now, to the left of the path. As I came up to it, I saw it was a Type 27 as at the Drift Bridge. This was the favoured pillbox type of the Outer London Line (*colour plate 12*).

The pillbox had a loopholed blast wall, serving as an entry porch, on its south side. I doubled up and went in. Small embrasures pierced each of the eight faces. Holes above the embrasures must have allowed the gun fumes to escape. Set in one face of the concrete wall running around the interior of the pillbox was a steel door approached by a short length of iron-rung ladder. This was the way to the central well, which had an upper lip slightly higher than the surrounding roof of the pillbox. At the centre was a concrete pedestal, with a steel fitting at its top, on which a Bren gun or Lewis gun would have been mounted for anti-aircraft fire. The pillbox was impressive, very well constructed and fitted out. This had been a strong position, and there were others positioned to right and left every few hundred yards.

40 Opposite: Sketch map showing the Outer London Anti-tank Line near Cheshunt

41 Above: Trailing ivy through the embrasure of a Type 27 pillbox near Cheshunt. The hole in the wall to the right was for the gases of the firing LMGs to escape

A little further up the slope I found the next pillbox, overgrown in a hedgerow at a corner of the anti-tank ditch where it had made a sudden 'V' to the south. And, by pacing the straw-like grass of the field to the left, I found another one, with a shed built against it beside a paddock full of horses. I returned to the footpath, and stood in the shade of some bushes by a stile. The heat was oppressive. The sun hammered down as if yellow beams were being physically pile-driven into the earth. There was no one about. I seemed to be the only thing moving in this landscape of field and hedge. Ahead of me I could see the roofs of houses. So I was not far from people. They must be lurking in the relative cool of their living rooms, or perhaps under sunshades in the garden. 'Only mad dogs and Englishmen ….' The words trailed unwanted through my head. I am not a great one for hot sun, and become easily irritated by excitable weather forecasters who regard it as the only sort of weather people should enjoy. Now I was the one who was out and about in it, and no one else was!

Concentrating once more on the reason I was here, I cast my eyes to the line of the ridge running away to my right and saw a row of some 10 anti-tank blocks running along a hedgerow. Such a line of blocks in support of an artificial anti-tank ditch was unusual. I wondered why it was considered necessary to construct them here. Unfortunately, there was no access, without considerable trespass, to the field where they stood, although I didn't really think on this hot, still day anyone was going to jump out shouting at me. But it was best to be responsible. The sight of these additional concrete defences reminded me that this section of the Outer London Anti-Tank Line had been mined as well. You tend to think of land mines being placed on the coast at the head of the beaches, but anti-tank mines were also used on inland stop lines, often being placed at roadblocks or around particular pillboxes standing at vulnerable points of the defence line.

I knew the positions of the minefields here, which a document at The National Archives had given me. There had been one at the point where the footpath came up the ridge. I had walked right through it, which gave me a momentary sensation of apprehension. As I have written earlier, I have found documentary evidence that the clearance of minefields was not always all that thorough. But I didn't recall reading about any ramblers who had disappeared in a cloud of earth in the middle of the countryside!

I was beginning to enjoy this tract of countryside crossed by the defence line. The blue sky and waving grass, and the long, droning heat, were lulling me into reflection. So here had been set the outer defence of London whose centre lay 15 miles to the south. These fields had been torn apart by the earth-moving machinery, the ditches scarring the green slopes, the army of construction workers building the pillboxes and the anti-tank blocks, the soldiers laying the mines, all under the Luftwaffe's constant watch in the sky. And then the defended landscape had been precisely measured, ranges and arcs of fire had been calculated – a battlefield was prepared, a 'battlefield that nearly was'.

I had found a document which listed the section posts of the 2nd/8th Bn Middlesex Regiment a little further to the east. One entry reads:

> H platoon area. Section 1. Section position: corner of field in front of hedge in front of stack 30 degrees west of black barn with corrugated-iron roof. Arcs, right: hangar – left: three white posts.

Yes, the ground was measured and death calculated in degrees and inches. Everything was prepared for battle. The gentle vista before me might have become a battlefield. Today that fact seems so incredible that people don't take the concept seriously, preparing to think of the period in terms of comic old men playing at soldiers in the Home Guard. One thing is certain: 1940 wasn't a game, a pretence, or a bluff. It was very real. And it very nearly happened.

At Gammon Farm I found some more anti-tank blocks and a smaller pillbox – a simple hexagonal Type 22, insignificant alongside those mighty Type 27s. A little further to the west is the wonderfully named Bread and Cheese Lane – one can only wonder at how it came to be given this name. Perhaps it was where the bread and cheese was brought out to the men working in the fields. Someone will undoubtedly know.

A rather overgrown Type 27 with a single anti-tank cube beside it (almost certainly the site of a roadblock) stood at one point of the lane, but the pillbox I really wanted to see was a little further to the north around a sharp-cornered double bend. Here where the ridge falls away to the north stood a very tall hexagonal pillbox, with embrasures set high in its walls to allow for a clear field of fire forwards, and also backwards over the crest of the ridge to the rear. This pillbox, a Defence of Britain recorder had told me previously, had been camouflaged as a small house, complete with windows, door, and drainpipe. It is worth coming a distance to see this unusual pillbox. But don't drive down Bread and Cheese Lane: it is very narrow, there are no passing points, and you will definitely be unpopular with the local farmers who use it for their work.

The trouble with stop line defences is that, having explored the line in one direction, you have to return to do the same thing the other way. Bread and Cheese Lane, I had decided, was to be the western border of my defence area, although I knew surviving defences continued beyond that point. Now, how was I going to be able to get to points on the Line in the opposite direction? The answer was the trackway (the former lane) I had crossed previously, which ran parallel with the course of the anti-tank ditch a little to its north. I strolled along it beneath welcome shady trees to Park Lane Paradise, the oddly named road where I had tried to find parking earlier; it seemed an age ago. I now had to walk up this road to where the defence line had crossed it, braving the oncoming traffic, with the faces in the passing cars peering out at me.

Sweating profusely under the heat, with my face and neck beginning to glow a healthy red, I came eventually to the gates of Cheshunt Park Farm at the point where the anti-tank ditch had crossed the road and where there had been a roadblock with lines of concrete cubes on the grass verges. A heavily-overgrown Type 27 pillbox stood by the side of the drive to the farm. The anti-tank line had run right through the farm, and the military engineers had undoubtedly taken advantage of the buildings here to turn the position into a defended locality. Air photographs showed pillboxes and anti-tank cubes around the farm. I had been meaning to anchor the eastern boundary of my defence area here, but my records told me the surviving defence works continued across Cheshunt Park beyond the farm. It might be worth including these if I could only get to them. I looked at my map. Cheshunt Park appeared to be the formal grounds of a great country house, probably (I thought) now demolished. It seemed too far to walk there on this boiling day, so I decided to return to my car and then drive back to see if there was any public access to the area.

42 Extra tall Type 22 pillbox in Bread and Cheese Lane, Cheshunt

It took me a good 40 minutes to retrace my steps to Thunderfield Grove, and I then passed through the shade of the woods to find the car, with the sun full on it, heated like an oven. I flung the doors open and waited for the inside to cool down. It didn't. So I set out once more, roasting gently, this time borne along by a turbo-charged engine to boost my own flagging energy. Off Park Lane, I found what I should have known about all along: there is a large car park at Cheshunt Park, which is now a public recreation area and a golf course. Perfect! Alongside the car park was an information board about the history of the place, but there was no mention of the 1940 defence line. Now where had it run? I was confused by the golf course and a maze of paths running away in all directions, and took the first path that seemed to be heading north. Soon I was in a wonderful landscape of grassland and trees, the lines and clumps of which I could see still retained the stamp of a formal layout. The information board had told me *Time Team* excavations to discover the line of Roman Ermine Street had been carried out in this park a few years ago. I thought I recalled the programme, but not its results – probably a surfeit of excitable running up and down.

It took me a while to locate the defence line. I was beginning to think the pillboxes had been removed as they were in the way of the golf course or were otherwise inconsistent with public amenities, but fortunately nothing like that had happened. After at last finding the northern edge of the golf course in the area of Candlestick Lane (another name to start the mind wondering), I suddenly spotted with a whoop of delight (heat does that to you!) two short lines of anti-tank cubes, probably from a block here. A bit further east was a Type 22 pillbox vandalised with graffiti and damaged by a fire that had been lit against it. I knew there should be a further pillbox further east, but I could not get to it. My knees began to buckle at the prospect of the wood, scrub, and barbed wire I saw ahead of me, so I struck west instead, re-crossed Candlestick Lane, and at the edge of a field bordering Cheshunt Park Farm which I could see in the distance, found a fine Type 27 pillbox. It was so overgrown, however, that access was only possible by being stung by nettles and ripped by brambles.

That's enough for today, I thought, as I contemplated the sting rash and scratches on my burnt flesh. However, with growing dismay I now realised I was lost: all the landmarks I had tried to recall had become merged into a confusing landscape of open, yellow grass bordered by thick hedgerows. Fortunately, a woman walking a dog hove into view and set me straight again. As I regained the car park, never did the sight of a glittering sea of metal seem so welcome.

13

HARTFORD END TO WAKES COLNE, ESSEX

We have now visited the majority of the defence areas I surveyed for English Heritage in the South-East of England, and will head off next towards the Eastern counties. We have only had a limited look so far at coastal defence, but that can be remedied soon in East Anglia. This was one of the areas considered most vulnerable to a German landing, in particular at the time of the German invasion of Norway when it seemed that a further assault across the North Sea against England was a distinct possibility. It was only with the build up of German forces in the Pas de Calais after their victory in France that the South-East became the most likely target. Today we have the hindsight of knowing the Operation Sealion plans, but at the time there was no flaw in German intelligence to reveal the German intentions to the British High Command. The breaking of the German Enigma codes by the brilliant decryption work at Bletchley Park was all in the future.

Even with the deduction that the main focus of the German attack was likely to be against Kent and East Sussex, there was always the danger of a subsidiary attack at any point along the long coastline of Britain. Germany's operations against Norway had shown what she was capable of with amphibious landings and air assaults. Although the distance involved in crossing the North Sea was considerably greater than that of the English Channel, an assault from the east could not be ruled out. There was always the possibility of a landing in East Anglia to attack London from the north while the main German Army was advancing against the capital from the south. Even the West coast of England was not considered safe. A sudden German descent on Ireland and an attack across the Irish Sea against the English North-West coast or into the heartland of

England via the British Channel was thought much less likely, but most certainly was not ruled out.

The first county in the East of England that I visited was Essex, although in many ways this county has more in common with the South-East than the East. To most southerners, however, even today, Essex is an unknown quantity, ridiculed absurdly by comics, but away from the fringes of London a county of wide and varied landscapes, little-visited by the hurly-burly world to the south, which suits the residents of Essex perfectly.

Certainly, the 1940 defences of Essex were as intensely organised as south of the Thames. Here too the whole landscape was prepared for defence, with stop lines, area defence, and, above all, around the long shoreline of creeks and marshes and remote land spits, coastal defence. The county was crossed as well by the GHQ Line, which we last saw through the summer haze meeting the Thames north of the Deangate ridge in North Kent.

Each region has its own variations in the defence works built against invasion, most commonly shown in the form of the infantry pillbox. In Essex, we are in the landscape of Eastern Command, and we will be meeting here a distinctive strong, square pillbox, known in the absence of a more official designation, as the 'Eastern Command-type'.

I was heading for a part of Essex, which, although I live not far away, was previously entirely unknown to me. It lay north of Chelmsford in a pleasant, gently undulating landscape watered by the River Chelmer. The GHQ Line followed the course of this river to Great Dunmow before marching across country to meet the infant River Cam on a route into Cambridgeshire. I had chosen the area because I had found a Luftwaffe air photograph at the Imperial War Museum that showed, by added triangles and other symbols, defence works along the banks of the Chelmer. By consulting maps, I had worked out that this area was around Ford End on the A130 road, in particular centred on a small settlement called Hartford End.

The area was the first that I surveyed for this project. It was on a sunny May day, with the rape crop yellow in the fields and the trees in young spring green, that I came here. I was full of enthusiasm and full of energy. As you will have seen, sometimes this drained away a little over the course of the next two years!

I parked in a lay-by on a sharp corner just outside Ford End to the west, and took a footpath running at the edge of an orchard: the spring growth was already blocking it with nettles. I pushed through them, and almost immediately began spotting pillboxes – Type 22s: the Germans had also seen them from a height of 2000ft and marked them on their air photograph. In a hedgerow was a larger pillbox, so overgrown I could hardly make it out. The Germans had termed this an anti-aircraft machine-gun post, and my own examination of RAF air photographs had shown it to have a central well, as with the Type 27s, for anti-aircraft fire. With much twisting and turning, and foraging about, I came down a slope to meet a path running by the south bank of the River Chelmer. Here was another hexagonal pillbox, looking like a Type 24, but which my work with air photographs also showed to have a central well. Once again, it was so overgrown I could not check to make sure.

I pressed on east along the river finding thick-walled (intended to be shell-proof) Type 24 pillboxes amongst trees just where the Germans had indicated they were. On the slopes behind them I could make out the shapes of other smaller Type 22s. The military engineers had placed the heavier pillboxes at the front edge of the defences by the anti-tank obstacle of the river, with lighter defence positions to the rear covering the ground in between with interlocking machine-gun fire. I stood on the river bank with the long, sloping fields before me, feeling the warmth of the earth and the force of nature all around, thinking that here would have been a killing ground if the enemy had tried to force these river positions. I don't normally like to think in terms of 'killing grounds': this is the language of excitable journalists rather than professional soldiers, but here it seemed apposite. There was something about this coloured landscape that seemed to attract the colour of red: it was indefinable, nothing that could be rationalised, but the thought was very real and sent a shiver through me.

I find there are some landscapes in which the past is very present as if it has been recorded on the earth around, reappearing with the growth of nature each season. This was a landscape where the past had never happened, but it still felt as real to me as if I was standing on the battlefield of Naseby or of Hastings; yet here it seemed even more immediate as if there is a quality in time where dual universes, of what has happened and what might have happened, brush against each other.

Further on, I found a perfect concrete-walled Type 24 pillbox, buried in grass, a really excellent example of its type, clean inside, and unspoilt by the usual attention of those people who love to leave evidence of themselves behind them (*colour plate 13*). The pillbox was unusual in that areas of its walls were still lined with sheet metal stamped with a strange design of crosses within boxes. I reflected that if a section of this metal turned up on an archaeological excavation at some distant future date, there would be learned pages written about the Christian ritual possibly carried out in this small building by the river. But the sheeting was probably just part of the stock of the contractor responsible for the pillbox, and used by him for its internal shuttering.

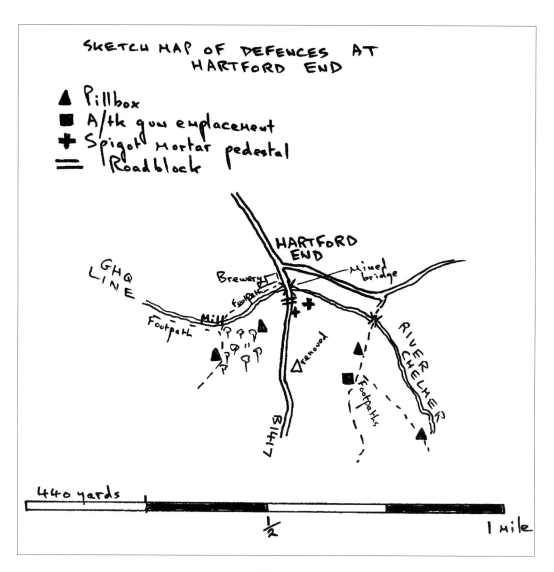

43 Sketch map showing the defences of the GHQ Line at Hartford End

44 Unusual metalwork used for interior pillbox-shuttering at Hartford End

I came to a lush green meadow, beyond which stood the buildings of a disused water-mill. It was not clear how the footpath continued here, so I vaulted a split-pole fence and marched on regardless, reaching a curving path beyond. If the owner had hailed me, it might have been interesting to talk to him. This house would almost certainly have been defended in 1940: there might be some surviving internal evidence he could have told me about. For the moment, however, my attention was taken up by the first of the Eastern Command-type pillboxes I was to find, heavily overgrown under trees just beyond the mill. Its square shape looked very solid, with embrasures in each face and a loopholed blast wall, detached by a few feet from the main structure, protecting the entrance.

The footpath led up the slope of a low ridge and I found I was walking into the arc of fire of a small concrete-faced Type 22 which stood in the corner of a field: on a rainy day on a later visit I sheltered for a while in the entrance of this pillbox facing a jumble of farmer's equipment while the rain lashed down on the back of my legs. But this day was bright with sunshine, and I came out onto the B1417 road leading to Hartford End at a point where yet another Type 22 pillbox stood up high on a bank. I was half-a-mile or so from the river: the defences of the GHQ Line had clearly been built in some depth.

Now I walked down the road to the bridge at Hartford End where Ridley's brewery stands by the river, as it had done in 1940. It is likely that defence positions would have been placed amongst the brewery buildings. Hartford End, in fact, was a Category 'C' 'defended place' with a garrison of two platoons from the 11th Bn Essex Home Guard. The bridge was mined for demolition, and with a Canadian pipe mine on its approaches designed to be exploded to create a blocking crater. There was also a roadblock here commanded by two Spigot mortar emplacements, the concrete pedestals of which can be seen in the meadow to the south-east of the bridge, and also by a massive double-chambered anti-tank gun emplacement to the south commanding the river crossing. Hartford End provides a fine example of a defended locality where the hardened (or concrete) defences largely survive. All you have to do is imagine the various additional slit trenches, sandbagged positions, and barbed-wire entanglements, and the roadblock with its concrete blocks and steel rails.

A track running south from a lane to the east of Hartford End enabled me to reach a further Eastern Command-type pillbox as well as the anti-tank gun emplacement I have just mentioned: the former is overgrown and inaccessible, but the latter I was able to go inside. It had sheets of corrugated iron used as shuttering still flapping on its interior walls. The main anti-tank gun embrasure faced towards the bridge 300yds to the north, and there was a side chamber as well with embrasures for Bren and rifle fire. The purpose of this was so that an infantry section could defend the emplacement while the Royal Artillery gunners were firing the anti-tank gun. The noise and confusion of men and equipment within the concrete interior under such circumstances can only be imagined.

Close to the anti-tank gun emplacement, a footpath led off to the left. When I was here once, there was a scrawled notice saying 'Beware of the bull', but the bull must have been hiding because, although I kept an anxious eye on the field, I did not see him. This reminds me of the question raised in a local newspaper some years ago about the purpose of pillboxes. One answer came back that they had been built as a refuge against bulls, probably a more practically sensible answer than it might seem at first.

The footpath climbed a slope and I came across two very well-preserved Eastern Command-type pillboxes close together actually on the path, which passed between their blast walls and their entrances. These I could go inside and inspect in detail. They had immensely strong walls, 4ft thick, and chamfered corners and roof edges to help break up the outline and make in-coming shells ricochet away. The interiors were also shuttered with corrugated iron, some of which survived.

45 Close-up of a stepped embrasure for LMG fire at Hartford End

I now came into a tract of countryside which seemed to me almost like parkland, fields and thick hedgerows in various shades of yellow and green under a warm spring sun, with nothing to hinder you wandering off across the landscape as you willed, or so it seemed. I had a sudden vision of frolicking satyrs and maenads and Dionysius passing in his garland-wreathed chariot: it was the sort of place where you felt such things might happen. The colours and the light, and the fecundity of nature all around, seemed to bring forth the ancient gods of the earth.

I stamped my booted feet as if to get them firmly back on the ground. And now I could see there were pillboxes everywhere, heavier shell-proof ones close to the river and lighter Type 22s behind in the same pattern as I had observed earlier. I saw one half-submerged in rape in the centre of a field, and another making a startling appearance at the division of a field of yellow with another of green. Great houses glistened in manicured loveliness on the far bank of the river. What a verdant, well-ordered scene this was upon which the defence works had been imposed 65 years ago. And almost all of these had survived. It is a wonderland for the pillbox seeker!

It will take you some time to see all the pillboxes, if you should wish to do so. They lie in hedgerows or abandoned now in the centre of fields. You can see them on the crests of the ridge or deep amongst the meadows by the river. And they stride off into the distance as well where you can see a busy road crossing the defence line ahead. Only one I know of has been destroyed – an anti-tank gun emplacement that stood alongside Warner's Farm, removed when the road was widened. And so I will leave you there to seek them out, while I take the long path back along the river bank to the lay-by where I left my car. For there are other defence areas to visit in Essex, but first I had to seek the help of the leading authority on this subject in Essex.

Chelmsford is a large, bustling city, with a pretty hideous centre, all concrete and glass with some of those derelict-looking shopping malls that characterised the 1960s when such things were considered the way forward in civic life. Now they are tatty, vandalised, and increasingly ugly, which is a pity because Chelmsford is otherwise a friendly, welcoming place with a history back at least to the Romans. Some say its Roman name (Caesaromagus, meaning something like 'the plains of Caesar') derives from the place where the Emperor Claudius received the surrender of the British tribes in AD 43, or perhaps even Julius Caesar 100 years earlier; that being by the way, I had come here to see Fred Nash at the offices of Essex County Council.

In a shining, marbled hallway of bustle and noise, Fred appeared suddenly from a bubble-like lift pod like a character out of *Star Trek* on the good ship Enterprise. He is a lean cadaverous-looking man, rather later in life than some, but with a hundred times more energy than most. He has been employed part-time for many years by Essex County Council to record the defence sites of the Second World War within the county. Like many archaeologists, a lot of his time is spent organising funding so that he can continue this work (no golden handouts for him) and he publishes his results, in a variety of reports and news-sheets issued by the Council's archaeology department. His energies, knowledge, and enthusiasm have put Essex in the front rank of those counties who pay more than lip service to their Second World War heritage and have an active programme of recording work, often using amateur volunteers. Their contributions were invaluable to the Defence of Britain Project.

Fred took me to his desk, a few square feet of space in a crowded office shared by the County Council's Waste, Recycling, and Environment Department. He has a desk, a filing cabinet, a share of another filing cabinet, a chair, and a waste paper basket, and little else. He does not mind these cramped conditions at all; indeed he seems to relish them. In any case, he is usually more out than in, exploring the defence landscapes of Essex. I think for any retired person to be back again amongst working people, doing something worthwhile and, above all, something you love, gives you a whole new lease of life. Fred has certainly found his niche.

Parking me on a borrowed stool at the side of his desk, and giving me a plastic beaker of surprisingly good coffee, he told me how he had started. While working in the computer industry in Hertfordshire, he had become interested in the 1940 defences that he found surviving in his local neighbourhood, and had made a record of these, extending this to a county-wide survey on behalf of Hertfordshire County Council. In 1993, he moved to Essex with a local government job, and soon made a start recording the profusion of defence works in that county. In this work for Essex County Council, Fred was aware of the lack of any documentation to help him locate the sites or recording those that had been destroyed.

A major breakthrough came, however, when a colleague at County Hall said to him, 'Are these of any use to you, Fred?' thrusting two large, heavy ledgers in front of him. 'We're about to throw them out.' They had the title written in large black letters across their cover, *Defence Contraventions*, and they contained a record, parish by parish across Essex, of all the Second World War defence works built on private land, with the owner's name and address, a grid reference, and details of the defence construction. The 'Contraventions' in the title referred to the contraventions of the usual planning laws by-passed by the powers of the Defence Regulations that had given the Army the right to enter land to build defence works. The ledgers related to the immediate post-war period when many of the defence works (termed temporary defence works or TDWs) were being assessed for removal. They were categorised A, B, or C in accordance with the importance of the need for their removal, for example public danger, obstructing roads, railways, and ports, interfering with agriculture, and so on.

Fred's document, saved from the skip, was a gold mine. He has used it ever since as the prime documentary basis for his fieldwork. Certain lists of TDWs are held by The National Archives, and some County Record Offices have files on the removal of individual structures, but, as far as I know, nothing as comprehensive and detailed as *Defence Contraventions* survives anywhere else. And yet, every county must have had similar ledgers after the war. The Lands Branch of the War Office would also have had similar records, itemising every parcel of land where defence works had been built. All were probably destroyed, perhaps in the 1960s and 1970s – whole storehouses of documents cast onto bonfires. A great loss. All this makes what survives increasingly valuable.

My purpose in coming to see Fred was to share information with him. He needed to be aware of the areas in Essex I was examining for English Heritage, as there would be a great deal he knew that he could pass on to me; and in turn he would welcome the results of my own research. What I most wanted from him were his site records: they would help my work appreciably.

I showed Fred the fruits of my field survey in the Hartford End area – all the pillboxes I had found tucked away, virtually invisible, in inaccessible hedgerows or hidden in undergrowth: I thought I had been the only person to visit them in years, and was a little miffed to find that he had records of them all. We compared our maps. They were virtually identical. There was little I could give to him about that area, although my German air photograph was new to him. He promised to send me the site records of the other Essex areas I was due to visit – Audley End and Wakes Colne – and a few days later these arrived by post, hefty packages of paper detailing every site. They were to prove invaluable. I left Fred surrounded by his busy local government colleagues in their Chelmsford offices, and took the road to one of those areas – Wakes Colne.

The valley of the River Colne runs from west to east towards Colchester, and in 1940 the river was followed by a Corps Line (that is a stop line designated by the defending Army Corps, in this case XI Corps) running from Colchester across Suffolk to join the GHQ Line in North Cambridgeshire. At Wakes Colne, the Line left the anti-tank obstacle formed by the River Colne, turning north and running for 4 miles until it joined with the River Stour at Bures. For this section of the Line, an artificial anti-tank ditch was dug alongside the railway that ran to Sudbury. That railway line had crossed the Colne Valley by a magnificent brick viaduct of 30 arches, 1066ft long (an easy number to remember), opened in 1847.

The defence area I was approaching lay around the Wakes Colne Viaduct (also known as the Chappel Viaduct after the small village that stands close by) at the point where the Corps Line turned north. Fred had given me directions. 'Take the road into Chappel village,' he had told me. 'Pass the Swan Inn (good for lunch), and you'll find an open grass area where you can park.' And so it proved. As I came down the A1124 I saw the great viaduct ahead of me, sweeping imperiously over the valley below – but, before I got to it, I had to swing off right, as Fred had told me. He was correct about the parking as well. This was a recreation area where people came to walk their dogs: it joined up with a new park known grandly as Chappel Millennium Green. I didn't mind what they called it. I was just glad to find somewhere to leave my car, and to see that there was public access to the defence works I had come to survey.

I followed a footpath that led me to the viaduct, which lay before me like a great, yellow, many-legged monster browsing in the green valley. Towards its centre its legs were longer, with its nose and its tail, widely-separated, touching the ground. I stood under its arches, seeing the beautifully crafted Victorian brickwork – what an engineering achievement this was, early in the period of the first great railway building. How the gangs of navvies must have laboured here over the many months of construction, bringing a combination of fear and

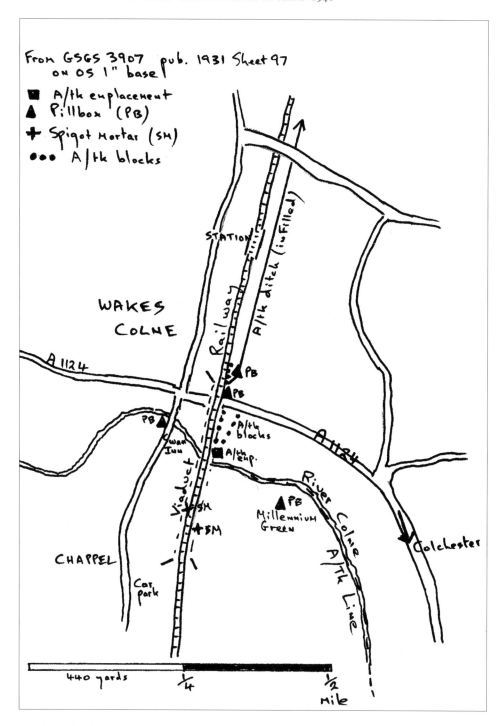

From GSGS 3907 pub. 1931 Sheet 97
on OS 1" base
■ A/tk emplacement
▲ Pillbox (PB)
✛ Spigot Mortar (SM)
●●● A/tk blocks

WAKES
COLNE

A 1124

STATION

A/tk ditch (infilled)

Railway

PB
PB

?PB

wan
Jun

A/tk
blocks

A/tk emp.

Viaduct

SM

SM

CHAPPEL

Car
park

PB

Millennium
Green

A 1124

River Colne

A/tk Line

Colchester

440 yards   ¼   ½
                            mile

46 *Above:* Sketch map showing the defences at Wakes Colne

47 *Opposite:* Infantry pillbox at the Wakes Colne Viaduct

awe to the neighbourhood as the iron road was laid above it. And in 1940, there had been more construction workers as another line was laid through the area; this one designed to keep German tanks at bay attacking from the east.

I followed the viaduct to the north and came to the first of the defence works: this was the pedestal of a Spigot mortar, that Home Guard weapon that could project a 20lb bomb at an approaching tank. Its firing is said to have been erratic. It was alleged that you were in more danger behind the weapon than in front of it, but I'm sure that view was unfair.

There is another pedestal on the other side of the viaduct. Wakes Colne and Chappel together, in fact, made up a 'defended place', so the Spigot mortar positions are undoubtedly survivors from those defences. I crossed the River Colne by a footbridge, and immediately came upon the main defence works of the Corps Line. They stood half in and half out of the viaduct's arches, dark grey and rather sinister like a growth on the yellow brick of the piers. I was startled when I first saw them. A great anti-tank emplacement, with a holdfast for a 6pdr gun, stood to the south of the road, with its hurtling traffic, and leading from it were rows of massive cubes and cylinders. These were in two separate alignments. It looks as if the military engineers changed their mind as to the exact alignment of the front-edge anti-tank obstacle at this point. The cylinders were probably built first, then that line abandoned, being replaced by the cubes running parallel with the viaduct arches, which continued on the north side of the road to meet the end of the anti-tank ditch there.

On the far side of the road an infantry pillbox could be seen sticking out from the piers of the viaduct. This site is difficult to get to, and is dangerous, with the heavy traffic rushing by at your heels, so, if I were you, I would be content to look at it from a distance. There is another pillbox (a Type 24) hidden by bushes further to the north, but others alongside Wakes Colne and Chappel Station were removed many years ago. It's worth driving to the station, as it's a wonderful survival from the great days of steam; there's a museum there as well, host to many events such as a beer festival every September.

If you tread the board walk around the Millennium Green, you will be able to see a rather eroded-looking Type 24 pillbox submerged in vegetation (*colour plate 14*). Another pillbox stands amongst scrub on the south-west side of Chappel Bridge close to the Swan Inn. Fred told me about this one, otherwise I would have missed it. Certainly, it's one to see either before or after refreshment at the Inn.

14

SUDBURY TO THE RIVER LARK AT JUDE'S FERRY BRIDGE, SUFFOLK, AND AUDLEY END HOUSE, ESSEX

Some 10 miles from Wakes Colne, over the border into Suffolk, lies the attractive market town of Sudbury, where the painter Gainsborough was born, surrounded by some of the most remote and unspoilt countryside I know. When I go for walks in the area (I live not far away) it is like stepping back into a previous, happier age. You can walk down the lanes with only the very occasional passing car. People smile at you from cottage doorways: they actually talk to you. Footpaths are overgrown and unmarked, the stiles broken, signposts twisted sideways or removed altogether. It may sound contrary, even eccentric, but I find this a refreshing antithesis to the labelled, packaged world of modern tourism.

I was driving to the north of Sudbury on the A134 road that takes you to the straggling roadside village of Long Melford, full of boutiques, pubs, and antiques shops. Just before this village, coming from Sudbury, a side road (the B1064) leads off to the left. Not far along it, there is a car park at Rod Bridge – Rod Bridge is the crossing of the River Stour by both the road and the former railway, and in 1940 it was a major defended point on the same Corps Line as we have just seen at Wakes Colne. A Type 27 pillbox (that's the type with the open central well to mount an anti-aircraft gun) stands by the lane a little further to the north. There was also a 6pdr anti-tank gun emplacement here guarding the bridges, but it was removed many years ago and I don't know its exact site: possibly it was between the river and the railway.

I walked from the car park to the road, and crossed the Stour by the road bridge, coming to a path on the left signposted 'The Valley Walk' – this runs south along the line of the former railway. You might like, however, to take a few further steps along the lane to view the Type 27 pillbox I've just mentioned.

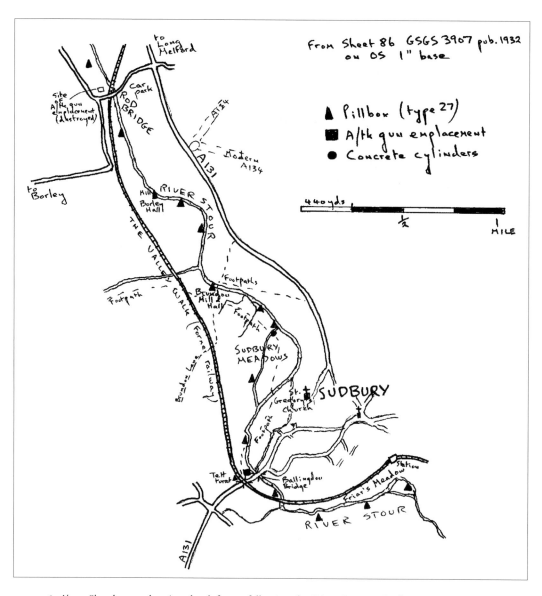

48 *Above:* Sketch map showing the defences following the River Stour at Sudbury

49 *Opposite:* Curious cow by a Sudbury Type 27 pillbox

If you do this, you will see as well a church tower on the crest of the slope ahead of you. This is Borley Church, the rectory of which was the scene in the 1920s/30s of one of the most famous hauntings in British ghost-history (if you can have such a thing). The rectory has long since been pulled down, and I find the churchyard calm and reflective, with long blowing grass and distant views, just as a churchyard should be. I go there often. It is a place in which to think.

Today, however, I was heading along The Valley Walk to see the Type 27 pillboxes that are scattered in profusion amongst the water meadows below Sudbury. After a couple of hundred yards, I took a footpath that led left from The Valley Walk taking a course around Borley Mill and Hall. I passed a couple of pillboxes, inaccessible because of high vegetation, but eventually came to one on the bank of the river by a footbridge over a side channel. With something of a scramble, I was able to climb onto it and inspect the central chamber with its concrete pedestal for the anti-aircraft machine gun. John Schofield of English Heritage, another colleague, and myself once had a picnic on this pillbox on a tour of inspection. It was a sunny day, I remember, with the river sliding away peacefully beneath us.

50 The central well and AA gun mount of a Type 27 pillbox

Beyond Brundon Hall, which was probably incorporated into the defences here (certainly its bridge was mined) I entered Sudbury Meadows and saw the buildings of the town ahead of me on a slight eminence beyond the river. I passed several more Type 27s: a good one, stripped of its exterior brick-cladding, stood across the footpath, in a field of cows and buttercups (*colour plate 15*). I put down my pack in order to take a photograph, and, when I looked behind me, I saw a cow was sampling the pack to see if it was tasty. Fortunately, it wasn't!

Just beyond this pillbox was a water channel full of concrete cylinders, some used to reinforce the banks, others scattered generally about the bed of the stream. As these are the type of cylinders often found at roadblocks, they were probably brought here from the town during a clear-up after the war. Sudbury was a Category 'A' nodal point and would have had many roadblocks set up around it.

I walked now across the meadows with the buildings of Sudbury rising like a low cliff to my left, the tower of St Gregory's church prominent amongst them. Below St Gregory's are locks and wharves from the days when the Stour was busy with barges. Robert Arbib, a soldier serving with the American forces, came here and described the pillboxes he saw looking out over Sudbury Meadows. He commented:

> Perhaps they will be left there to gather moss and then grass and then to be split up by the roots of trees, as relics of an age, a strange, incongruous footnote to Suffolk history.

Arbib's book from which this passage comes is *Here We Are Together: The Notebook of an American Soldier in Britain*, published in 1946. Although it has long been out of print, I do recommend you find a copy as it is one of the best accounts of life in wartime England that I know. Arbib described everything he saw, often in lyrical and moving language. He was particularly struck by the girls of Sudbury, saying they were the most beautiful of any place in England, an impression which a glance at the busy market place on a Saturday morning will confirm today.

The water meadows narrow as the river bends to flow through the southern suburbs of the town, and I saw that the embankment of the former railway was now close on my right. This embankment acted as a secondary defence to the front-edge anti-tank obstacle of the river, and various gun positions were prepared against it. The locations of these are known from an immensely detailed Defence Scheme for the Suffolk Sub-Area at The National Archives, which records the defence works from Sudbury to Bury St Edmunds. I aimed now for the point where railway and river converged and where I could see the gardens of houses across a small side stream from the Stour. In one of these gardens I found an anti-tank gun emplacement, with its main embrasure blocked up, now used as a shed. It covered the important Ballingdon Bridge where the road heading out of Sudbury to the south crossed the river.

I left the water meadows by a footpath past an old pumping station and emerged onto Ballingdon Street with the railway bridge to my right. Passing through the bridge, I came to a builder's yard on the far side of the embankment. Until recent years, a very rare Tett Turret could be seen here, but it has now been removed and probably destroyed. These prefabricated defence components were made by a company in Surrey, and consisted of a concrete pipe set into the ground over which was a revolving concrete cupola allowing fire from one rifleman or a Bren gunner. It would have been a death trap! It's a pity the Sudbury example could not have been preserved as it would have made a good museum item. Very few, in fact, survive. However, the concrete shaft of the Turret may yet remain buried in the embankment.

I now climbed a flight of steps to the top of the railway embankment, and followed the path there (a continuation of the Valley Walk) until I came to a further bridge, this one passing high above the Stour. Just before the river, there is another Type 27 pillbox amongst thick bushes at the foot of the embankment to the left. Descending from the railway, I entered the beautiful grassy expanses of Friar's Meadow from which I could see yet more pillboxes lining the far bank of the river (*colour plate 16*). I had a record that one also stood on a small island formed by a looping branch of the river, but I was unable to reach the island to check.

The pillboxes continue to the south, but we have probably come far enough for today. You might like to do the return journey to Rod Bridge, as I did, by walking into the town from Friar's Meadow. Like me, by now you will probably have built up an excellent appetite and thirst which can easily be assuaged at one of Sudbury's excellent pubs. While here I would also recommend a visit to the Gainsborough Museum. Robert Arbib stayed here during the war when the Gainsborough birthplace was run as a small hotel, and he describes many amusing incidents in his vivid style. Certainly you can while away several pleasant hours in Sudbury, before tackling the route back to Rod Bridge, perhaps crossing the river below St Gregory's to regain the water meadows.

The Corps stop line we looked at crossing the water meadows of Sudbury continued north to Barton Mills (just south of Mildenhall in Suffolk), from where it followed the course of the River Lark, as an Eastern Command Line, eventually making a junction south of Littleport with the River Great Stour, which here carried the main GHQ Line towards the north. West of Mildenhall, the River Lark passed to the south of the small village of West Row, being crossed by a narrow lane leading to the village at a place called Jude's Ferry Bridge. Who Jude was, I have been unable to ascertain, but a few cottages and, what documents term, a hotel (now a rather fine riverside pub) grew up on the north bank of his ferry crossing. By the Second World War, the ferry had been replaced by a bridge, and in recent years that bridge has been removed and another built a few yards to the east. It was here that a defended locality, with all-round perimeter defences, was established in 1940 to protect this bridge crossing of the stop line.

As I approached Jude's Ferry Bridge from the south, I was aware of a pillbox standing tall against the flat skyline to my left. This was a Type 24, standing close to the south bank of the Lark: it looks exceptionally tall because drainage has caused the underlying peat of this former marshland to shrink in the years since the Second World War, resulting in the ground surface dropping by a foot or more. The lane now does a little twist as it approaches the bridge (previously it ran on a straight course a few yards to the left) and, having crossed the river, you can drop into the car park of the Judes (they drop the apostrophe) Ferry public house immediately on your left. I am sure you will want to pay a visit to this excellent hostelry a little later to justify your use of their car park.

I walked back to the bridge, and ahead of me, some 200yds away across the flat fields, I saw the familiar square-block shape of an anti-tank gun emplacement staring at me with the black, unblinking eye of its main embrasure. I wanted to inspect and photograph it so I continued along the road from the bridge, and took a track that ran past the emplacement. It was a square Type 28, with a single chamber for a 6pdr Hotchkiss anti-tank gun.

Walking back towards the river crossing I could make out clearly where the original bridge had stood before they built the present one. In 1940, like so many others it had been mined for demolition, and there had been a roadblock at its northern end by the pub, and another at the southern end. Looking north, I could see a block of vegetation to my left on the south bank of the river, which when I inspected it more closely revealed a heavily-overgrown pillbox, a small Type 22. This is now a few yards into the field from the road, but when built stood close to the original bridge. I was able to reach it from the bridge approach without too much difficulty, and, as I passed around it to its far side, had the sudden surprise of finding a Spigot mortar pedestal present as well – a very fine specimen. On its domed top by the steel pintle, I could read a name inscribed in the concrete, 'Sgt Rolfe'. Who Sergeant Rolfe was, whether a Home Guard soldier (the Spigot mortar, as we know, was essentially a Home Guard weapon from mid-1941) or a regular, can't be determined now. But whoever he was, he certainly assured that his name would come down to us and live on, a clever expedient simply by doodling in drying concrete! (*colour plate 17*)

The hidden Spigot mortar pedestal is not the only surprise on the south bank of Jude's Ferry Bridge. On the same side of the road, and close to its edge, are a couple of trees that seem to rise out of carefully prepared circular bowls. On closer inspection, I found that each of these is made of concreted sandbags, still piled six or seven layers deep. They were weapon pits, defending the south of the bridge approach, probably alongside the roadblock itself. Today they are to the west of the road, but they would have been on the east side of the original bridge approach. It's remarkable that they have survived, and this is probably purely because they have trees growing out of them: it seems likely these trees were deliberate post-war plantings rather than chance seedings. Surviving examples of 1940 infantry earthworks, reinforced by sandbags in this way, are so rare that you can number them on your fingers, and here were two side-by-side.

51 Anti-tank gun emplacement firing towards Jude's Ferry Bridge on the River Lark

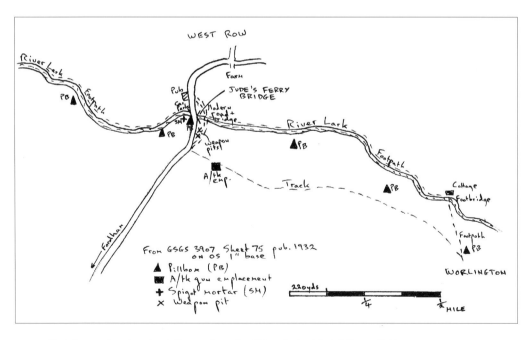

52 Sketch map showing the defences along the River Lark at Jude's Ferry Bridge

53 The concreted sandbags of a 1940 weapon pit, Jude's Ferry Bridge

You can walk from Jude's Ferry Bridge along the north bank of the river in both directions, and see pillboxes facing you across the water. To the west, there is one with a strange thin, overhanging roof that must be part of its original camouflage. Unfortunately, without permission, it's not possible to approach it on the opposite bank to inspect it more closely. To the east, you can walk towards Worlington, crossing the river by a footbridge at Kings Staunch Cottage where you tiptoe on a path running through someone's back garden, and see three further pillboxes. The return journey can be made by the track that passes the anti-tank gun emplacement. Although this is not a public right of way according to the Ordnance Survey map, I doubt if anyone would object to you using it. If accosted, always follow the golden rule of apologising first, and pleading your case afterwards.

We return now to the GHQ Line, to Audley End House, near Saffron Walden, in fact, back in Essex in 'Fred Nash territory'. This defence area is just right for a leisurely Sunday afternoon visit, for you will be coming to see the house first and foremost, I am sure. You can build the Second World War defences onto the visit, without too much extra effort or upsetting any member of your party who is perhaps not as interested in concrete defence works as yourself.

Audley End House is now managed by English Heritage, and stands on the western edge of Saffron Walden. It is one of the great Jacobean houses of England, built on the site of a suppressed Benedictine priory acquired by Henry VIII's Chancellor, Thomas Audley, and was the home for many centuries of the Howard family, Earls of Suffolk. The River Cam flows through the grounds and the farmed estate beyond, and it was this river that the GHQ Line was following as its main anti-tank obstacle as it approached Cambridge lying 14 miles to the north.

If you park your car at the house, as directed by the smart English Heritage attendant, you can walk over the lawns towards the Adam Bridge (named after the architect, Robert Adam) where the River Cam, broadened into an ornamental lake designed by Capability Brown, is crossed by the road from Saffron Walden. This bridge was blocked by roadblocks on both sides in 1940, and the bridge itself mined. The explosives for this purpose were not just strapped to the outside of the bridge, but packed into carefully prepared chambers within the fabric of the bridge connected by the electrical circuits that would detonate them. Fred Nash told me that the manholes at each end of the bridge covered these detonation chambers, which had been specially bored by the Royal Engineers. And this happened at hundreds and hundreds of road and rail bridges, as well as other strategic structures, throughout the country. It is one of the most remarkable, and little known, facts about the 1940-1 anti-invasion defences. We have to hope that the detonation chambers were emptied of their explosives at the end of the war: as we have seen at Sarre, this was not always fully carried out.

On the north-west side of the bridge, on the smooth green turf of Audley End's park by a clump of trees, stands a concrete-faced, square Eastern Command-type pillbox, of the pattern we met at Hartford End. It is a perhaps surprising sight here amongst the loveliness of these manicured grounds, with the rich facade of the house in the background. It always seems remarkable to me that this pillbox, and the other defence structures we shall see, were not cleared away after the war. The house was requisitioned for the Ministry of Works in 1941, and remained in the care of that department (a predecessor to English Heritage) after the war. We have seen how the defence works built into the structure of Pevensey Castle were preserved, but I cannot imagine anything similar happening here for historic reasons alone: it must have been the expense of removal that has allowed their survival. The Second World War structures are now regarded as part of Audley End's overall historic landscape, but such a view has only been prevalent in recent years.

If you follow the lake, or river, to the north, passing through the grounds in front of the house, you will come to Stable Bridge, crossed by one of the main drives. There was a pillbox here that has been removed, but the block at the bridge survives with two enormous concrete cubes on its west side. They would have had one or more steel hawsers stretched between them, an unusual method of creating a block. A small bridge stands a little way to the north, and this was blocked similarly: the concrete cubes again survive. Further north still, at the very edge of the formal grounds, is yet another bridge, known as the Tea House Bridge – a beautiful ornamental footbridge, a further example of Robert Adam's work. On its western side is a circular detonation chamber with a concrete slab across it. From here the explosives of all the last three bridges would have been fired. Very few visitors walking in these grounds, crossing and re-crossing the bridges, have the faintest idea of the tense watching and waiting that would have taken place here in those critical invasion danger weeks of 1940. It seems an unlikely place for a prepared battlefield, with its lawns and flower beds, fruit trees, cascading water, and long rows of glass houses. The expected German attack would have been from the east, from a landing on the Suffolk or Essex coasts, to break the GHQ Line into the Midlands or to swing left against the north of London.

You should now walk to find the organic kitchen garden because in the high brick wall that borders it to the north you will find some 12 holes knocked through the wall, some lined with steel: these were undoubtedly loopholes made to allow rifle fire from a Home Guard detachment stationed here. By June 1941, Saffron Walden had been designated as a Category 'B' nodal point, and one of the responsibilities of the 12th Bn Essex Home Guard manning its defences was to send a patrol to Audley End to guard the mined crossings of the River Cam.

These are all the defence works you can see within the grounds of Audley End House. Before leaving, however (after you've seen the house, of course) you should pause at the Polish memorial, erected to commemorate the Polish soldiers who trained here with Special Operations Executive before being sent on missions into German-occupied Eastern Europe. Much of their training was carried out in the grounds, which would have echoed with explosions and small arms fire, at a time when the invasion danger had receded.

On the far side of the Audley End Road is the miniature railway. When I first came here to survey the defences I had an appointment to meet with the man who ran the railway. He took me down the track to the south until we came to a bridge that crossed the Cam. Here are more massive anti-tank blocks and another Eastern Command-type pillbox. The bridge as well has chambers that were once filled with explosives. What amused me was that the bridge parapet was lined with cuddly toys, as were the embrasures of the pillbox. 'The children see them from the train,' explained the man. 'They love them. We put them away each winter and bring them out in the spring.' What a happy development for a stop line, I thought. Where German tanks might have manoeuvred to cross the river, we now have carriages full of laughing children.

54 Above: One of several loopholes in the north kitchen garden wall at Audley End House

55 Opposite: Bridge south of Audley End House (now crossed by a miniature railway), once mined and defended by a pillbox and concrete blocks

There are other pillboxes (Type 24s this time) to the south, and also alongside the B1383 road to the west. Two more lie at another defended bridge crossing to the north. But please note that you need to gain permission from the Audley End Estate to go there. You approach the site by a footpath running towards the outskirts of Saffron Walden from the B1383 road (you have an even better view of the loopholed wall from this path) until you come to the bank of the river at the edge of a field. At this point, there is yet another block on the river bridge: its matching block is actually on the other side of the wall, which was demolished at this point and rebuilt after the war. If you examine the wall carefully you can see the outline of the break. There is even a length remaining of the steel hawser that used to be stretched between the blocks.

The day I came here it had been raining in the night. For some unknown reason, I did not think I had to change into boots, and I set up along the river bank to the north in a pair of brand new shoes. It looks easy from a distance, but this is difficult walking, half on an overgrown bank and half at the edge of a field of wheat. Soon my shoes were caked in mud, and my trousers soaked. I pressed on regardless, and the sight of two solid shell-proof Type 24s at the west end of the bridge, angled towards each other, with more concrete blocks on the other side of the river, made the uncomfortable trek very worthwhile. Later, I had to balance that worth against the cost of a new pair of shoes!

15

BAWDSEY POINT TO WALBERSWICK, SUFFOLK

I was going to the coast again. It's a long time since we've been to an area by the sea. Cuckmere Haven was the last, and that seemed 1000 miles away now as I headed into the flat lands of Suffolk. This is an area I call the 'Robert Arbib country' after the American soldier we met at Sudbury, whose book I have already quoted. Arbib had been a sergeant with a US Army unit building an airfield at Debach north of Woodbridge. His descriptions of this area are particularly memorable – the camps, the dances, the women, the visits to the pubs, in particular The Dog at Grundisburgh which was drunk dry one memorable evening when the Americans first arrived. I was now passing on the A12 the places he had known, and swinging around Woodbridge to take the road to Bawdsey Point.

This narrow road over the heathland expanses of the Suffolk coastal region leads past the site of Sutton Hoo (the famous Saxon ship burial) where the National Trust have recently opened a new visitor centre. I have to confess that I preferred the site as it was formerly, when you came to the burial mounds down a long sandy track to have the place usually to yourself. Yet progress we are told is good, and it probably is here making the site more accessible to many thousands of people.

There is a link with the Second World War because the Sutton Hoo area was a training ground and various slit trenches were dug by troops amongst the burial mounds. Earlier, in 1940, long lengths of anti-landing trenches had been dug to stop German aircraft using this flat, open landscape to bring in men and supplies to support an invasion on the East Anglian coast. An information board on the new viewing platform in front of the famous ship barrow excavated in 1939 refers to anti-glider trenches. They were not 'anti-glider' so much as 'anti-powered aircraft'. There was little you could do to stop gliders landing, although admittedly the obstacles might cause them to crash. The main purpose of the trenches, however, was to stop powered transport aircraft being able to land, and then take off again to bring in more men and equipment.

I came through the village of Bawdsey and on down the narrow lane to Bawdsey Point itself, a triangular spit of land separated by the River Deben from the outskirts of Felixstowe to the south-west. On the far side of the river, a squat Martello tower told of a previous invasion danger during the Napoleonic Wars. If you come here in the winter months, this is a lonely place – just a row of houses, a car park, a jetty, where a small boat will take you to the far shore if you summon it for long enough, and Bawdsey Manor, which I shall come to just now. In the summer months, however, it is a popular place for visitors. There is a sandy beach north of the jetty, which children love, paddling and building sand castles, and watching the boats on the river. You can walk to Bawdsey Point itself, the beach here being shifting shingle so you can feel your leg muscles being worked in a way that no exercise machine could ever simulate.

When I rounded the Point this breezy day, with rain just beginning to spit in my face from a bank of clouds drifting in from the sea, I saw the late Victorian pile of Bawdsey Manor above the low cliffs that line the shore towards the north. This highly ornate brick house was built in the late nineteenth century for Sir Cuthbert Quilter. It is a mixture of towers, turrets, and gables, in a variety of styles from Tudor via William and Mary to Gothic and French Revival. It did not serve long as the Quilter family home, for in the mid-1930s it was sold to the Air Ministry, and an Experimental Station for radar development was built in the grounds. At the beginning of the war this became RAF Bawdsey, the country's first Chain Home Radar Station, an important Vulnerable Point in 1940 with its own all-round defences. There were eight transmitter and receiver masts which used to tower over the Point in a lattice-work of steel. The last of them was removed only a few years ago.

When I visited, the house and its estate were being used as an English language school. I had obtained permission from the owners to conduct my survey. A little later the school closed for a while, but I understand it is now functioning again. There is a great deal to see in its grounds if you are a Second World War buff; the buildings of the former radar station are widespread – stores, accommodation blocks, guard houses, and the transmitter block itself, the latter the subject of one of the BBC's recent 'Restoration' programmes. But what I wanted to find were the defence works. The grounds of Bawdsey Manor were surrounded by pillboxes, and on the cliffs were anti-aircraft gun positions, with all possible gaps in the defences blocked by anti-tank cubes. You can see some of the pillboxes from the lane outside: they stand high on strange podiums of surrounding brick, or at least appear to do so from a distance.

56 Bawdsey Manor. In 1940-1 this beach was lined with anti-tank blocks and tubular steel scaffolding

Having checked in with the reception to the school, I plunged off into the interior of the grounds, following the winding drive with the turreted facade of the Manor to my right. Straightaway, I began finding pillboxes, one by a playing field, another by one of the former accommodation blocks of RAF Bawdsey, now termed the school's 'Girls' House'. Although they were heavily overgrown, I could see these were of a Type 24 form, but with the distinctive podiums (or 'skirts') of surrounding bricks and concreted sandbags that I have already referred to.

I hastened away from the Girls' House as I felt a bit awkward lingering there with a camera, and pushed further into the grounds. It began to rain. Now if there are two things that don't go together, it's long, wet grass and pillbox recording. I had to cross large, open fields of grass that had once formed part of the RAF Bawdsey estate, and soon became soaked somewhere to the level of my waist. But I found two of the pillboxes that I had seen earlier from the road. One, in a tangle of woods, had clearly been illicitly visited, for it was filled with beer and cider cans, water oozing from its green, slime-covered walls. I could not wait to get out. It was surrounded by concreted sandbags, a cheap and cheerful method of 'hardening' your defence position, by spraying earth-filled sandbags with a covering of concrete so that they dry as a solid shell.

57 Pillbox in the grounds of Bawdsey Manor

The second pillbox stood on the side of a ridge, in the middle of a sea of grass. I arrived at it, with the water running from me like an explorer deep in a tropical rain forest; only I was not nearly so warm. I examined the pillbox's surrounding brick wall, which was beginning to fall away, showing that it was not part of a solid plinth but merely surrounded an earth core into which the pillbox itself was set. I wondered why the builders had gone to this trouble. Probably the encircling wall was designed so that attackers could not easily reach the pillbox to lay explosive charges against its walls or to lob grenades through the embrasures. There had possibly been barbed wire and earthwork defences around the pillbox as well.

I walked to the top of the ridge passing some enormous concrete blocks in a group upon which the legs of a radar transmitter mast had once been set. Standing under a clump of trees, with the rain pattering on the branches, and a forlorn, overgrown and dripping landscape of greens and browns all around me, I reflected on the quick rise, and equally quick fall, of man's interests when applied to the business of making war. Only a relatively few years ago, the spot that I stood upon had glistened with high-tensile steel, anchored into grey concrete, ordered, tended, security-patrolled, the high antennae overhead part of a critical electronic frontline for the nation's survival; and now here it was abandoned and already nearly forgotten, the rain running in rivulets from the concrete blocks, and the ivy and the lichen creeping inexorably over their surfaces. All around me was silence where once hundreds of men and women had worked and lived in a disciplined and uniformed environment. Now there were just the long bands of grass bowing to the rain and a huddle of distant roofs seen through the gloom.

I was so wet that it seemed immaterial whether I pressed on or not. I was trying to reach the top of the cliffs where I knew there was a line of Second World War defence works – anti-aircraft gun posts and pillboxes. I cast backwards and forwards in increasingly impossible conditions, trying to penetrate tangled thickets of nettles and brambles, until I had to give up. I came back towards the Manor. The rain was easing, but I slopped along as if my body had been filled with water. The owner of the school passed in her car, viewing my bedraggled figure with concern and readily assenting to my request to return on another day and complete my survey. The journey home was long and uncomfortable, but the hot bath at the end was wonderful!

A few weeks later I returned on a day of gentle sun which put a whole new complexion on things. Before I went up to the Manor, I explored the beachfront areas of Bawdsey Point, which I had not had time to do on my previous visit. North of the jetty there is a surviving row of anti-tank cubes at the head of the beach, tumbled over by the sea from their original position. They make an evocative sight (*colour plate 18*). Once there had been minefields and beach scaffolding here. The framework of the scaffolding is still in place beneath the sand and shingle, and, I am told, is sometimes revealed after a storm.

At the jetty, on the present site of the car park, there had been a gun emplacement in 1940, and the area had been lined with scaffolding, cubes, and barbed wire, which had continued around the Point. I walked there now, passing the concrete base of a gun position, seeing the sea surging on the shingle which had once been covered with steel, wire, and concrete defences. A pillbox stood just inside the fence at the edge of the Bawdsey Manor grounds, and, close to it, was a short line of cubes that had miraculously survived here, although the scores of others to which they had once been linked have long since been cleared away. Amongst the wooded cliffs below the Manor I spotted two concrete emplacements. These I needed to survey, and I could only get to them from inside the Manor grounds.

I reported once more to reception, and was accorded a guide this time, who appeared in the guise of an athletic young man who taught physical education at the school. He took me at a fast pace through the formal gardens of the Manor telling me that most of the overseas students who came here were so unfit they could scarcely keep up with him on even a short walk. As I struggled along beside him, beginning to puff a little, I was not surprised. I don't know what he thought of my state of fitness. I suspected that with the young foreigners lethargy was probably a major factor rather than bodily degeneration. In my case, it was definitely the latter!

58 Anti-tank blocks at Bawdsey Point

We rounded a large, circular feature in a walled garden. 'That's the base of a Martello tower,' my guide told me. An interesting survival, I thought. It had been one of a line of Martello towers along the coast here built to keep Napoleon at bay: I have already pointed out another. In 1940, numbers had been pressed back into service as observation posts or with machine guns in their tops. I had even read a German report on their re-fortification. The Germans took our defences very seriously. They had had too much bitter experience of fighting us. Today we snigger at 'Dad's Army' jokes, but we have forgotten how close we came to losing everything.

My PE companion brought me to a locked, wooden door across an opening in a group of large rocks. At least at first glance they looked like rocks, but we were, in fact, in what was a carefully contrived grotto formed in the late nineteenth century from a type of concrete applied most realistically. Sir Cuthbert Quilter had evidently been one of those Victorians who loved the romance of the grotto, festooned with ferns and hung with lamps, the place to take the ladies after dinner to look out over the sea and see the ships sliding by. But on the other side of the door was a high open area, with a reinforced concrete face pierced by two loopholes, for in 1940 Royal Engineers had turned the grotto into a strongpoint. It provided a highly unusual example of military architecture. One of the most fascinating aspects of the Second World War anti-invasion defences, I think, is the way existing buildings and their surroundings were adapted for defence. There are still a number of good examples up and down the country, and I shall be taking you to one or two later.

'We have to keep the door locked,' said my companion. 'Or the kids get in.' It was certainly a wonderful spot for youthful expression, although I preferred to think back a hundred years or so when the ladies and gentlemen of the Manor had come here and held hands, on a warm summer's evening, with the shining, moon-washed sea before them and the smell of herbs and heather heavy on the air. Or was I being carried too far away on flights of fantasy?

My PE man pushed on at an even increasing speed, flinging himself between the artificial rocks, and hauling himself up by his fingertips onto a concrete shelf. My pace behind him was much more sedate. 'An old injury,' I muttered by way of explanation, pointing pathetically at my right leg as if to explain my slow progress. My companion said nothing; he did not seem impressed. He stood fearlessly on the concrete platform with the earth cliff falling away sheer beneath him. I scrambled up painfully beside him, realising I was on the roof of a pillbox with the mounting for an anti-aircraft machine gun beside me. The pillbox had been built snugly in a cleft in the cliffs. Having taken my photographs, I took a long time getting down: Mr PE was already disappearing into the distance.

59 Strongpoint set in the cliffs beneath Bawdsey Manor

I caught up with him as he stood to look up at a bird on a branch overhead. 'Green woodpecker,' he said. 'Very rare here.' Nature studies were evidently part of his curriculum as well. He brought me to more defence sites deep in the undergrowth – an anti-aircraft gun mount, a further pillbox, and a line of concrete blocks blocking a path leading to the cliff edge. No wonder I hadn't been able to find these sites before. There was only one route in and one route out if you did not wish to be torn to bits by the undergrowth.

The defences had clearly been very thorough. After 1940-1, the main threat had not been of a full German invasion assault here, but of German raiding parties coming ashore from a U-boat to launch an attack on the radar station, to damage it and perhaps capture personnel for interrogation. These were the sorts of raids the Allies carried out against German-occupied Europe. It's remarkable in fact that no comparable raid (as far as we know) was ever carried out by the Germans against the British mainland, although the danger of such raids was recognised throughout the war. After our own successful raid against the German radar station at Bruneval on the French coast in February 1942, extra defensive measures were put into place at British radar stations in case the Germans retaliated. It was at this time, I think, that a long defensive ditch was dug on the north side of Bawdsey Manor, beyond the road, connecting up various loops of the existing waterways. Several pillboxes were built in this area as well, a number of which survive.

I limped away from Bawdsey Manor, expressing my thanks to my companion for giving up so much of his time to take me around. 'No trouble at all,' he said 'But I'd better get back to that lot.' He waved his hands in a dismissive way in the general direction of the Manor where small groups of students in tee-shirt and jeans could be seen slouching by. I wished him well. When I learnt that the school had temporarily closed, I wondered what had happened to him. I hope he has found a good job somewhere with people that are willing to keep to his pace. It must be frustrating to teach the half-hearted.

Later the same day I drove into Walberswick, the next of my Suffolk coastal areas. Walberswick is a village that lies south of the River Blyth, well known for its artistic community and for its fresh seafood, once a quite considerable port but now dwindled away. To its north, over the Blyth, is Southwold, with its pier and lighthouse and much fought-over holiday huts beneath the cliffs. During the war these huts were uprooted and placed on the fields as anti-landing obstacles, which probably caused more upset to their owners than Hitler ever did. There are holiday huts at Walberswick as well at the head of the beach by the car park that you come to at the end of the long road through the village. Here you will see lines of anti-tank cubes that once formed part of the anti-invasion defences, designed to divide the beach into sectors to stop German tanks moving laterally along it and to keep them penned to the shore (*colour plate 19*). The cubes disappear beneath the huts, and many must be buried under the sand. I tried to trace them, and met with

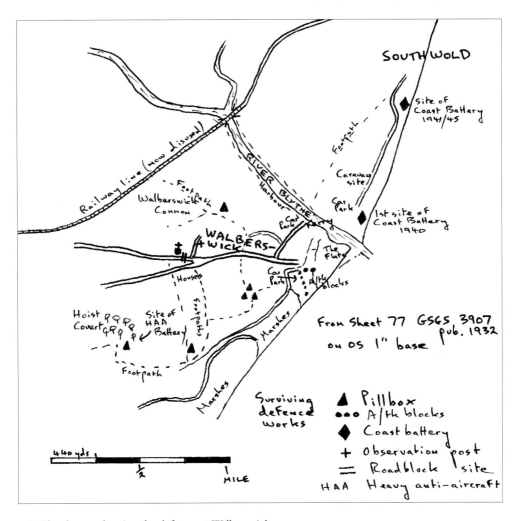

SOUTH WOLD

Site of
Coast Battery
1941/45

Footpath

Caravan
site

Car
Park

1st site of
Coast Battery
1940

Railway line (now disused)

Foot-

Walberswick
Common

RIVER BLYTHE

Harbour

WALBERS-
WICK

Car
Park

The
Flats

Houses

Car
Park

A/tk blocks

Footpaths

Marshes

From Sheet 77 GSGS 3907
pub. 1932
on OS 1" base

Hoist
Covert

Site of
HAA
Battery

Footpath

Marshes

Marshes

Surviving
defence
works

▲ Pillbox
●●● A/tk blocks
◆ Coast battery
+ Observation post
= Roadblock site
HAA Heavy anti-aircraft

440 yds

½

1

MILE

60 Sketch map showing the defences at Walberswick

some disapproving looks from hut owners taking in the first proper sun of the new sunbathing year.

I once gave a talk on the Walberswick defences at an archaeology conference held in rooms on Southwold Pier, and was pulled up short by a couple of members of the audience when I got my facts wrong. That is fair enough: it's the way you learn, and shows the importance of surviving local testimony. But it's an object lesson never to talk on so precise a subject to a local audience unless you have lived there yourself for an appropriate number of years and done much more fieldwork than I had been able to do. There will always be someone who knows more than you, or thinks he or she does, which is probably worse.

When I came to Walberswick from Bawdsey, the sun that shone on the beach hut people soon faded from the sky and was replaced by a dark bank of clouds racing in from the sea. The rain was brief but fierce. I sheltered under some bushes in an area between the coast and the village, and a lady in raincoat and wellington boots came past with her dogs. Seeing my maps and camera, and deducing I was perhaps not the average visitor to quiet Walberswick, she asked in an interested, friendly manner what I was doing. Her dogs sniffed at me, equally friendly. When I mentioned pillboxes, her eyes lit up and she became quite animated. Without hesitation, she told me where they all were, and led me off into the still-falling rain to show me the position of one 'that you'll never find by yourself'. She was probably right. It was dug into the ground and heavily overgrown in an area of waste land. It was dangerous as well, I thought: a passageway to the deeply sunk entrance formed a concrete cliff it would be easy to fall off.

Hearing me prattle on about my English Heritage work, the lady said: 'My husband will be interested to hear something is being done about these pillboxes. He was at D-Day, you know.' It always comes as something of a surprise to talk to people of the war generation, often looking still so youthful, someone to whom the remains lying about today were once real and meaningful, not buried, forgotten relics to be exhumed and pondered over. I had spent so long in my research that it was easy to forget that there were people around who still knew everything about what I was studying. It is so vital to capture this evidence before it is too late.

61 'Suffolk Square' pillbox at Walberswick

The lady disappeared up the track, evidently pleased by her 'find' of the morning (me and my project) and I was left to record the pillboxes she had pointed out to me. These were of another variant type, known unofficially as the 'Suffolk Square', the walls made of concrete blocks, with two embrasures side-by-side in each face, apart from that with the entrance which was protected by an attached blast wall. This area, overlooking marshes in front of the shingle beach, had been one of the defended localities by which the shoreline was defended. I had a note that a battalion of the South Lancashire Regiment had manned the defences here, later replaced by the Cameronians. One of the pillboxes had been a command post, and this may have been the one that was now sunken and dangerous.

The marshes to the south had been re-flooded as a defence measure in 1940, and they have remained flooded to this day and are now a nature reserve. The rain had ceased, and I had a lovely stroll on boarded walkways through these marshes, and found more pillboxes at the edge of the higher land that overlooked them. My work with air photographs had shown me there had been a heavy anti-aircraft battery positioned in this area as well, at the eastern edge of Hoist Covert. I also had a Luftwaffe air photograph taken in August 1940. This showed the lines of anti-tank blocks, and the sites of various pillboxes around the village. It did not show, however, the anti-tank scaffolding that had lined the beach in both directions, running to Dunwich in the south and beyond Southwold to the north, as this had been erected later in 1941.

On the far side of the River Blyth, the two 6in gun emplacements of an Emergency Coast Defence Battery that had been constructed at the head of the beach in May/June 1940 were clear on the German photograph. Emergency coast batteries were the first defence works to be rushed into place in May 1940 to protect Britain's coast, even before the disastrous results of the fighting in France were known. In 1941, the River Blyth battery was moved further north to a site on Gun Hill at the southern edge of Southwold. I drove here later from Walberswick and inspected the coastline from Southwold to the Blyth river. Nothing survives now of the lines of anti-tank cubes, the pillboxes, and the coast battery that once stood here. They have all been cleared away as clean as a whistle, which makes what survives south of the river at Walberswick all the more important. Long may these Second World War remains stay there around the sacrosanct beach huts. They are an important reminder of the defences that once stood on this stretch of East Anglian coast, and the purpose behind them.

16
LUDHAM BRIDGE TO ACLE, NORFOLK

Inland from the east coast of Norfolk, you come into that landscape of waterway and lake known as The Broads, created, we are told, by centuries of peat digging. Through the western expanse of those Broads flows the delightfully named River Ant, passing to the west of the small market town of Ludham. The A1062 road from Ludham to the west crosses the Ant at Ludham Bridge, and it is here that we are coming next.

Spot, whom we met at Cuckmere Haven, was with me this day in the car, looking as if he owned it and the road and everything else we passed. Jack Russells are very proprietorial. They love the power that is accorded them by being in a vehicle with their master beside them. They will snap at everything that approaches, be it an old lady with a shopping trolley, a crop-haired kid, or a traffic warden. They like to be seated up high in lorries, tractors, or Land Rovers, where they can enjoy a wide view of the world they are passing through – that lower world of peasant and shop girl and poodles with clipped tails and checked coats. When they emerge onto the plebeian pavement from their privileged place by the steering wheel, they will sniff suspiciously around for a few moments, and then go for the first thing that moves. They have to be dragged back on a lead, rising on their rear legs, snarling and snapping at some sweet little girl or a blowing piece of newspaper. After a while, they quieten down, content that they have cleared the way for their master, and that all will now be well.

And so it was with Spot when we came to Ludham Bridge. I had parked in a lay-by a little way beyond the bridge, and walked back with Spot on his lead and my pack with my recording gear over one shoulder. It was summer and it was busy. It was the first time I had been to The Broads, and I had not known what to expect. What I saw on the River Ant was motorboat after motorboat, of different sizes, queuing to moor at the bank by the bridge. Earnest young ladies in shorts and tee-shirts leapt ashore with ropes in their hands while their partners played Captain Hornblower, fiddling with the rudder as the boats slid along the bank. On the towpath were hoses for fresh water and pumps for fuel, and a short distance away alongside the road was a cafe and stores where you could fill up the interior of man, woman, and boat to your heart's content.

Spot hated all this activity. As I descended from the bridge to the towpath running beneath, he went for the heels of a buxom wench in a pneumatic yellow vest, and then attacked the jugular of a small, black shaggy dog who had been lying peacefully in the sun. A fierce battle developed, which I ended by jerking Spot bodily upwards by his collar and carrying him like that, feet dangling down like a carcass hung outside a butcher's (in the good, old days) until we were clear of the war zone. It had probably not been a good idea to bring Spot.

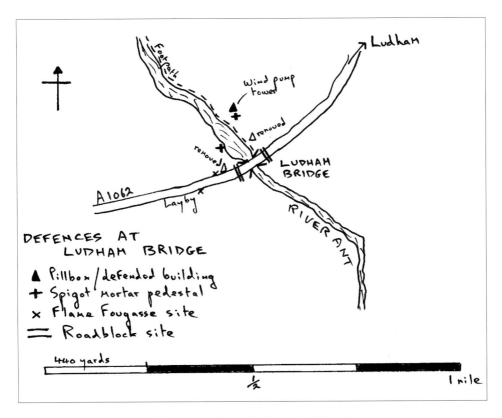

62 Sketch map showing the defences at Ludham Bridge on the River Ant

I tied Spot's lead to the branch of a tree, and looked around. Ludham Bridge had been a defended locality on a demolition belt running broadly parallel with the coast 15 miles away. Every bridge crossing of this belt had been mined for demolition, and Ludham Bridge was no exception. It had also been defended by two roadblocks, one on each side, and by pillboxes, Spigot mortars, and flame fougasses. We haven't looked yet at the latter category of site, which was one of those imaginative and thoroughly nasty inventions of the Petroleum Warfare Department. A steel drum hidden at the roadside was filled with a mixture of petrol and tar, and was fired by an explosive charge so that it leapt into the air to discharge its flaming contents all around. A similar unpleasant device, probably even more effective, was a tank of petrol by the side of the road, fed by gravity to flood the road surface in the face of advancing enemy troops. The petrol would then be fired by a grenade. Two such sites are recorded to the west of Ludham Bridge, one on each side of the road.

The major defence site, however, at Ludham Bridge is the red-brick tower that can be seen rising from the east bank of the river a short distance upstream from the bridge. This once housed a pump to drain the surrounding land, with sails turned by the wind supplying the motive power. The sails have long since been removed, and just the tapering brick tower remains. In 1940, it had been fortified by inserting concrete loopholes at two levels in the circular walls and by adding a brick blast wall at the doorway.

63 The defended wind-pump tower at Ludham Bridge, loopholed and with a blast wall added to its doorway

I picked my way with Spot over the marshy ground to the tower, stamping a path through chest-high nettles. In front of the doorway was a Spigot mortar pedestal, from which anti-tank bombs would have been fired towards the bridge, supported by machine-gun fire from behind. The inside of the tower was impressive. There were eight loopholes in all on the two levels, which during the war would have been divided by a wooden floor, now removed. I could imagine the men manning this position: the documents show that in 1940 they came from the 9th Bn Royal Berkshire Regiment, although I suspect that their place was taken later by the local Home Guard unit at Ludham, only a mile and a half away. Ludham was a Category 'B' nodal point, and Ludham Bridge would probably have formed part of the defence scheme of the town. Even Spot was impressed by the evocative atmosphere of the tower, subsiding to the floor and lying still. This is one of the best surviving examples of a 1940 defended building in the country.

On the opposite bank of the river is another Spigot mortar pedestal. I returned to the bridge and crossed over to it. I found the pedestal sunk in the ground so that only a few inches showed above the grass. Around its shining steel pintle was the mooring rope of a boat. The boat occupants looked at me sternly from their lofty position on the quarter deck as I photographed it. I doubt if they knew what it was, but they didn't have the curiosity to ask me, and I knew enough of the difference between landlubbers and seafaring folk not to speak unless I was spoken to. When I saw Spot lifting his leg against their mooring rope, I made off quickly.

On a Saturday morning, Elizabeth and I came to Acle, which is a small market town on the edge of The Broads close to the River Bure. The Bure joins with the Ant, which we have just come from at Ludham Bridge, so the boats we met there are likely to have passed here too. For this is most definitely boating country, and there is a small marina at Acle connected to the Bure by a waterway called the Acle Dike. A railway runs to the south of the town on its way to Great Yarmouth, and this is one local line that survived the dreaded swingeing axe of Dr Beeching in the 1960s. Running just north of it, the new Acle by-pass carries the A47 around the town. It makes a junction with another main road that heads off to the north-east, crossing the River Bure at Acle Bridge where there is yet another marina. We shall be going there later.

Elizabeth was with me not through any renewed desire to get to grips with reinforced concrete again, but because she was visiting a friend who lived on a farm nearby. But first we drove into the town centre for a cup of coffee. As we manoeuvred to park in The Street close to the broad area of The Green (once, I think the market place) she saw suddenly a site which, together with the wind-pump tower at Ludham Bridge, I would place in the top 10 of anti-invasion

England. All her fluctuating enthusiasm returned. It would be hard to miss this one; it did not really require Elizabeth's superior pillbox spotting skills. Here was a massive loophole at one side of a red-brick building, staring at us down The Street. You almost flinched as you looked at it, as if the gun behind it was about to fire. It would certainly have made a mess of the Saturday morning traffic in the same way it was intended to make a mess of the invading German soldiers advancing up this Norfolk street.

Acle was a Category 'A' nodal point in 1940, in a most important position at a junction of routes behind the coastal frontline defences some 8 miles to the east. The town also contained the headquarters of 213 Infantry Brigade defending this area of Norfolk. Possibly there was also an underground battle headquarters as at Sarre, but, if so, there is no clear evidence of it today. Along the line of the River Bure ran another of those demolition belts that we found at Ludham Bridge. As at that place, the road crossing of the river was a forward defended locality (FDL): this bridge a mile north-east of Acle was known at the time as Wey Bridge.

As a nodal point, Acle had all-round defences, and a surprisingly high number of these survive. But the chief site is the one we had just spotted – the defended seventeenth-century manor house on the green at the heart of the town: I noted it was now offering bed and breakfast. An addition had been added to the right end of this building – a pillbox, but disguised with matching red-brick walls and a pitched roof so that it looked like an extension to the house (*colour plate 20*). Two embrasures stared out, facing south and east. Elizabeth and I peered into them. It looked like the pillbox was being used today as a boiler house. What a useful addition to your property, paid for by the tax payer: it was not surprising no effort had been made to remove it. It looked good and it was useful, and it was also a valuable historic structure. But you wouldn't think so when you read a plaque affixed to the manor house wall. The 1940 addition wasn't even mentioned.

There is still a climate of opinion in the country that is almost embarrassed by the Second World War when it comes to a consideration of the part our home landscape played in the defeat of the Nazis. It sees the period as ugly and brutal, the physical remains of which, and even the memory, should be removed, smoothed over, or forgotten, certainly not promoted and advertised. Ugly and brutal it certainly was, but it was also part of the mainstream of history, receding now to take its place with the other great happenings of the past. Indeed, for many towns and villages throughout the country, there has probably been no greater event in the whole march of history than the Second World War. The soldiers from many nations who came to defend the land, and later to train for battle upon it, lived in billets and camps, passed in convoy, manned the searchlights and the anti-aircraft guns, marched with the Home Guard, and flew in the great bombers overhead, gave numbers of tiny and scattered settlements a place in history. The home landscape of the Second World War should be commemorated, not hidden away. And at Acle, there is no better memorial than this splendid pillbox staring down The Street. The people who live there should be proud of it.

Elizabeth disappeared for her appointment, taking both the car and Spot, and I was left in the centre of Acle, pondering my next move. As a nodal point, Acle had been required to hold out, if attacked, for a minimum of seven days. The southern defence perimeter of the town was the railway line, the embankment of which, east of the station, was lined with anti-tank blocks. There was at least one anti-tank gun (a 6pdr) for which earthwork positions were prepared on either side of Old Road. The garrison of the nodal point came partly from the 14th Bn South Staffordshire Regiment, replaced in 1941 by the 9th Bn Royal Berkshires, and partly from the 6th Bn Norfolk Home Guard.

I walked from The Green along Pyebush Lane heading towards the area of the northern defence perimeter, beyond the houses of the town. I knew at least one pillbox survived here, and I found it after a few hundred yards, by the side of a track – a Type 22, heavily overgrown. When I had examined post-war air photographs, I had spotted what I felt sure was another pillbox further on, past isolated St Mary's Church, at the sharp corner of a lane, but I did not know if it survived. Certainly no one had recorded it for the Defence of Britain Project. So, as I came closer, I felt a sense of triumph when a concrete shape hove into view, just where it should have been. The eye of one embrasure stared directly at me as I approached, with the flat countryside stretching away on all sides. I stopped and took a photograph, which came out well. I have made it my first slide whenever I give a talk. It seems to symbolise the idea of these defence works in the landscape (the aspect of the subject which appeals to me most), part of a linked system, sited to take advantage of the natural topography, and blending with it – the defended landscape of 1940.

There were roadblocks, Spigot mortar emplacements, loopholed walls, and fougasses within Acle, all long since cleared away. One Spigot mortar pedestal, in fact, has been preserved within a garden off New Road, moved, I think, from its original site. Two further Type 22 pillboxes survive, one on the north side of the railway to the south-east of the town. Nearby, close to where Weavers Lane (now an overgrown footpath) crosses the railway, I found some brickwork and concrete in a dense thicket, with a void going down into blackness close by. I had a note that a pillbox had stood here, which is probably what these remains were, but I couldn't get out of my mind the fact that there may have been an underground battle headquarters somewhere in Acle. Was this the site? It was impossible to do more than speculate. The thicket was impenetrable and the void looked dangerous. Perhaps a local resident knows what stood here.

64 Spigot mortar pedestal at Acle Bridge

I headed north along Weavers Lane, and came to the Acle Dike, which is lined with all manner of motorboats and yachts ready to slip down the waterway to the River Bure, and out into The Broads. A pillbox stood here until at least the 1970s, but was then removed. This was also one of the bases of The Broads Flotilla, a Home Guard unit consisting of three boats armed with Lewis guns which patrolled the lakes and waterways of The Broads. Another of its bases was at Wey Bridge (Acle Bridge) where I was heading next.

It's a mile or so along the Old Road (now the busy A1064) to Acle Bridge. I had arranged to meet Elizabeth there at the Bridge Inn, a pleasant pub on the bank of the river. If I got my timing right I could get in a drink before she arrived. But there was still a good way left to tramp.

The pillboxes that once stood at the defended locality of Acle Bridge have long since been destroyed. The bridge itself has been replaced recently, removing the evidence of the detonation chambers that could previously be seen cut into the structure of the old bridge. What do survive, however, on the south bank of the river are three Spigot mortar pedestals of a particularly large diameter topped by their stainless steel pintles. There used to be another as well on the south-west side of the bridge, but that has now been removed. Four Spigot mortars is an impressive armoury, assuming of course that each emplacement with its pedestal had its own gun. Documents show that the garrison of the Wey Bridge defended locality in 1941 was a platoon from the 9th Bn Berkshire Regiment with a section of the battalion's anti-tank company. Possibly the Spigot mortar supplemented the still limited number of 2pdr anti-tank guns that were available to the Field Army in 1941.

One of the Spigot mortar pedestals stands in the garden of the Bridge Inn by the bank of the river. It seemed a convenient place on which to balance my pint glass as I waited for Elizabeth to arrive, looking out at the bridge less than 100yds away. By the time I spotted a small Jack Russell pulling its owner purposefully on a lead across the car park, I was well into my second pint. I wondered if this pub had been serving pints for the thirsty soldiery in the hot summer of 1940. If so, we may have to add a whole new meaning to the idea of fighting to the last round!

17

WEYBOURNE, NORTH NORFOLK

I had made several visits to Weybourne on the North Norfolk coast: it was one of the largest, in terms of size, of the defence areas I was surveying for English Heritage. I kept going back because it was such a lovely place to visit, and the walks were so good. Spot loved it, and so did Elizabeth, and the many defence works merged into a background of beach and sea, heath, hill, and headland, and the long line of the cliffs to the east.

An old rhyme dated to about 1700 runs, 'He who would Old England win, must at Weybourne Hoop begin'. Certainly, there had been a fort built here at the time of the Spanish Armada. Weybourne Hoop (or Hope as it is spelt today) is the point where the cliffs from the east finish and a flat coastal strip of salt marsh running through Cley to the west begins. It was formerly an anchorage for ships with deep water close inshore. This was one of the factors that made it dangerous as a point of invasion.

In the First World War the coast here had been defended by earthworks and the cylindrical concrete gun posts that had provided the name 'pillbox'. In the mid-1930s an army camp for training with anti-aircraft guns was established here, lying on land to the west of Weybourne Hope. This camp was used throughout the Second World War, and was only closed in 1959 after a generation of National Servicemen, the brave 'blanco and bullshit brigade', had passed through it. Much of the camp site was cleared in the 1980s and returned to agriculture, but part of it was purchased by the Muckleburgh Collection (named after the hill behind the camp) which opened a museum of Second World War arms and armour in the old NAAFI building. Some 300 acres of the surrounding land are also owned by the Muckleburgh Collection, and used for a variety of purposes including tank driving and displays of military vehicles. Many defence works survive on this land. This August day I was coming to see them and to meet the Muckleburgh Collection's owner, Michael Savory.

I arrived early in the morning before there were many people about. The museum is a popular venue on the tourist trail, attracting many visitors, both young and old. It is a hands-on museum where you can touch and experience exhibits, going for rides on armoured vehicles, for instance, and watching re-enactments. This is the best way to stimulate interest, although most people have an inherent fascination with war and warfare anyhow – unfortunate, and even unhealthy, perhaps, but built into the psychology of the human race. I am not a great one for dwelling on the machinery of death, but I think it is right that we should be proud of our nation's achievement in battle and the courage of our soldiers, and we should respect the similar qualities shown by our enemies. That sort of thing does not generate future wars. It makes us more aware of the need for vigilance in our own defence, and provides a scorn for politicians who create wars for their own ambition, as we have seen so recently.

Michael Savory met me in the museum's café. He is a lean, wiry man of tremendous drive and energy. He was immediately interested in the research I had already carried out and the copied air photographs and documents I had brought with me. We spread them out on the café table.

'Here's the site of the army camp,' I said perhaps unnecessarily: the grid pattern of roads and huts was very clear. We were looking at an air photograph taken in 1946. I traced a line running around the camp site. 'That's the line of an anti-tank ditch that was dug to protect the coastal front as far as Kelling.' Michael hadn't known about the ditch. He pored over the photograph, fascinated. 'It passed across the entrance to the camp,' I said. 'Very close to where we are now, in fact. There was a block there formed of concrete cubes.'

'We cleared them away,' said Michael. 'There're a couple of Spigot mortars close by. Let's go and see them.' We were up and about, Michael fired with enthusiasm, before I had even had a chance to gather my papers together. I jammed them back into their envelope and joined him outside. The sun was lighting the green slopes of the hills beyond the camp site. Beyond us across a field there were a few original huts from the camp. Some cars were trickling into the car park, disgorging a mixture of mums and dads, teenage girls with their habitual pose of boredom, and excited small boys who immediately began running vigorously about, peering at the anti-aircraft gun that stood by the car park, 'Cor, Dad. Can I shoot that?'

Michael showed me the pedestal of a Spigot mortar to one side of the drive to the camp. 'We moved it there,' he said. 'The other one's in its original position.' We plunged into some bushes, scrambled over a barbed-wire fence; at least I scrambled, tangling one foot in the wire, while Michael moved with the spare ease of a poacher. I struggled to keep up with him. A Spigot mortar pedestal

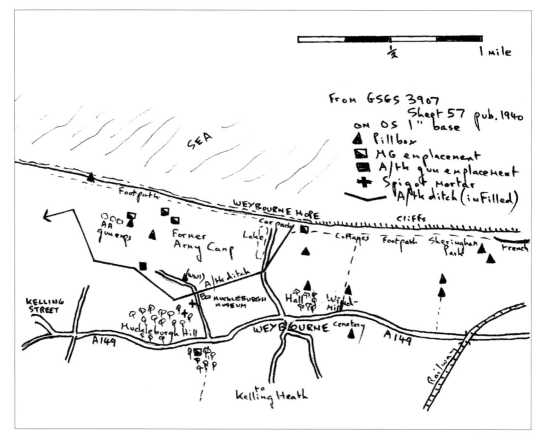

Map annotations include: ½ — 1 mile (scale bar); From GSGS 3907 Sheet 57 pub. 1940 on OS 1" base; ▲ Pillbox; ◨ MG emplacement; ◨ A/tk gun emplacement; ✚ Spigot Mortar; A/tk ditch (inFilled); SEA; Footpath; WEYBOURNE HOPE; Car park; Cliffs; Cottages; Footpath; Sheringham Park; Trench; ◯◯◯ AA gun emps; Former Army Camp; Lake; KELLING STREET; (now) A/tk ditch; MUCKLEBURGH MUSEUM; Hall; Wind-Mill; Muckleburgh Hill; A149; WEYBOURNE Cemetery; A149; Railway; to Kelling Heath

65 *Above:* Sketch map showing the coastal defences around Weybourne

66 *Opposite:* First World War pillbox in the grounds of the Muckleburgh Collection Museum – the original shape that gave the name 'pillbox'

rose out of the undergrowth by a fence like a Mayan temple stone deep in the jungle.

We returned to the drive, and walked along it past the museum into territory where the general public are not permitted on their own. There beside the track was one of the archetypal pillboxes from the First World War, circular with five embrasures and with an iron door. Michael unlocked the padlocked door and pushed it open. I peered inside. There were big cracks in the roof. 'It needs some money spent on it,' Michael said. 'Or it'll collapse in time – a pity.' It was indeed a pity. If ever a structure deserved the benefit of a little public money, it was this, abandoned in these grassy wastes by the North Sea, a defence work approaching 100 years old that gave us the name 'pillbox', a term still used by the military today.

We returned to the museum. 'We need to drive now,' Michael said. I thought he was going to lead me to some powerful army vehicle, perhaps one of the big-wheeled American 'gama goats' that are used to give visitors rides, or a tracked vehicle, or at least a Land Rover, but instead he opened the door of a low-slung, mud-coloured saloon car of an indeterminate make and I squeezed inside, pushing aside a jumble of newspapers and computer disks so I could sit down. With a roar from the broken exhaust we disappeared once more up the track past the First World War pillbox.

After a short distance, we left the main track, and picked our way over broken ground, lurching over ruts and pot holes, until we came suddenly to an anti-tank gun emplacement with a brick observation post close by. The emplacement had probably held a 2pdr gun. We inspected the interior briefly, and then it was back into the car which Michael drove between the hummocks of grass, rocking into hollows and over ridges of buried concrete, as if we were on some 4-wheel drive expedition, only the vehicle we were in did not look as if it would stand up to such treatment. Still we slid with aplomb in and out of pools of mud and water, and rose up grassy slopes with great grace and only a moderate increase in the note of the engine.

We stopped again, and trekked through long grass and nettles until I realised I was standing above a large, circular concrete pit. 'This is one of the 3.7in anti-aircraft gun emplacements,' said Michael. 'We dug it out a while back. See how perfectly preserved it is, with its ammunition lockers around the circumference.'

I saw a series of concrete recesses around the edge of the emplacement, looking something like small, open-fronted burial recesses, the sort of thing you see hacked out of rock in the catacombs, only these were formed of concrete slabs and had held the shells for the gun.

'There are two more of these emplacements in a line here,' said Michael. 'The other two are buried: I'd like to excavate them all so the public can see them. These guns were still firing into the 1950s. They must be amongst the best-preserved anti-aircraft emplacements in the country.' He waved his hand at the sky. 'It's finished now – the age of guns protecting England's air space and her coasts. All missiles today, of course.'

'Don't we still need coastal artillery?' I asked.

'There'd be no need. They'd all come through the Channel Tunnel anyhow. The island fortress is no more.'

The car took us a few more bumpy yards over the open hill slope. In front, beyond a series of grass ridges, was the shingle beachfront, with its foaming lines of surf. The wrinkled, sunlit sea stretched away to the horizon. A brick-shuttered pillbox stood on the grass above the shingle. Behind it was a sunken concrete emplacement with a large embrasure for the fire of the Vickers medium machine gun. More than 60 years ago soldiers had crouched here, looking out, waiting for the German fleet to hove into view – but it had never come. In front would have been barbed-wire entanglements, and, at the head of the beach, a continuous line of anti-tank scaffolding, a high, criss-cross structure of tubular steel-rods. The hillside would also have been mined; here, where I walked, anti-tank and anti-personnel mines had been laid, some 250, the records said, in this small sector alone in front of the army camp.

'What my ambition is …' began Michael, looking out over the sea. The sun was warm on our faces, the sound of the waves on the shore lulling and dream-inducing. Small white butterflies moved from flower to flower amongst the grasses.

'…What my ambition is, is to reconstruct a section of these beach defences, and display it to the public. We could erect the scaffolding and the barbed wire, clean out and camouflage the pillboxes, dig fire trenches, set up command and observation posts. We could re-establish the whole system of coastal defence that stood here in 1940, with the anti-aircraft guns and the camp behind. It would be a grand project, would it not?'

'It would indeed,' I agreed. 'And very much needed. There's no museum anywhere, I think, to the 1940 defences. There would be a great deal of interest from the public, I'm sure. And what a fine memorial to the men who served in home defence.'

'Ah,' said Michael thoughtfully. 'We just need a little funding from somewhere.'

He returned me safely to the museum in his unlikely rough-ride car, which had behaved impeccably. We shook hands.

'I hope something can come of that idea to reconstruct the defences,' I said.

'It's all down to finance,' he said.

I would have thought the Heritage Lottery Fund, for instance, might support a project that had such an important public educational role. After all, for a few short weeks in 1940 it seemed that our very survival as a nation might depend on those defences dug into the hillside above the sea at Weybourne. Public money, however, might not run to erecting them for a second time! I must return to the Muckleburgh Collection one day soon and find out if Michael has been able to take his ideas any further forward.

There is much more to see of the anti-invasion defences of Weybourne, and a quick tour follows:

Drive down Beach Lane from Weybourne village to the car park on the sea front, from where the anti-tank ditch running south of the army camp started. From this point you will see the cliffs rising to the east, and a machine-gun emplacement is dug into them, now perilously close to the cliff edge. This is one of a number of defence works that stood here – gun emplacements and a command post, with underground chambers. They have been removed, although it is likely that there is much that has just been filled in and will still survive under the ground. Other structures have fallen over the eroding cliff, and bits and pieces of concrete and brick can be seen at low tide on the shingle banks beneath.

To the south, a brick-shuttered Type 24 pillbox now stands in the middle of a cultivated field: in 1940, it stood on the line of a hedgerow. Further to the east are the wall footings and concrete floor of an observation post, with another hexagonal pillbox near by. You reach next a track running between the Old Coastguard Cottages and the windmill: the latter, without its sails, was used as a Home Guard observation post. Two pillboxes, and a Spigot mortar pedestal, survive in this area close to the boundary to the grounds of Weybourne Hall, which served as an army headquarters. On the cliffs by the Coastguard Cottages, a 4in gun emplacement was constructed, which necessitated the demolition of six houses. The gun emplacement has long since gone (perhaps fallen over the cliff) as has probably the site of the six houses.

If you press along the footpath east of the Old Coastguard Cottages, you come eventually into the National Trust land of Sheringham Park where more pillboxes survive: one has been converted into an observatory for a local bird-watching group. This was a strongly defended part of the coast, with, remarkably,

67 *Opposite:* Machine-gun emplacement on the cliffs above Weybourne Hope

68 *Above:* Cut-off beach scaffolding protrudes from the shingle close to a pillbox west of Weybourne Hope

what would be termed in another location an anti-tank ditch, dug parallel with the cliff edge (*colour plate 22*). You can still see this as it was never infilled: its position today is much closer to the eroding cliff than in 1940. It was clearly more of a linear earthwork for infantry defence than one with an anti-tank role as such. It's hard to imagine tanks being hauled up the cliff here. Certainly it's recorded as being filled with barbed wire, so I imagine it was part of a cliff-top defence with the aim of preventing German troops scaling the cliffs to outflank Weybourne Hope itself. An oblique air photograph shows a considerable group of defences here – slit trenches, pillboxes, barbed wire, and even what looks like an Allan Williams Turret. South of these was a rifle range, the numbered targets of which can be clearly seen in the photograph I have referred to.

Back at Weybourne Hope, you might like to explore the beachfront to the west, walking at the head of the beach below the army camp land where we have just travelled with Michael Savory. The defence works overlooking the beach can be seen from here, and it can be imagined how dramatic a section of reconstructed defences would look. If you walk beyond the margins of the land of the Muckleburgh Collection, and that of the small radar station of RAF Weybourne (the modern inheritor of the defence tradition of Weybourne Hope) you will find a Type 22 pillbox that survives remarkably on the beach, although it is washed over at high tide and must be hammered by the seas in bad weather (*colour plate 21*). Alongside it, when I was last there, I spotted fragments of anti-tank scaffolding protruding from the shingle, a sight that I found evocative. It is the only time I have seen scaffolding still in situ of the hundreds of miles erected along the coastline of England in 1941: here its base had been cut off and left buried on the beach. Perhaps after storms, when the shingle has been scoured by the waves, more is revealed. The sight, I thought, was worth the long walk along the seafront, and the invigorating tramp back along the shingle produced its own reward in terms of expanded lungs and improved leg muscles.

There is more to see at Weybourne of the 1940 defences, and also in the areas to the east and west (it has to be remembered that these coastal defences were continuous and there are remains in many other places), but for this visit, I feel, we have done enough, and we will say now farewell to East Anglia. Next we will be travelling into the heartlands of Southern England where further battlefields were prepared.

18

SULHAM VALLEY, BERKSHIRE

I am heading for Berkshire, to be precise to the Sulham Valley which runs from Pangbourne on the River Thames to the River Kennet further south. The broad southern part of the valley is crossed by the M4 and by the main railway line to the west, with the suburbs of Reading spreading almost to its eastern flank. It is the upper and central part of the valley, however, that concerns us, around the small settlement of Sulham itself. This is an attractive farmed landscape, with woodland on the valley slopes, and with the gentle stream of the River Pang meandering through broad pastures. In July 1940 a main branch of the GHQ Line (Line Red) was routed through it.

We have looked at the GHQ Line so far in its route across Surrey to the south of the North Downs, and also in Kent, where it met at Penshurst the branch running from Newhaven across the Weald to the River Thames on the North Kent coast. We have followed it as well as it crossed Essex and entered Cambridgeshire on its way to the north. Now it is time to introduce you to the other branches of the GHQ Line that ran from the West Country into the Central South of the country.

GHQ Line Green (these colours are the Army's official designations: the relevant colours were crayoned onto a map I found at The National Archives showing their routes) ran from the North Somerset coast near Burnham-on-Sea in a great loop around Bristol, rejoining the River Severn near Longney west of Strood. Its main purpose was the protection of the port of Bristol, but it also provided a westward extension of GHQ Lines Blue and Red which branched from it, the former at Whaddon in Wiltshire and the latter at Great Somerford south of Malmesbury. GHQ Line Blue followed the course of the Kennet and Avon Canal to a point just west of Reading where it met GHQ Line Red which had just passed through the Sulham Valley (the area we are going to look at now) having crossed southern Oxfordshire into Berkshire. GHQ Line Blue, linking with Line Green, formed the principal anti-tank barrier against a German advance north from a landing on the Dorset or Hampshire coast, while Line Red acted as a rear defence should Line Blue be crossed. In that eventuality, the section of Line Red south of Pangbourne (the Sulham Valley) was of critical importance, for it not only defended against an enemy advance to take the important anti-tank island of Reading from the north but it also protected the western approaches to London. The intense system of defence there that we are coming to see is explained by this strategy.

A busy, narrow lane crosses the Sulham Valley, running east from the village of Tidmarsh. There is little opportunity to park in this lane, so I recommend you make use of the car park of The Greyhound public house at Tidmarsh (it gives you the opportunity to enjoy their excellent facilities, which I recommend you do first), or you might find a space in a pull off by the lane a short distance away. This, in fact, was where I managed to park my car, and I took a footpath from the lane at the nearby bridge over the River Pang. You will see the river is only some 15ft wide with shallow banks, hence the need to dig an anti-tank ditch along the valley to provide an obstacle the Germans could not simply drive their tanks across.

I crossed the river by a footbridge, and followed a footpath running along a hedgerow. Suddenly, under a tree, I saw the first of the anti-tank gun emplacements that stud this valley – a rectangular Type 28A, with two main embrasures, both now blocked with brick, for the fire of the 2pdr anti-tank gun. The emplacement is used as a cattle shelter, so I had to disturb its bovine occupants to inspect the interior. There was a dividing wall separating a side-chamber for light machine-gun fire from the main space occupied by the anti-tank gun. The embrasures faced north and east across the line of the anti-tank ditch which would have bisected the field in front of me.

I walked on down the path, and came to a marshy place by a small stream where I found two more rectangular emplacements close together in front of me (*colour plate 23*). I was standing now exactly on the line of the anti-tank ditch, which crossed the field to my right where I could see the buildings of a farm in the distance. This is Oaklands Farm, and it is highlighted in history because documents at The National Archives record that in July 1940 its owner, a Miss Wrench, wrote to the Berkshire agricultural authorities requesting them to put pressure on the Army to bend their defence line around her farm rather than going straight through it, rendering much of it useless for agriculture (remember that at this time farming was a front-line activity and state-controlled). The Chief Engineer replied, 'I regret that exigencies of defence do not permit of moving the line eastwards', and so Miss Wrench had a ditch 800yds long and 55ft wide (from spoil heap to spoil heap on either side) cut across her land. By early in 1944 it had been filled in. Miss Wrench does not mention the concrete emplacements in her letters, but the one you have seen and the two in front of you she also inherited. It's nice to think that at least she got some free shelters for her cows out of this exercise in the nation's defence.

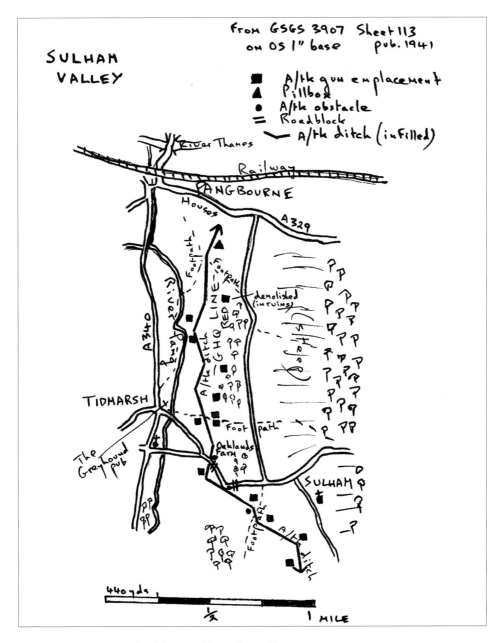

69 Sketch map showing the defences of the Sulham Valley

70 Above: Double-chambered anti-tank gun emplacement, with blocked up main embrasure, in the Sulham Valley

71 Opposite: Interior of an anti-tank gun emplacement in the Sulham Valley, showing the main gun chamber with two embrasures (now bricked up) and a side chamber for LMG fire

I inspected the two emplacements, and saw that they had been positioned back to back, their anti-tank gun embrasures pointing in opposite directions along the anti-tank ditch. Each also had a side Bren gun chamber. These emplacements north of Oaklands Farm clearly formed a particular strongpoint on GHQ Line Red. Although the main purpose of the line was to defend against an anticipated German attack from the west, the fact that emplacements were on both sides of the anti-tank ditch (not only here but elsewhere in the Sulham Valley) indicates that the line was designed for a two-way defence; for example, against a German attack west from London *after* the capture of the capital.

As the field to the immediate north was not in crop, I followed a hedgerow at its edge until I came to a small copse in one corner. Here, under the trees, I found another anti-tank gun emplacement. This one was even larger with two main embrasures and two side chambers. On its outer walls I could see evidence of damage caused perhaps by shell-fire or by explosives placed at the embrasures: I had already noted similar damage on the other emplacements I'd looked at. Now, don't hasten off to write your best-selling account of a German ground attack on England that really did happen, for I think this is evidence of tests carried out before D-Day of the effectiveness of Allied weapons against German reinforced concrete bunkers. Such experiments were often undertaken in assault training areas at the coast, but they seem to have been carried out inland here as well. One emplacement in the northern part of the valley was blown up entirely, and now lies in shattered sections at the side of a field.

I returned to the footpath and followed it past the twin emplacements I had already inspected until after a couple of hundred yards I came to Sulham Lane. Here I turned right, passing through a lovely landscape of farms and stables, and houses with perfect flowering gardens, lying beneath the wooded slopes of the valley to my left. I came to a T-junction with another lane (this, in fact, is the lane from Tidmarsh that I left at the bridge over the Pang at the beginning of the walk) and saw a stile to a footpath that crossed the field beyond.

As I pushed through the thick grass of the field, I saw to my right on the opposite side of the hedgerow an anti-tank gun emplacement with two main embrasures. I couldn't reach it without trespassing, so I recorded it from a distance, and then headed at some speed for a stile I saw ahead of me at the far end of the field. The reason for my increase in pace was a bull which had appeared through an opening in the hedge by the emplacement and was now taking a considerable interest in me. Even when I had reached safety on the far side of the stile, he continued to regard me steadily from a distance of about a foot, eye-balling me with a look that was distinctly unfriendly. Perhaps he suspected some intent by this strange forked creature on his attendant cows, or perhaps he just wanted to investigate the things held out that clicked and flashed in the sun, but I was glad to see on my return that he had wandered back into the other field to check on outliers of his harem.

From the stile where I had reached safety, I made a short detour to the leafy hedge on my right and found (as my records told me) two vertical rails set in a concrete base, part of a block at a point where there had been a short break in the anti-tank ditch. There may have been other rails further along hidden in the dense thickets of the hedgerow. Why there was a gap in the ditch here, I'm not sure, but it shows clearly on an excellent series of air photographs taken in August 1943 that I had seen. A little further on, 100yds or so to my left, I spotted a further anti-tank gun emplacement, with two blocked main embrasures. The doorway has also been bricked up so there's little point in trespassing into the field to visit it; best to view it reflectively from a distance, and reconstruct in your mind the course of the anti-tank ditch that cut through the field between the emplacement and the footpath. The emplacement's twin embrasures would have enabled fire to be aimed across the ditch both to the north and south.

The line continues along the valley to the south-east, on its way to join with GHQ Line Blue at Theale. There are 24 of these massive anti-tank gun emplacements between Pangbourne and Theale, and you will be able to spot several more of them if you continue the walk to the south. For today, however, I had reached the southern limit of my area, and wanted to return now to explore more of the valley to the north.

When I got get back to the lane, I turned left along it. At a sharp right-handed bend I found amongst bushes on the left two pimples or dragon's teeth from a roadblock here. The anti-tank ditch had just touched the corner of the lane at this point as it passed through the fields to the left. Further to the north, it turned once more towards the lane, and by a farm gate on the right (Oaklands Farm again) I came upon four massive anti-tank cylinders from another roadblock where it crossed. These cylinders were made by filling segments of concrete drainage pipes with concrete and adding a domed top of concrete. The purpose of the domed, or sometimes pyramidal, tops to anti-tank blocks was probably to make it more difficult for them to be surmounted by placing balks of timber upon them to create a ramp.

To the left, there was an overgrown emplacement amongst trees that commanded the roadblock. It had two main embrasures that fired in opposite directions along the anti-tank ditch, which made a bend here passing in front of it. A record received by the Defence of Britain Project stated this emplacement was camouflaged as a house, being painted brown with white windows. I don't know where the recorder obtained this information (probably from a local resident) but once again it shows how important the gathering of oral history is for this subject. Landowners and villagers saw the defence works being built, and some of the most keen-eyed observers of the scene were children whose memories are often amazingly fresh. However, even the youngest witnesses to the 1940 defences (those who saw them when they were still in use) will now be in their mid-seventies.

I passed the gate to Oaklands Farm, wondering how many years Miss Wrench farmed here, hoping things improved for her after the anti-tank ditch was infilled in 1944. A few hundred yards further on I came back to the bridge crossing of the River Pang and re-found my car at the side of the road.

You can continue the walk further to the north as well, and find many more defences near the banks of the Pang. A footpath leads to the right from the A340 not far north of The Greyhound, and wanders delightfully at the back of large houses close to the river, until it eventually crosses by a footbridge. Here the valley opens out into a broad area of grassland. You will see further anti-tank gun emplacements in the distance, and be able to find the one I have already mentioned that was blown apart: it lies in a hedgerow not far from a path leading to Sulham Lane.

Further north you will come to outlying suburbs of Pangbourne where by houses here is a variant on a Type 22 pillbox that's worth a visit. It's an example of a small pillbox that was given thickened walls and a chamfered roof edge to deflect enemy shells. Unfortunately there's no internal access, but it's in good condition and makes a change from the anti-tank gun emplacements. There were only five similar pillboxes in this entire sector of GHQ Line Red such was the reliance on the anti-tank gun emplacement. By the way, the concrete structure set low in the ground by this pillbox has nothing to do with it. It's a former drainage channel: there are several others in the area. I have to confess that, when I first saw it, I did ponder about it for a while. It just goes to show that not everything made of grey, lichened concrete is necessarily associated with the Second World War.

19

FRILFORD AND FYFIELD, OXFORDSHIRE TO DUNMILL LOCK, BERKSHIRE

We have just seen GHQ Line Red at its very strongest, with huge anti-tank gun emplacements every few hundred yards alongside a machine-cut anti-tank ditch, in the section south of Pangbourne. North of that town, however, the line followed the course of the River Thames into what is now Oxfordshire, but which at the time of the Second World War was still part of Berkshire. At Abingdon, the Thames makes a great loop to the north incorporating Oxford, and GHQ Line Red cut off that loop by running across its base. Here, another artificial anti-tank ditch was necessary.

I came to the Oxfordshire villages of Frilford and Fyfield, west of Abingdon, to find the surviving evidence of the Line as it ran between these two places. It was a late summer's day with blue skies, and a hot sun striking down on a flat landscape of open arable fields that were the colour of straw from the harvest just in. As I drove, I could see combine harvesters in the fields, progressing like stately battleships through a sea of wheat, a great cloud of chaff and dust billowing behind them.

At the western of the two villages, Fyfield, cut off from the rest of the world now by the A420 trunk road curving around it to its south, it was a bit of a problem to work out the way into its centre – a bit like one of those children's puzzles where you have to try different lines to see which one takes you to your objective. When at last I had succeeded, I found a sleepy place of stone-built houses nodding under the sun, apparently empty of inhabitants. I saw not a soul, and drove slowly to the western side of the village thinking perhaps the whole place had been evacuated in some sudden emergency.

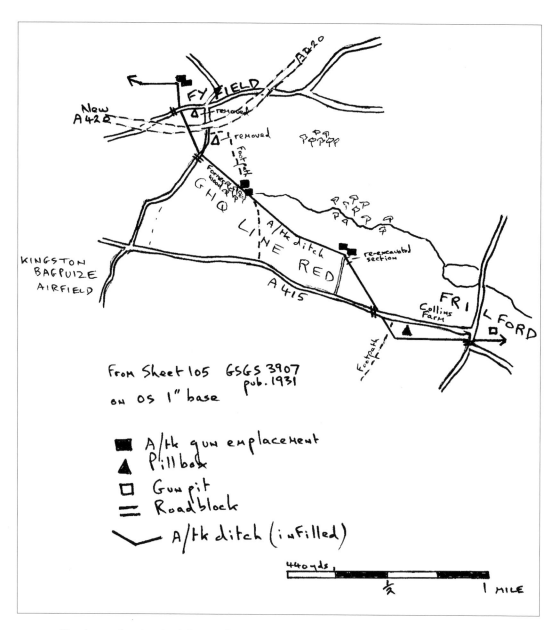

72 Sketch map showing the defences of GHQ Line Red between Fyfield and Frilford

I parked at the side of a deserted road that had once been the main street through the village before they built the A420, and looked over a farm gate at two familiar concrete rectangles in the distance – Type 28A anti-tank gun emplacements, set back to back like those we have seen at Oaklands Farm in the Sulham Valley. The anti-tank ditch had approached them directly from the south, now running under the houses of the nearby estate at St John's Close, built since the war and about the only recent addition to Fyfield that I could see. At the emplacements, it had then turned a right-angled corner and shot off to the west. I knew all this from a superb series of air photographs taken in 1944 by the United States Army Air Force, which had been based at nearby Kingston Bagpuize airfield. They show the zig-zagging course of the still open anti-tank ditch, the blocks where it crossed roads and lanes, and the anti-tank gun emplacements set in twos at strategic points of the line.

There was no public access to the emplacements at St John's Close, so I set off to the south to find some I could examine close up. Having braved the crossing of the A420, I found myself in a strange strip of unused land bordering the modern road, with the old road blocked off and a footpath running through a glorious wilderness of long grass and scarlet poppies. I found my way to a quiet, tree-lined road called Digging Lane, and passed a row of cottages where the air photograph showed a pillbox had stood (there was no sign of it now).

The anti-tank ditch had crossed Digging Lane a little further to the south, and then taken a course south-east towards Frilford. A footpath running behind the cottages would take me to meet its line, and so I set off over the dusty, reddish earth towards that distant point. In the field to my right they were burning the stubble; there was a flickering line of red fire with the smoke rising like a billowing wave against the sky. This is an elemental sight, as ancient as man, and good to see. I thought that under European Regulation 2569E/5087/2207 the practice of stubble burning was now banned, so it was encouraging to see that here in Oxfordshire they take no notice of silky-suited bureaucrats in glass palaces.

I reached an overgrown area at a bend of the track where the anti-tank ditch had crossed, and found two concrete emplacements, so overgrown with vegetation trailing over their roofs and hanging down their sides that it was like a scene from a movie when the hero discovers an ancient temple deep in the jungle. But there was no Indiana Jones here, just a red-faced Englishman bearing pack and camera and clutching a crumpled copy photograph in one hand. This air photograph showed me that during the war the emplacements had stood at the eastern edge of a narrow block of woodland that stretched for a short distance to the west. The wood had been grubbed out and its land merged with the field around, but I could still see where it had been because the area had been left as thin grass surrounded by yellow stubble.

The southern of the two emplacements was less overgrown than the northern, and its roof line was clear of the growth that clung to the walls. There were chamfered edges between the walls and the roof (on all sides except the rear) so that incoming shells striking them might ricochet away. The corners of the walls were also cut off for the same purpose. I pushed my way through the veils of vegetation hanging over the doorways of the two emplacements and looked inside each in turn. The interiors were in good condition with dividing walls between the main anti-tank gun chamber and the side chambers for light machine-gun fire. Something I had not seen in the Sulham Valley were slots in the concrete floors to take the trail of the 2pdr anti-tank gun.

I continued my journey along the track, with the course of the anti-tank ditch now crossing the fields to my left. At last I came to the A415 road, and I followed its broad, grassy verge, relatively safe from the traffic, towards Frilford. To my right was a large garden centre which offered the feature of a maze cut in a field of sweet corn (a maze amongst maize, you might say). An individual was seated on a tall ladder at the centre. Clearly, no one was to be allowed to get lost for too long: these days there are probably worries about compensation claims for the trauma caused.

I passed a track on the left leading off at right angles to the road. I knew it led up a slight rise to the line of the anti-tank ditch and the site of two more emplacements, but it was private land and I would have to ask permission to go there. A board close to the track proclaimed 'Collins Farm. Murray Maclean. Grower of hedgerow trees and shrubs'. Records I had received at the Defence of Britain Project referred to this farm and its farmer. He had done work several years ago re-excavating the anti-tank ditch near the emplacements on his land, and I understood he had left open the section he had dug so that its profile and depth could be seen, the only such archaeological work on an anti-tank ditch that I had heard of. I hoped I would find him at home.

I came to the gates of the farm, and wandered up a drive between stone buildings rising from banks of bright flowers. I came into a yard and stood uncertainly not knowing which of many doors I should approach. Just then a man appeared around the corner of a building and asked politely if he could help me. I was most fortunate. I had come straight to Murray Maclean; doubly fortunate, in fact, for I had caught him just before he was about to go out. Very kindly he gave me the permission I sought, and took me into his office where he kept a collection of books and papers to do with the Second World War history of the area. These included a map made by the local Home Guard showing the defences of Frilford and those of GHQ Line Red. I made some hurried notes, noting that the map showed a pillbox I did not know about to the south of the main road, not far from where we were. I asked Murray Maclean about it.

73 Shell-proof Type 22 pillbox on GHQ Line Red at Frilford

'Oh, that's in the garden of Mrs X', he said, naming a lady. 'She's here at the moment painting. I'm sure she'll let you go and see it'. And he took me across the farmyard to a building where there was a group of women painting; not whitewashing the walls, which had been my first bewildered thought, but a water-colour class of gentile ladies in earnest pursuit with brush and palette of a still-life subject.

When the subject of pillboxes was dropped into the tranquil assembly, there was a buzz of interested conversation. I have often commented upon the word 'pillbox' as a conversation opener; it acts like a magic spell. Mrs X charmingly gave her assent to my visiting her garden in her absence, and I backed out of the room with profuse thanks and a trill of chattering 'goodbyes' in my ears. I extended my thanks to Murray Maclean, and set off to find Mrs X's pillbox.

It felt strange wandering up the front drive of a large, unknown house and picking my way amongst someone else's property. Emboldened by the permission I had gained, however, I pressed on resolutely past tennis courts and summer houses and at last found what I was seeking by a wood store – a perfect Type 22 pillbox inasmuch as it was small and six-sided, but more of a Type 24 in terms of its thick shell-proof walls and chamfered roof edge, with a small rifle loop each side of the entrance. On the anti-ricochet wall seen through the doorway was the stencilled number '261'. Such is the prevalence of anti-tank gun emplacements on GHQ Line Red, that (as in the Sulham Valley) it's good to find an ordinary pillbox. I wish I had one in my garden. But then I probably wish I had a tennis court as well.

Next I set off up the track from the main road towards the two anti-tank gun emplacements on Murray Maclean's land. That statement, in fact, is not quite correct, for one stands just over the fence on his neighbour's land, as it did in 1940. I hope the neighbour doesn't mind, but I stepped over the fence to visit it. It's a particularly good clean example, with its main embrasure facing south across the anti-tank ditch that turned here to cross in front of it. Again, it was divided into a main anti-tank gun chamber and a side light machine-gun chamber with three embrasures. Murray Maclean's emplacement had been fitted with wooden doors and converted into a chemicals store, so no entry was possible.

74 Main gun chamber of anti-tank gun emplacement near Frilford

75 Section of an anti-tank ditch re-excavated on land of Collins Farm at Frilford. The anti-tank gun emplacement, now used as a chemicals store, is in the background

What can be seen, however, in front of it, is the preserved section of the anti-tank ditch excavated in the early 1990s. This is at the point of approach of the ditch from the south-east just before it turned in front of the emplacements: I though it was a pity the excavation could not have incorporated the angled turn as well. The ditch section is now grassed and has lost something of its original sharpness, but it was still impressive, confirming the documented standard dimensions of an anti-tank ditch at 8-10ft deep, with a flat bottom about 5ft wide, and 15-20ft wide from lip to lip at the top. The ditch had been re-excavated to show equal sloping sides, whereas ditches generally had a near-vertical face on the defended side: the aim was to allow the tank to descend into the ditch, but then to become stuck against the steep face and be unable to reverse out. I wondered, in fact, if the re-digging had been done carefully enough, and whether any evidence of timber revetment had been located. Even if this section of GHQ Line Red had been planned for defence from the north as well as the south, and the ditch had therefore been engineered for a two-way defence supported by the spoil thrown up as a bank on both sides, one wouldn't have expected a double-sloping profile such as this.

I had one more site to see at Frilford, and this meant returning to the road and walking past Collins Farm again and through the village. On the far side, on wasteland beyond the junction with the A338 road, is an open concrete gun pit, with a holdfast to take the 6pdr Hotchkiss gun. Very few of these structures were built and their survival is rare. This example survives in excellent condition with its holdfast in the centre of a circular, concrete-lined pit with recesses for ammunition around its inner circumference.

Here we must conclude our exploration of this section of GHQ Line Red. I would have liked to have surveyed the line further, but time and the need to set boundaries to the defence area precluded this. For example, to the east at Marcham there are five more anti-tank gun emplacements and a line of massive anti-tank cubes which cry out for further investigation. One day I shall go back and see some more of this Oxfordshire section of GHQ Line Red.

We are now going to find a section of GHQ Line Blue, which I have already referred to as running from its junction with GHQ Line Green at Whaddon, near Trowbridge in Wiltshire, entirely along the course of the Kennet and Avon Canal to Theale just west of Reading. Here, as we have seen, it joined with Line Red coming south through the Sulham Valley.

GHQ Line Blue was much recorded by Defence of Britain Project volunteers, several of whom had evidently taken boating holidays on the Kennet and Avon Canal during which they made notes of the defence works seen along its banks. One record even bore sad witness to a family dispute over a surfeit of reinforced concrete for it stated plaintively, 'Not allowed to stop to inspect this pillbox.' I received something similar once from a recorder in Northamptonshire who wrote of a chorus of disapproval from within the family car when he wanted to record a concrete block spotted by the roadway. 'Some people just don't understand,' he set down despairingly.

Such stories are at variance with the remarkable enthusiasm for the subject that can be found amongst all manner of perhaps unlikely people, a phenomenon I have already referred to more than once. But possibly being cooped up in a small cabin cruiser on a canal on a wet summer's day and expecting the crew to leap out to brave sopping grass and tearing brambles in order to record a wall of dull grey concrete, is pushing the expectations of enthusiasm too far.

I drove along the old A4 Bath Road towards Hungerford, pleased to have escaped from the M4 that I had been following earlier through a harsh blaze of sunlight. The sunlight continued, but it was now dappled by trees and it was possible to relax a little and enjoy it. I turned off the A4 down a narrow lane that leads to Denford Mill. The lane twisted to the left and bridged the River Kennet; I rattled across a cattle grid and over another channel of the river, and then suddenly I crossed the Kennet and Avon Canal (I could see lock gates to my right) and now there was a bend to the right and I was looking straight into the great embrasure of an anti-tank gun emplacement ahead of me. I approached it in some awe, and then the road made an abrupt turn to the left and over the hump of another bridge, this time crossing the railway line, and I thought I had escaped from the monster which had fixed me with its eye. In my rear-view mirror, however, I saw a second concrete embrasure, set in red brick, glaring down at me ready to blow my car off the road. Undeterred, I turned the vehicle around, and returned, staring fully into the eye of the embrasure as I came over the bridge and spinning off to the right into a broad car park carved out, white with chalk, from the land between the railway and the canal.

I climbed out of the car and wiped my brow. I had found this sudden view of the anti-tank gun emplacements at Dunmill Lock most impressive. I had seen pictures of them before, and knew they stood close to the road, but the reality of coming upon them that summer's morning quite exceeded my expectations. I wandered back up the road to inspect them.

There were two emplacements set back to back with their doorways facing each other in the manner I had already seen on GHQ Line Red. They had been built on top of the bank that fell away to the canal below. The right hand of the emplacements, when seen from the road, was the largest. It had the two mighty stepped embrasures I had already seen when I drove past, one pointing in each direction along the road as it bent to cross the railway bridge. Its forward face was dug well into the bank which was eroding away so the foundation was revealed, although it was hard to see this clearly as the ground was covered in thick bushes and one slip would have meant an abrupt journey downhill to the canal.

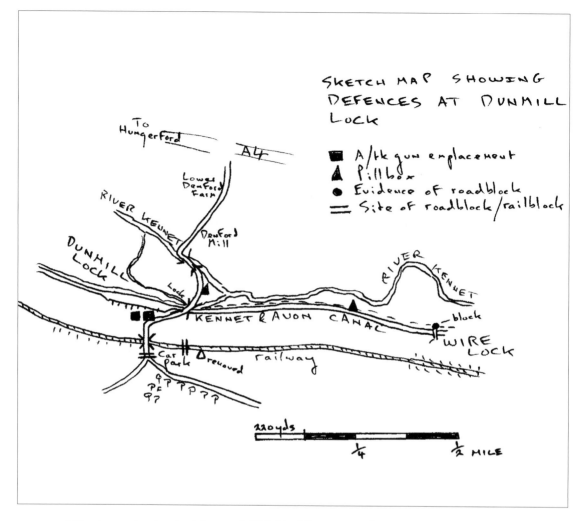

76 Sketch map showing the defences of GHQ Line Blue at Dunmill Lock

I entered through the wide door built to take the 2pdr anti-tank gun. The emplacement was used as a cattle shelter: the floor was thick with dung and rubbish. There was also a certain amount of recent graffiti scrawled on the walls. The emplacement was enormous: there were two side chambers with dividing walls for light machine-gun fire. As I exited, I saw the number '339' painted on a wall at the entrance. I looked at the external brick-shuttering. The bricks were of a particular hollow type set end on that are found at many sites in this part of the country. Many were badly eroded, and some small sections of shuttering had fallen completely away revealing the concrete and iron reinforcing bars beneath.

77 One of a pair of massive anti-tank gun emplacements at Dunmill Lock

78 The companion emplacement at Dunmill Lock – now used as a shelter for cattle

I walked over to the second emplacement, which was considerably smaller than the first, with one main embrasure only facing west and one side chamber with two Bren embrasures. A small black cow stood in the entrance watching my approach anxiously. As I looked, it lifted its tail and did its business … splot, splot … on the concrete floor. What a way to treat such an important, historic structure! The emplacements had become a part of the farmer's landscape, used by him for their value as free cattle shelters. Once many of the historic buildings of England had been similarly treated – the castles and abbeys, and Roman forts and villas, now so lovingly tidied up and cared for by English Heritage.

The two anti-tank gun emplacements protected a major defended locality at Dunmill Lock, firing west and east along the line of the Kennet and Avon Canal and also forward at a roadblock just south of the railway bridge. The defences of the Line were organised around these defended localities that protected the bridges over the canal and the river behind, which were all prepared for demolition in the event of invasion. The locks, in particular, were strongly guarded for if they were captured and the gates opened, then the canal would be drained and rendered less effective as an anti-tank obstacle.

My study of wartime air photographs of Dunmill Lock showed that the two anti-tank gun emplacements had been given pitched roofs as part of their camouflage scheme. From the air they looked like a couple of houses at the bend in the road. So, when I read later that there was a proposal to turn the emplacements into a restaurant, presumably linked together in some way, I wondered sardonically if they would resurrect the pitched roof-look again. Pillboxes had certainly been disguised during the war to *look like* cafés and snack bars, but I thought it was going a bit far to actually turn one today into a functioning restaurant. I believe the idea has fallen through, which is probably a good thing because, however skilful the conversion, it would have wrecked these two emplacements, which are relatively rare structures, and particularly so in their paired relationship on GHQ Line Blue. Anyhow, there was something about the memory of that cow in the doorway that would have put me off ever eating there.

The restaurant proposal had become a very real issue with the residents of Dunmill by the time I visited to do my survey. Not surprisingly, they were against it, not so much because it would have meant the loss of the fine lines of the emplacements and their dominating embrasures, but because it would have brought a further weight of visitors into an area that was ill-equipped to cope with it. I learnt about this first-hand when I walked down the lane in search of a pillbox that I knew stood close to one of the river bridges.

79 Small pillbox covered by blackberry bushes close to Dunmill Lock

I found the pillbox. It stood by the cattle grid I had clanked over earlier, a small Type 22 shuttered with the same type of hollow end-on bricks as used on the anti-tank gun emplacements. Other than for the side facing the road, it was completely covered with blackberry bushes. As I recorded it, I picked a few of the ripening berries, and stood there munching them as a lady passed by trailing a small, white dog. With my pack over my shoulder and a clip board in my hand, I thought I looked efficient and purposeful. The lady obviously thought so too for she called across, 'Are you thinking of starting a chain?'

'I beg your pardon.' I was surprised enough to drop the remaining blackberry from my fingers.

'A chain of restaurants. Aren't you the developer?'

Suddenly I understood. She was referring to the proposed restaurant at the anti-tank gun emplacements. I was flattered. Clearly I looked entrepreneurial, with my open shirt, my camera, and that clip board, so obviously taking notes for the conversion of a pillbox into a burger bar in the middle of a Berkshire village. Anything was possible these days.

I soon put the woman straight; told her I was surveying these things for English Heritage, that I was, in fact, the 'Man from the Ministry' who would be delivering the right judgement on these matters in due course. I smiled reassuringly, puffing myself out to tell her that 'between you and me' I would be recommending the emplacements be 'preserved in their present form'.

The lady smiled sweetly, although she did not look wholly convinced. Later I learnt that she had phoned English Heritage to check on this man with blackberry juice on his hands who said he was one of their officials.

'I remember when you could play in this lane and there was never a car,' she said, as she hauled her dog away from my ankles – probably he was attracted by something I had picked up at 'the restaurant that was not to be'. I felt sorry for her. Aren't we all trying to keep the modern world away, appalled at the changes that threaten to blast away all our familiar landmarks? Compared with the destruction done to certain parts of England, however, some people might settle for a trendy, themed restaurant and a bit of extra motor traffic.

20

THE BASINGSTOKE CANAL AT CHEQUERS BRIDGE TO EWSHOT, HAMPSHIRE

Close to the Hampshire/Surrey border lies the garrison town of Aldershot. The Army was attracted here at the time of the Crimean War by the open heathland all around, land of little agricultural value but providing ample scope for the building of camps and for the training of troops. Soon the military presence grew to such an extent that Aldershot (previously a small village of few pretensions) became known throughout the Empire as the home of the British Army. In 1940, it formed a separate Army Command – Aldershot Command. Other places famous in British military history fell within its area – Farnborough, Camberley, Sandhurst, Bisley, Chobham, Pirbright, Fleet. Many hundreds of thousands of men in two world wars passed through the camps of Aldershot, fired on its ranges, undertook exercises on its heaths and commons. The military lands extended to the south as well – Hankley Common, Ockley Common, Thursley Common, and further west at Bramshott and Woolmer Forest. Even today, with the more limited needs of the modern Army, it is still one of the busiest military landscapes in the country. In 1940, the area was given a special protection against an anticipated German attack from the south.

From the junction of GHQ Lines Red and Blue at Theale south-west of Reading, the main course of the GHQ Line (known now as GHQ Line 'A') continued south-east towards the Surrey market town of Farnham, passing to the south of Aldershot which was thereby protected against attacks from the south. For the additional defence of Aldershot from the west, however, a spur line was constructed from GHQ Line 'A' through Crookham village to the main London railway line. A similar line also defended Aldershot to the east.

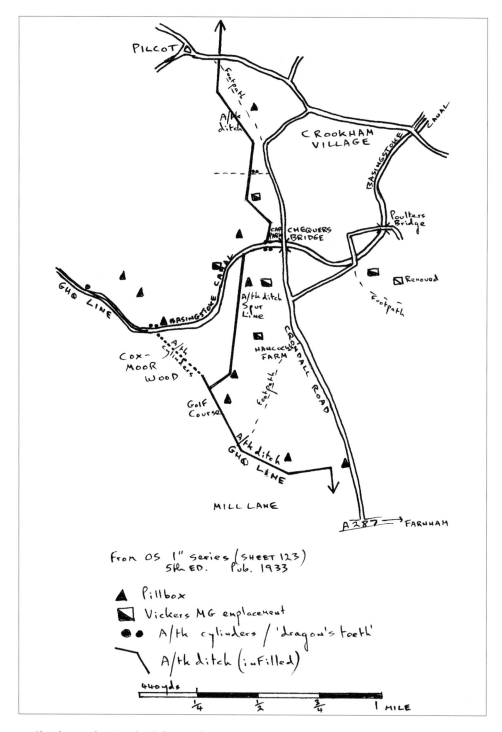

80 Sketch map showing the defences of two joining stop lines in the vicinity of Chequers Bridge, Crookham

It was to survey that spur line west of Aldershot from its junction with the GHQ Line that I was now travelling through Surrey, along the A31 Hog's Back (the North Downs ridge) west of Guildford, and through the complicated road system at Farnham, until I was on the A287 heading towards Odiham, where I entered into Hampshire. I love this landscape. Perhaps it was because my boyhood was spent nearby, but I find a particular familiarity and closeness with its pattern of hill and ridge, of hedgerows and woods dark with leaf, of sunken lanes and flint-parapeted bridges, and of large houses set well back behind screens of evergreens and dense thickets of rhododendron bushes.

So it was with a sense of great pleasure that I entered the network of lanes north of the A287 road. I had taken a wrong turn, and found myself in roads, bordered with hedgerows, that looked as if they ran between fields, but in fact behind those hedges were houses, each perfect within its own large plot of well-tended land. The roads were also set with obstacles as if it was some great game you were playing where you had to pass between narrowed openings, and over a series of bumps, before an on-coming vehicle got there first; often this was a van driven with speed and skill by an assorted range of builders, landscape gardeners, plumbers, burglar alarm installers, and television repair men.

After several wrong turnings, I found myself at last in Crookham village, and by good fortune took the road (the Crondall Road) that brought me to Chequers Bridge, a crossing of the Basingstoke Canal. In an instant I recognised where I was, and, although tail-gated by an impatient van whose driver in the mirror seemed to be sitting in my rear seat, I was able to fling the car into a most welcome parking area thoughtfully provided on the canal's north bank.

I breathed a long sigh of relief as I tumbled out of the car and walked to the canal side. An information board told me that the Basingstoke Canal had been completed in 1794, and ran for more than 30 miles from Hampshire into Surrey, joining with the River Wey and, eventually, the Thames. After lying derelict for many years, it had been restored in the 1970s and 1980s. At Chequers Bridge there had been a wharf on the north bank at the point where I now found nine anti-tank pimples (dragon's teeth) arranged in three rows in bushes by the towpath. Looking across the canal, I could see a further eight pimples on the south bank. This was the point where the machine-cut anti-tank ditch of the western spur line protecting Aldershot had crossed the canal, having started from GHQ Line 'A' about half a mile to the south. To the west, the GHQ Line joined with the canal and followed it for several miles before turning north towards Reading.

Another board close to the pimples provided information on the 1940 defences along this section of the Basingstoke Canal. Although some of the details are slightly inaccurate, it is nevertheless heartening to see information set out in this way, the sort of thing I would like to see done at many other sites. I took a photograph of the board, and continued along the tree-lined towpath. In a field beyond the canal to the right, I knew was a square, or possibly, rectangular pillbox. I could not get to it as there is no public access, and I am not sure of its exact form or what type it is, but I had seen its position on air photographs.

A little further along, I scrambled up the wooded bank overlooking the canal and disappeared under the trees at the top. Here I found a Vickers machine-gun emplacement, a purpose-designed structure for the fire of this weapon, square with thick walls and roof, and here brick-shuttered with cut-off corners to its forward faces and with a detached blast wall. Most examples to be found in England are either within the area of Aldershot Command or further west along the course of the Taunton Stop Line – a Southern Command Line crossing the waist of the South-West peninsula. The large main embrasure of the emplacement I was examining faced away from the canal, defending Chequers Bridge and the spur line from attack from the west.

I continued my journey along the towpath, enjoying the walk on this mild winter's day, with the canal a ribbon of silent, greenish water to my left. Thick woodland now stretched away from the canal on both banks. At the edge of the wood by the towpath, I spotted a Type 24 pillbox, but it was so overgrown with a barbed-wire fence across its front that I could not reach it. From my notes I knew that I had reached the point where the GHQ Line met the canal, and, as if to confirm this, a few yards further along the towpath, I came upon two massive concrete cylinders at least 3ft in diameter, and 5-6ft high with domed tops, of the type made from concrete-filled drainage pipes that we last met in the Sulham Valley. On the far side of the canal, I spotted other cylinders peeping through the trees close to the bank. And this was all I could see of what I suspect is one of the finest surviving examples of linear concrete anti-tank defences in the country – a double row of cylinders forming the front-edge obstacle of the GHQ Line running through this woodland (Coxmoor Wood) south of the Basingstoke Canal.

There used to be a bridge across the canal at this point, but it has been removed. There was absolutely no way I could get into Coxmoor Wood to inspect the lines of cylinders. One record received by the Defence of Britain Project said there were 360 cylinders 2ft apart in two lines, running for some 500yds through the wood, with the lines themselves separated by 3ft. I would have loved to have been able to view the cylinders myself, but, when I was able to track down the landowners later, permission was not forthcoming. I was told they would think about it and contact me later, but I never heard a thing. I think they were worried about game birds that were breeding in the woods. Of course, it is their absolute right to control entry to their own land, but it was a great pity from my point of view – the only significant site I was unable to reach in all my travels.

81 Anti-tank cylinders reaching the Basingstoke Canal at the edge of Coxmoor Wood

From the point where the cylinders finished at the south-eastern edge of Coxmoor Wood, the GHQ Line was continued to the south by an artificial anti-tank ditch. Within the wood, however, it was clearly considered easier to construct parallel lines of cylinders than clear a wide blaze and dig a ditch. However, the labour required and the logistics for erecting 360 cylinders (if that indeed is the correct figure) through dense woodland must have been daunting. An air photograph taken in January 1946 shows the cylinders running through the wood, so a clearing for the line, albeit narrower than that needed for a ditch, must have been hacked out anyway. In other locations, anti-tank ditches were dug through woodland, for example at the edge of Hog Wood on GHQ Line Green near Bath and through Epping Forest on the Outer London Anti-Tank Line.

Many defence works line the Basingstoke Canal further to the west, but these were beyond the boundaries I had set for my defence area, so I returned along the canal to Chequers Bridge. The bridge formed an important focus of the defences, mined for demolition as indeed were all crossings of the canal. On the far side of the Crondall Road, a footpath, joining with a lane, took me to the next bridge to the east – Poulter's Bridge. A low, grassy hill rose above the canal to the south, and on the flank of this, by an old quarry pit, I found a Vickers emplacement, with a large, stepped embrasure facing west so that fire could have been laid down to enfilade the canal. A free-standing blast wall on the southern side protected the entrance. Inside, I found the concrete table on which the Vickers gun would have been positioned complete and undamaged, although it was surrounded by a litter of beer cans.

I scouted around for a while on this hill top trying to find a companion emplacement which I knew had stood here, but all I could locate were a few chunks of concrete, so clearly it had been removed relatively recently. I could not understand why this had been done because there did not appear to be any particular purpose for such a difficult and expensive piece of destruction. Why remove the one emplacement, in any event, and leave the other? I was off the public footpath, and in sight of a neighbouring farm, where horses were grazing in the fields below me, so I did not stay to debate the point with anyone that might see me, but trudged off disconsolately to the Crondall Road.

My spirits, however, rose once more when I came to Hancock's Farm on the right of the road leading south from Chequers Bridge where I knew several pillboxes and Vickers emplacements stood. Seeing a head moving back and forth behind a hedgerow I hailed this phenomenon, which resolved itself as the farmer seated on a small Ferguson tractor ploughing the field. Describing what I was in search of, I gained a friendly permission to go where I would on his land. I was even given a guide (the farmer's small son) who led me away through a maze of farm buildings until I emerged on a spine of land south of the canal. The boy pointed out the positions of the pillboxes, and then left me to my own devices. He was a smart lad, knowing much about the defence works on the farm and why they had been built, a representative of a new generation growing up with knowledge and interest in this subject.

What a wonderful place it was on this fine winter's day, with a strong breeze tugging at the grass, so that the sweep of the land rippled like the sea. Looking north, a dark curving line of trees marked the course of the canal, and over to the right was Chequers Bridge. To my left, the anti-tank ditch of the spur line had cut its deep course across the fields. I wandered over to a small red-brick pillbox half-smothered in vegetation. It was a highly unusual eight-sided pillbox with an embrasure above its doorway. It had stood right on the edge of the anti-tank ditch which passed in front of it, and fire would have been laid down from it across the ditch towards the canal. Close by, but set further back from the anti-tank ditch, was a Vickers machine-gun emplacement, much overgrown and with bits and pieces of farm equipment piled around it. Its main embrasure faced south to enfilade the ditch. Fixed into its exterior brick-shuttering were rows of iron hooks that were probably used to fasten camouflage netting. Further to the south, close to the farm, I found another Vickers emplacement, also piled high with rubbish. It too fired to the south-west across the line of the anti-tank ditch.

I skirted a large slurry pond, and came to lower, boggy land at the edge of a wood. Here was another pillbox, this time a Type 24 with an attached blast wall that looked as if it had been damaged recently by machinery. It was buried to the level of its embrasures, and the farmer told me later that this had been done when the anti-tank ditch which ran close to it was dug *after* the pillbox had been built: the spoil from the ditch was simply dumped around the pillbox. This story provided me with an insight into the hurried and piecemeal construction of these defence lines in the desperate days of 1940. Standing by the pillbox and looking up the slope ahead of me, I could see a darker strip of grass amongst the pale winter grass, and this, I knew, had to be the line of the anti-tank ditch on its way to meet the Basingstoke Canal (*colour plate 24*). As ever with earthworks, I found the sight most stimulating; the ditch, infilled after only three or four years in use, and now 'archaeology', as with any ditch from any age, its line revealed as a crop mark.

82 Vickers machine-gun emplacement on land of Hancock's Farm near Chequers Bridge

83 The concrete table on which the Vickers MMG was positioned

I walked around the edge of the wood, and came to a pillbox that stood by a water-filled ditch on the far side of the farmer's fence. Beyond it was smooth green grass, with people moving in the distance in the steady, relaxed way that golfers have. The pillbox, in fact, lay just inside the land of Bowenhurst Golf Club, a course so new it was not even on my maps. As I did not think the golf club would mind, I climbed the fence, and approached the pillbox, which was another Type 24, shuttered in red brick. What was remarkable, however, was that at each embrasure was an asbestos shutter that still swung open on its hinges. A group of golfers was quite close to me; if they saw me they were supremely indifferent, which I have found is generally the way of golfers whenever I have strayed into their territory. I felt like shouting out to them: 'Come and see this! This is a very rare survival. Do you realise you are playing golf at the junction of two anti-tank lines?' – but I didn't, which is probably just as well!

My point about the junction of the spur line with the GHQ Line, however, was worth making. About 100yds from the pillbox, amongst what had then been fields bordered by woods, had been the unusual sight of two branching anti-tank ditches. How wonderful, I thought, it would be to find that exact point and to re-excavate it. But I don't think the golf club would share my excitement because, as far as I could make out, it lies under one of their greens!

Having thanked the farmer profusely, I headed back north to Chequers Bridge, crossed the canal, and walked on up the Crondall Road towards Crookham village. The anti-tank ditch had made a zig-zag course through the fields to my left. Coming to a narrow road, leading to some houses sitting solidly behind their evergreen hedges, I wandered along it and, after a few yards, came to the point where it bridged the infant stream of the River Hart flowing towards the north. On the grass verge of the near-side bank of the stream I counted six dragon's teeth where the anti-tank ditch would have crossed.

Further on, at the end of this short length of road, I found a footpath that offered a pleasant route along the edge of woodland. I decided to follow the path because, although I had no record of any defence work in this immediate area, I had nevertheless spotted a suspicious square shape on an air photograph that I thought might be a Vickers machine-gun emplacement. After a short distance, I came to a grass paddock on my left, and here with a jab of excitement I found my suspicions were confirmed: there was indeed an emplacement, heavily overgrown, at the edge of the paddock close to the backs of houses that faced onto Crondall Road.

It is always deeply satisfying to find something new that has not been recorded by anyone else. And none of the Defence of Britain Project recorders seemed to have located this structure, which was a particularly important one having been built at one of the angles of the anti-tank ditch. What was remarkable was its large size, and the fact that it did not have just one large, stepped embrasure for the fire of the Vickers, but two – and, I thought (it was so overgrown I could not be sure) just possibly three. If the latter, it is unique: two main embrasures are extremely rare anyhow. An additional bonus was that all the embrasures I could see had hinged asbestos flaps in place which would still open and shut.

I decided to push my way through the overgrowth to the entrance of the emplacement to see if I could resolve from the interior the question of the number of its embrasures. I went down three or four steps, peering into darkness ahead, and found myself suddenly up to my knees in water. Horrified, I made an immediate retreat. There is a lesson here. Do not go inside concrete structures like this, in particular sunken ones, unless you can see clearly what you are doing. If I had stumbled and fallen on some hidden object, or if the water had been deeper, perhaps over some shaft, I might have been in real trouble. As it was, I emerged with soaking wet legs, aware of two people watching me over their back garden fence. Affecting nonchalance, I retreated along the edge of the paddock with cold water oozing from my boots, conscious of the stares that followed me every inch of my way. It seemed a very long 100yds back to the public footpath. This is a good illustration of how *not* to go about approaching and recording Second World War defence works! Yet, despite my foolishness, I felt it was still a great discovery.

My chilled and soaking feet put a literal damper on the rest of my explorations. I found one more pillbox, a Type 24 by the side of a public footpath that led off the Crondall Road north of a sewage works. It was so overgrown, it was impossible to inspect it closely, and I moved on to emerge eventually on the Pilcot Road close to the point where it bridged the River Hart. There had been a roadblock here, part of a defended locality at Pilcot with defences manned by the 25th Bn Hampshire Home Guard. I had a record of a pillbox and a Spigot mortar emplacement amongst houses south of Pilcot Road, but I could see no sign of them, and there was no one to ask. Some workmen were laying a pipe in a trench at the side of the road, and they looked at me curiously as I squelched up and down. Faced with their stares, I decided to call it a morning. The idea of marching up to people's front doors, anyhow, to ask if they had a pillbox in their back garden was not the sort of thing you did with wet legs. I did not want to frighten the Pilcot housewives.

It had been an extremely active day so far, and I still had another area to see close by. I hoped my enthusiasm and my energy would return, and there would be time to complete the work before it grew dark.

Fortunately, I had a change of both socks and trousers in the car (brought for just such an eventuality) and I managed to pull these on in the car while cramming down a hasty sandwich. I consulted my maps, had a drink of coffee from a thermos, and rearranged my notes for the next area. Then I was off again.

A mile south of Chequers Bridge is the A287 road which the Crondall Road meets in an area known curiously as the Bowling Alley. This was a defended locality on GHQ Line 'A', crossed by an artificial anti-tank ditch, some lengths of which were hand-dug by troops from Aldershot Command. The anti-tank ditch runs east to Warren Corner, another defended locality. In August 1940, these defended localities were manned by troops from the 1st Pioneer Battalion, Royal Canadian Engineers. The headquarters of that unit was at Seymour Farm on Ewshot Lane to the north, and it was to Ewshot Lane that I was now driving.

Ewshot is another of those places where I feel instinctively at home. It consists of a straggle of houses around church, farm, and pub, with some recently added estates, in a rolling landscape, part forested and part small enclosed fields, the approach lanes narrow and dank, houses and fields alike hidden behind thick hedgerows that do not look as if they have been cut for many years. It is the sort of place where you can walk the lanes, and not really see where you are, or understand the landscape around you as your horizons are so limited. The sky is a small window above you, your view restricted by the surrounding woods and the hills, so different from the all-round, all-seeing bowl of the sky that I have become used to in East Anglia. On the northern side of Ewshot village, an uncultivated landscape, almost like parkland, still owned by the Ministry of Defence, stretches away to the southern suburbs of Church Crookham. Here there are areas of former barracks, some destined to be redeveloped as housing much to the concern of Ewshot residents who fear the impact on their community.

Just beyond the Bowling Alley, I came to a narrow lane (Dare's Lane) leading north from the A287, and followed it to its junction with Ewshot Lane. I was able to find a pull-off place for the car almost opposite Seymour Farm. The lane was running with water from recent rains. The stone buildings of Seymour Farm seemed almost overwhelmed by over-hanging trees and thick hedgerows which gave the place a somewhat forbidding appearance. There was no one about, certainly no bodies of troops now marching along the lane or the sound of Canadian accents, but just the dark winter trees and the gurgle of water running into a drain. I knew I was in an exceptional 1940 defence area, lying to the rear of GHQ Line 'A' but containing defences set in depth to protect the military lands to the north as well as the western approaches to Aldershot town. This was one of the most heavily defended inland areas in the country, and the subject of a particular mystery, as we shall see.

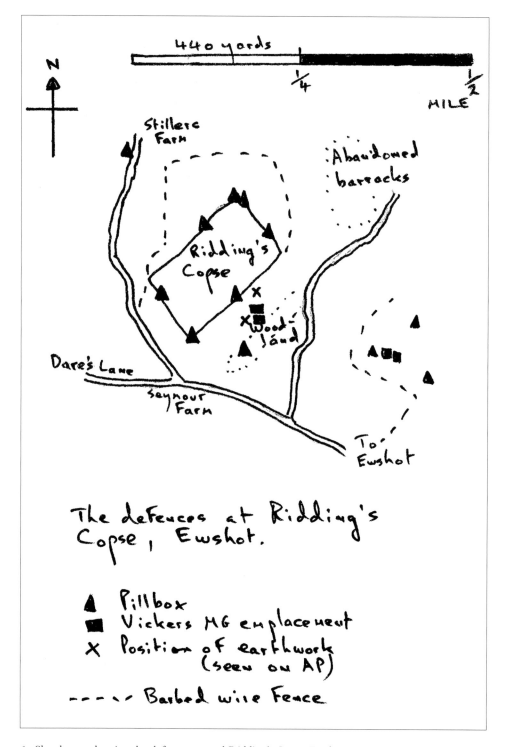

84 Sketch map showing the defences around Ridding's Copse, Ewshot

The first thing to do (as ever when arriving in a new area) was to work out where exactly I was in relation to the defence works that I had already mapped from the Defence of Britain Project database. I knew there was a scattering of pillboxes both to the north and south of Dare's Lane and Ewshot Lane, but it was impossible to get to them without requesting permission, and it was far from clear who owned this land. I decided I would make my first priority Ridding's Copse, which was a rectangular block of woodland surrounded on three sides by lanes. I walked along Ewshot Lane and saw the wood rising above me running along the crest of a low ridge. The fields around were uncultivated and unkempt with long, yellow grass. The black edge of Ridding's Copse stared back at me, looking mysterious and forbidding. I even felt a shiver down my spine. I sensed it concealed some sort of secret.

On the eastern side of the Ridding's Copse ridge, I found a narrow lane, running with black water, bordered by overgrown hedgerows. At various points by the side of the lane, there were dumps of rubbish tipped out by fellow citizens – TV sets, rolls of carpets, decaying sofas, and indescribable things spilling from black bin liners. Steering a course well clear of this pollution, I came to a gateway on my left through which I could see a slope, grey with last summer's grass, framed behind by the black trees of Ridding's Copse.

After going a few yards into this field, I was able to make out two overgrown shapes on the top of the rise about 50yds away. These were Vickers machine-gun emplacements almost entirely buried beneath overgrowth, and with turf on their roofs that probably originated from their wartime camouflage. They were brick-shuttered, each with one main embrasure for the fire of the Vickers. What was strange, however, was that the two emplacements were angled towards each other so that their fields of fire would have converged about 20yds in front of them. Now why should they have been sited to do that? Why were they not positioned to provide a wider field of fire that would have swept the entire width of the slope ahead between Ridding's Copse and a strip of woodland to the south?

The mystery was compounded by a strange shape I had noted on air photographs in front of the emplacements – an earthwork of a broadly oval shape with a straight entry trench on its far side. Another earthwork, this one making a half-arc, stood between the emplacements and the edge of Ridding's Copse. These earthworks could still be made out on air photographs taken in the early 1960s, but there is absolutely no evidence of them on the ground today. An expert on military fieldworks, whom I had consulted, thought they might be of First World War origin, possibly constructed in training by troops from the nearby camps. The earliest air photograph available that shows them is dated December 1942 so it is not possible to say if, in fact, they pre-dated the war or were dug contemporaneously with the construction of the Vickers emplacements, probably in July 1940. If they were earthworks from some 25 years earlier, why should the concrete emplacements have been positioned so carefully in relation to them with their converging fields of fire? It is a mystery.

There were other mysteries at Ridding's Copse as well. I walked through the long, rank grass to the edge of the trees, and found a Type 24 pillbox there positioned to fire along the margin of the wood to the west. However, fire could also have been laid down from it across the open area towards the Vickers emplacements. I walked around three sides of the rectangular block of Ridding's Copse, and found five other pillboxes all firing outwards from the wood. The fourth (north) side of the wood I could not get to as it bordered fenced-off farming land, but there were probably further pillboxes there as well. I did find one more pillbox, however, in the narrow block of woodland to the south of the emplacements. It faced north to fire at Ridding's Copse itself. All very strange.

85 Twin Vickers machine-gun emplacements with converging fields of fire: Riddings Copse is in the background

Something had evidently been going on within Ridding's Copse that it should be protected in this way. I did not want to venture into the wood itself as it was fenced off with barbed wire. The land around was uncultivated and there seemed to be no problem walking there, but the woodland might be a different matter. So whether anything still shows within the thick trees and undergrowth of a wartime use I do not at present know, but it is possible. Although I had found at The National Archives a document that listed a large number of sites within Aldershot Command, such as ammunition dumps, battle headquarters, observation posts, and firing ranges, there was no site included even close to Ridding's Copse, or indeed Ewshot itself. What had been going on there, and how did that relate to the strange earthworks seen on the air photographs?

Another indication that this area was defended for a particular purpose, over and above its general importance as part of the defence in depth towards Aldershot behind the GHQ Line, was that on the 1942 air photograph I could make out a dark line running through the fields surrounding Ridding's Copse, and this is very likely to have been a barbed-wire fence erected to delineate the military area. The fence line had crossed to the far side of the lane by which I had approached Ridding's Copse, and it was here that I decided to go next.

The ridge occupied by Ridding's Copse continues to the east above Ewshot village, and here is open grassland, uncultivated as around Ridding's Copse, and interspersed with small stands of woods and thick clumps of bushes. To the south, it sweeps in a broad, gently falling slope to Ewshot Lane. I pushed my way through thick, wet grass and undergrowth so that my legs were soon once more soaked, and came to the top of the ridge, seeing on its open summit two more of the familiar, overgrown mounds that again proved themselves to be Vickers machine-gun emplacements. These two were even more buried in vegetation than those at Ridding's Copse, and were dug deep into the slope of the hill so that I was able to step onto the roof of one. One embrasure stared out through such a tangled mass of wicked brambles that, although I could see it, I could not get anywhere near without ripping my clothing and my flesh to shreds. My searches for 1940 defence works, many left virtually untouched since the war, have shown me vividly how soon sites become totally overgrown, almost to the extent of invisibility, and how formidable nature's own defences are.

On the western side of the Vickers emplacements there was also an immensely overgrown Type 24 pillbox. I could just make out that it had asbestos embrasure shutters in place, as I had seen at Chequers Bridge. Behind it, under trees on the top of the ridge, was a further Type 24, brick-shuttered, with some of the bricks falling away. Metal hooks in the brickwork were probably attachments for camouflage netting, similar to those I had seen earlier on Hancock's farm.

I found another pillbox to the east, also under trees, at the edge of a slope that fell away to Ewshot village. It also had hooks in its outer faces.

I startled a lady walking her dog here, who must have wondered at my sudden appearance with pack and camera bearing down on the overgrown pillbox where her dog was sniffing. Apologising for making her jump, I told her (as was my wont) that I was surveying them 'in an official capacity', at which she seemed genuinely interested.

'There're many more pillboxes around the village,' she said, gathering in her dog and preparing to retreat.

'I'll get around to them tomorrow,' I said. Time had been flying past. The light was already fading from the cloudy sky.

'Good luck,' she said, and hauled her dog away. She would return home, I thought, and recount her meeting with the strange pillbox-hunter in the woods.

I walked back to the Vickers emplacements on the ridge, looking down the long grassy slope they commanded to the south. What a powerful defence position this had been. The emplacements and pillboxes on the ridge top had stood behind the perimeter fence which I could see on the air photograph curving across the slope in front. It had been a position of strength, but for what exact purpose? I looked at my watch. What I had told the woman had been true. There would not be enough daylight left to complete the area, so I would have to return tomorrow – a nuisance, but unavoidable. It had been a long day, and I was tired. That night, I slept like the metaphorical log.

There was rain in the night, but the following day dawned clear, with a glorious sunrise that filled the eastern horizon with bars of deep red and blue. I was away early from my Farnham hotel, eager to resume my acquaintance with the defended Ewshot landscape. This time I drove into Ewshot village itself, and parked by the recreation ground where the first person I saw was my lady of yesterday evening, now taking her dog for its morning walk. She smiled brightly at me.

'How's it going?'

'Finishing off today.'

'Don't miss the one above the village hall there,' she said, extending her arm towards a wooded knoll at the edge of the clipped grass of a playing field.

86 The pillbox was here before the house – Ewshot village

It was not a site I had amongst my records. I thanked her, aware as ever that most knowledge of these sites (hardly surprisingly) is held by local people, and that, if I had only had more time to exploit this source fully, then it would have been to my great advantage. I followed her direction and pushed up the slope to the knoll, finding a Type 24 pillbox under the trees in excellent condition, with a very clean interior. Through an embrasure I looked out on Ewshot below. I wandered how the site had been missed by previous recorders as it stood by a footpath. If it had not been for the woman, who I could see on the playing field below throwing a ball for her dog, I would have missed it.

At the junction of Ewshot Lane with Church Lane close to the village hall, I found a Type 24 pillbox, shuttered with deep-red brick, set into the roadside bank that now formed part of the front garden of a recently built house. I recorded and photographed it, and then turned up Ewshot Lane where there was yet another Type 24, again dug into the bank of the lane. It seemed reasonably certain that a roadblock would have been positioned close to it, although I had no evidence for this. Walking back into Ewshot, I turned up Church Lane and found a further pillbox on a slope beside Homecroft Farm. To my imagination, its embrasures each side of the doorway looked like a face, with the embrasures forming the eyes and the doorway the nose and mouth. Vegetation covering the roof created a mass of unruly hair. Clearly, I was becoming pillbox-happy!

Although I could not see them, my examination of air photographs indicated there were (or had been) further pillboxes in the gardens of houses and at the edge of woodland on the far side of Church Lane. I walked up Tadpole Lane, and found one Type 24 pillbox on the right at the edge of a farm track, firing towards the south. Further to the north on Tadpole Lane, I could see another in the distance facing towards the lane with its back to woodland. I was now at the eastern border of my defined defence area, but beyond it I knew there were many more pillboxes, in particular on the high, forested land to the east. Without doubt, here was one of the densest concentration of pillboxes and machine-gun emplacements anywhere in the country, with almost all of them surviving. If anyone asks you where to go to see pillboxes, you can tell them to come here.

I had done as much work at Ewshot as I could for my survey, but it is clear a more detailed study should be carried out, in particular to evaluate the reasons for the defence of Ridding's Copse. Here is a perfect project for a local historical or archaeological group to take up. It could combine documentary research with oral history, and have a programme of field survey and possibly even excavation. Hopefully one day we shall solve the Mystery of Ridding's Copse.

21
WAVERLEY ABBEY, SURREY

Waverley Abbey was the very first defence area I researched for this project: in fact, it had formed part of a pilot project that had preceded the full one establishing the various methodologies to be used. And so it seems appropriate that I conclude my journeys here in company with John Schofield who commissioned this work for English Heritage. I have come to Waverley Abbey on several occasions, in fact, and each time I have learnt something new about its 1940 defences, which is what invariably happens when you look in increasing depth at a particular area. It shows that people who are able to study this subject at a local level have the best chance of pulling together all the relevant field and documentary evidence, taking advantage as well of the memories of people actually living within their study area.

Waverley Abbey was the first house of the Cistercian Order in England, built early in the twelfth century in a loop of the River Wey south of Farnham. The Abbey was dissolved in 1536, and its ruins now spread attractively across a green meadow by the river and are in the care of English Heritage. On the other side of an adjacent crescent-shaped lake is Waverley Abbey House, now a Christian teaching centre. Just after the war, a new owner took up residence there and proposed demolishing the Waverley Abbey ruins to lay out a racecourse. Fortunately, English Heritage's predecessor, the Ancient Monuments Branch of the Ministry of Works, threw out this outrageous proposal in record time. A mile north of Waverley Abbey stands seventeenth-century Moor Park House where Jonathan Swift met the 'Stella' – Esther Johnson – of his Journal. The house became a school last century and is now a business centre. At Waverleymill Bridge, where the road from Farnham crosses the River Wey, stands Stella Cottage, where Esther is said to have lived.

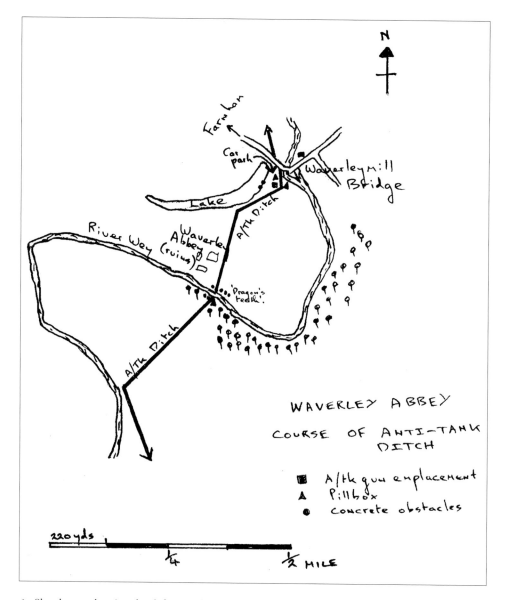

87 Sketch map showing the defences of the GHQ Line at Waverley Abbey

From June to August 1940, GHQ Line 'B' was constructed south of Farnham, following the River Wey past Waverley Abbey to Godalming, and then on to Shalford south of Guildford from where it ran east below the North Downs to Penshurst (where we have already seen it). A series of defended localities was established along the River Wey, and the one north of Waverley Abbey was named 'Stella Cottage' from the house at Waverleymill Bridge.

When I came to Waverley Abbey with John Schofield it was a hot summer's day. I picked John up at Farnham station, which lies at the head of the lane that leads to Waverley, and in the rush hour can be a very crowded place to negotiate. A level crossing, where the barriers fall repeatedly, adds to the traffic queues, holding up vehicles that are seeking to get out onto the Farnham by-pass. Of course, John's train was late, and there was no car parking at the station, but in the end the train came in and I was able to scoop him up, hotly pursued by irritable taxi drivers who have territorial instincts akin to Barbary apes. We escaped into tree-lined Waverley Lane, seemingly idyllic in the summer heat under its green canopy of leaves, but in fact a narrow rat run, like many places in the over-crowded South-East, used by VW Golfs, white vans, and HGVs, all driven at tumultuous speed, so that there is no tolerance for anyone wishing to cruise quietly along through the gentle English countryside.

At Waverleymill Bridge, the road makes a sharp left-hand turn to cross the River Wey. Here, if you are prepared enough and, with the Tesco's home delivery van 3in behind you, have the nerve, you can make an equally sharp turn to the right into a small car park provided for visitors to Waverley Abbey. At one side of this parking area is a structure that is among the most remarkable of the anti-invasion defences I have seen – a gun emplacement with a single main embrasure facing south that has an open courtyard attached to it, its brick walls pierced with loopholes. Impressed in metal in the concrete surround to one loophole is the date, '1940'. Piles of roughly cemented bricks at intervals on the tops of the walls, looking somewhat like the crenellations on a castle parapet, are a unique survival, and must have been intended to break up the outline of the walls for camouflage purposes (*colour plate 25*).

John and I inspected the gun emplacement, which I am told by Mike Osborne[*] was for a field gun rather than an anti-tank gun, and then walked across a nearby paddock to an adjacent Type 24 pillbox. Between this pillbox and the emplacement, a length of anti-tank ditch ran from the road, making a sharp-angled turn to pass across the front of the field gun embrasure. It was very hot, and we braved the crossing of the road to lean over the stone parapet of the bridge and gain at least a sense of coolness from the rushing water beneath. Like so many other bridges, this one too had been mined for demolition, and it had had a roadblock on its eastern side. A short length of anti-tank ditch continued from the north bank, and survives as the water-filled drain that can still be seen here. Further north, the river provided the main anti-tank obstacle, but sections of anti-tank ditch were cut across a number of loops to straighten and strengthen the line.

---

[*] Read his essential book, *Defending Britain* (Tempus, 2004), published while this book was being prepared.

88 The date '1940' punched in metal into the concrete of a loophole at Waverleymill Bridge

89 Anti-tank pimples (dragon's teeth) by the lake of Waverley Abbey House. The ruins of the Abbey are in the background. The meadow to the left was crossed by an anti-tank ditch

On the left-hand side of the road as you walk east away from the bridge is Stella Cottage, which is a fine stone house rather than the small rustic dwelling its name implies. Its gardens stretch down to the river bank, and, if you peer through the thick hedge, you will see the rectangular shape of a large anti-tank gun emplacement facing towards the bridge. On my first visits to Waverley, I did not know this emplacement was here: it was a discovery notified to by me by another Surrey researcher, which goes to show that there can be new sites to locate anywhere. Please note that it is in a private garden and there is absolutely no public access.

Beyond Stella Cottage is a footpath that leads between houses and follows a route along the wooded river cliffs above the Wey to Moor Park House. It makes a most pleasant walk, and there are a large number of defence works to be seen as well as Mother Ludlam's Cave, reputed to have once been the haunt of a witch. John and I had followed this route on a previous visit, which was probably just as well as I don't think either of us would have had the energy to do so today under the hot sun.

If you undertake the walk, however, a few hundred yards along the footpath you will find another gun emplacement with an attached walled courtyard at the rear for infantry defence similar to the one at the Waverley Abbey car park. Close to it is a brick-shuttered Type 24 pillbox. As you follow the driveway past Moor Park House (on the public right of way) you will see two massive anti-tank cylinders with metal rings on their tops so that a steel cable could be stretched between them. Reaching a junction of lanes by the gates to the house, an unusually tall Type 24 pillbox stands at the edge of the field on the north-west side. It fired west towards the river and covered a roadblock a short distance along the lane to the west: you will find a single cylinder from this overgrown by ivy on the north side of the lane. Next, if you walk back along the lane and past the junction, on the right there are some 10 concrete cones lying on the grass verge at the edge of woodland. This is an unusual form of concrete obstacle, and presumably came from a nearby roadblock. On the lane to the north of the junction some eight dragon's teeth also lie between the lane and the river.

You can make a round trip of this walk by returning to Waverleymill Bridge by footpaths to the east of Moor Park House. I wouldn't recommend that you return along Waverley Lane, as to do so is to court instant extinction. I survived the ordeal on one occasion by squashing myself razor-thin against the hedgerows, but I do not recommend the experience.

On our present visit, however, having inspected the anti-tank gun emplacement by Stella Cottage, John and I were content merely to take the path that strikes across the fields from the cool waters of the Waverley Abbey House lake to the Abbey ruins. We could see these in the distance, spread across the green meadow by the far river bank, their grey shapes outlined against the darker green of the woods behind.

By the lakeside were nine dragon's teeth, probably moved here subsequently from the point where the anti-tank ditch had met Waverley Lane. These concrete pimples were generally used to block the gaps between the ditch and the roadside.

The anti-tank ditch had crossed the fields to the Abbey in two angled lengths, passing the ruins on their eastern side to meet the river. I have seen the line of the ditch still showing as a mark in the grass even on quite recent air photographs. There is no evidence that the ruins themselves were utilised as defence positions, although it is reasonable to suspect this. Certainly, nothing of concrete seems to have been constructed amongst them, but there may have been slit trenches or sandbagged infantry posts. The ruins actually stood in front of the Line, and in a real battlefield situation they would undoubtedly have been levelled so they did not provide cover for an enemy attack. Whether charges were prepared for this purpose is not recorded.

A field of at least 25 large pimples (dragon's teeth) in three rows (and possibly more under the grass and stinging nettles) survives on the bank of the Wey by the Abbey ruins. This is one of the largest surviving groups of these concrete obstacles that I know of anywhere. A further 12 line the bank opposite: you can just make them out through the vegetation – easier to see in the winter. Also on the south bank is a Type 26 pillbox (a square type), dug deeply into the slope of the bank at the rear and almost totally hidden by trees. It was positioned to enfilade the line of the anti-tank ditch to the north.

The landscape of the Wey Valley north and south of Waverley Abbey formed a constricted battleground between the river and the heights behind which favoured the defenders. The Royal Engineers who laid out GHQ Line 'B' here took maximum advantage of the topography, but also adapted it to suit the defence. They clearly decided that neither the curving loops of the river or the river cliffs behind represented a satisfactory front-edge anti-tank obstacle. An artificial anti-tank ditch was constructed, therefore, which cut across the river loops ensuring that the Germans would have to cross an obstacle that was in the open at the centre of the valley where it could be covered by fire from the wooded heights behind. The river, of course, formed an additional obstacle, but where a loop faced west towards the direction of enemy attack, it also presented a danger that an assault could be made along the river itself, passing through the defence line in that way. To guard against this, cables were strung across the river between the dragon's teeth that we have seen on each bank, some of which have iron loops set in their tops for this purpose. We have already viewed a similar defence provision on the River Mole below Box Hill.

It was cooler under the trees by the green, sliding river, with the concrete dragon's teeth standing on the bank amongst the tangled vegetation like a gigantic honeycomb. John and I looked hard at the tree trunks, trying to make out an inscription that had been carved 65 years ago and which was legible until recent years. However, time and decay had now played their part, and we could not even make out for sure which tree had borne it. The inscription had read, 'Bond, Sgt Pioneer Corp [sic]. 1941'. Here was another soldier aware of his place in history, and seeking to commemorate his presence here. One wonders what Sgt Bond was doing in 1941 with time on his hands to carve his name and unit into a tree trunk. Presumably the construction work on the concrete defences had been completed months before, or wet cement might have provided a more long-lasting memorial, as it has done for Sgt Rolfe at Jude's Ferry Bridge. Yet, what seems permanent of a time and place, will nonetheless in the end prove transitory. The Cistercian brothers in their white habits, at prayer in their Abbey church, or seeking shelter from the hot sun within the stone cloisters of the outer court, could not have guessed that their sense of permanence, their order, and their rituals would be suddenly overthrown and their buildings razed virtually to the ground.

I find it satisfying looking at the defence works of 1940 in conjunction with other more remote historic landscapes. It shows that the material remains of recent events are but the latest in the long flow of history that has passed over the landscape. Everything is changing, and being replaced. Land use alters; there are new ideas, new needs. Nothing – the stone Abbey walls or the concrete defences – will be here indefinitely. For instance, within the far river loop south of Waverley Abbey gravel was quarried in the 1950s, destroying one pillbox and obliterating all trace of the anti-tank ditch. For a while we preserve what we value, but in time all will assuredly fall, and what will come in its place it is impossible even to guess at. But for the moment, it is right that we save the best of what we have, partly as a commemoration of what was done and partly for future generations to appreciate and to understand.

At Waverley Abbey, we have some excellent examples of defence works illustrating a 1940 anti-tank line. It is to be hoped now that they will receive statutory protection equivalent to that which ensures the Abbey ruins are preserved for the future. This was the principal purpose of the two-year project I was now completing, and it was of this that John Schofield and I talked as we walked through the Waverley meadows along the line of the infilled anti-tank ditch back to the car park. John would like complete defence landscapes to be preserved where the landscape itself adds meaning to the surviving works. In other words, a pillbox positioned at a hedgerow should be preserved with that hedgerow; the edge of a wood that determined the terminal of an anti-tank ditch should retain that boundary; a trackway flanked by roadblock supports should retain its width. There is a vast amount of work to be done to achieve these things, to preserve the legacy of Britain's ground defence in 1940. The survey I have undertaken is in many ways just the beginning.

What I have described to you has been the first half of the fieldwork for this project. Later I moved on to survey the North of the country as well, and then the South-West where there is a particularly fine survival of sites. By the time I had finished, I had visited some 75 separate areas, inspected 1000 individual sites, and walked upward of 500 miles. In addition, I had examined some 1500 documents (1200 at The National Archives alone), and around 15,000 air photographs.

Before I could have a holiday from the subject, however, there was a great deal that needed to be written up, including, of course, this book.* In fact, it has proved an enjoyable process setting down in this informal way what I have seen and learnt, and I hope you will have found my travels interesting. You might be stimulated to follow in my footsteps, or perhaps seek out new areas for yourself. There is still a great deal of basic recording work to be done, and, if you feel the urge to be involved, you should find all the requisite information in Chapters 3 and 4 to get under way. The subject might become just a hobby for you and you will probably want to keep it that way, but, should you start to produce real results and locate new sites, in particular as a result of original research, then you should consider liasing with your local county archaeology service so that they can be added to the appropriate Historic Environment Record (formerly known as Sites and Monuments Record). Many enthusiasts also set up their own web pages providing details and images of defence works within particular areas.

John and I had a wonderfully refreshing beer at a pub in Tilford, and then I braved Farnham railway station again and dropped him off for a train that would bring him into London in the rush hour. I didn't envy him. In my time I have had my fill of daily commuting.

As I drove home, I thought of some of the places I had been and some of the sights seen during this survey of the South-East and Central South of England. It would be hard to pull out a particular favourite. It is often the landscape itself, as much as the defence structures, which remain in the memory.

I recalled the multitude of pillboxes at Hartford End seen against a countryside yellow with fields of rape; the verdant valley at Sulham studded with the great, grey hulks of the anti-tank gun emplacements; the wide spring-green fields of the Hoo peninsula, with the slight hollow of the anti-tank ditch coming towards me like an arrow in the grass; the shining band of the Royal Military Canal with the flat expanse of Romney Marsh seamed by innumerable watercourses and bordered by the hills behind; the rising smoke from the burning stubble in

---

* The full project has been published as a CBA Research Report – see 'Bibliography', Foot, W. 2006

the great, straw fields of Fyfield; the dark, wet woods at Ewshot, and at Cripp's Corner, where the lanes ran in streams with the rain; the high, stone ramparts of Pevensey Castle with the gun embrasures like half-opened mouths against the sky; and at Cuckmere Haven, the white cliffs, and the sea breaking on the shingle shore, and the concrete blocks and the anti-tank ditch and the pillboxes set back from the sea's edge defending the great heart of the land of England beyond.

'We shall fight .... We shall never surrender.' The defence works were built to give effect to Churchill's defiant speech; in case the Germans could cross the Channel or come out of the North Sea, the battlefields were prepared. Thankfully the Battle of Britain was won in the air, but the thousands of defence works of 1940-1 still to be found across England are a testament to the spirit of our nation at that time. The ground battles never took place, but they so nearly did. We shall never know if we could have driven the Germans back had they landed. But one thing is certain, had the enemy come, we would have fought them, and gone on fighting.

We would have fought for our land.

APPENDIX

INFORMATION ON THE AREAS DESCRIBED

Sketch maps for many of the areas are provided with the text, but, if you are planning to visit these places, you will probably wish to arm yourself with the appropriate Ordnance Survey sheets. For convenience, the numbers of these are given below – LR (Landranger 1:50,000); EX (Explorer 1:25,000); OL (Outdoor Leisure 1:25,000).

BERKSHIRE

Dunmill Lock (pp210-6). 1m east of Hungerford on the Kennet & Avon Canal. NGR: SU 351682 (LR 174; EX 158).

Sulham Valley (pp195-202). 1m south of Pangbourne/5m west of Reading. NGR (Oaklands Farm): SU 639745 (LR 175; EX 159).

ESSEX

Audley End (pp161-5). 1 mile west of Saffron Walden. NGR: TL 521380. Audley End House is in the care of English Heritage and there is a fee for entry. Enquiries to Audley End House and Gardens, Audley End, Saffron Walden, Essex CB11 4JF. Tel: 01799-522842 (LR 154; EX 195).

Hartford End (pp141-7). 6 miles south-east of Great Dunmow. NGR (Hartford End bridge): TL 688174 (LR 167; EX 183).

Wakes Colne (pp149-52). 7 miles west of Colchester. NGR: TL 896284 (LR 168; EX 195).

HAMPSHIRE

Chequers Bridge (pp219-26). 5 miles north-west of Farnham. NGR: SU 791517 (LR 186; EX 144).

Ewshot (pp227-234). 3 miles north-west of Farnham. NGR (Ridding's Copse): SU 811507 (LR 186; EX 145).

HERTFORDSHIRE

Cheshunt (pp133-9). 2 miles north-west of Cheshunt centre. NGR (Cheshunt Park): TL 344044 (LR 166; EX 174).

KENT

Deangate Ridge, Hoo (pp122-7). 4 miles north-east of Rochester. NGR (Deangate): TQ 775735 (LR 178; EX 163).

Farthingloe, Dover (pp26-33). 1.5 miles west of Dover town centre. NGR (Little Farthingloe Farm): TR 294404 (LR 179; EX 138).

Penshurst (pp99-105). 5 miles north-west of Tunbridge Wells. NGR: TQ 526437 (LR 188; EX 147).

River Medway, Maidstone (pp119-22). 1.5 miles north of Maidstone town centre. NGR (Allington Lock): TQ 748581 (LR 188; EX 148).

Royal Military Canal (pp11-20). 8 miles west of Hythe. NGR (Ruckinge village): TR 026336 (LR 189; EX 125).

Sarre (pp34-40). 8 miles north-east of Canterbury. NGR: TR 257650 (LR 179; EX 150).

NORFOLK

Acle (pp181-85). 8 miles west of Great Yarmouth. NGR: TG 401105 (LR 134; OL 40).

Ludham Bridge (pp178-181). 1.5 miles south-west of Ludham village. NGR: TG 372170 (LR 134; OL 40).

Weybourne (pp186-194). 3.5 miles west of Sheringham. NGR (Weybourne Hope): TG 111436. Information on the opening times of the Muckleburgh collection military museum is at <muckleburgh.co.uk> Tel: 01263-588425. (LR 133; EX 251 & EX 252).

OXFORDSHIRE

Frilford – Fyfield (pp203-10). 4 miles west of Abingdon. NGR (Collins Farm): SU
438972 (LR 164; EX 170).

SUFFOLK

Bawdsey Point (pp167-74). 2 miles south-west of Bawdsey village. NGR (Bawdsey
Quay): TM 331379. Bawdsey Manor is in private ownership and its grounds should
not be entered without permission (LR 169; EX 197).

Jude's Ferry Bridge, West Row (pp158-61). 2.5 miles west of Mildenhall on the River
Lark. NGR: TL 677748 (LR 143; EX 226).

Sudbury (pp153-8). 15 miles south of Bury St Edmunds. NGR (Brundon Mill): TL
864422 (LR 155; EX 196).

Walberswick (pp174-77). 1 mile south of Southwold. NGR: TM 500746 (LR 156; EX 231).

SURREY

Dorking Gap (pp106-12). 1.5 miles north of Dorking town centre. NGR (Burford
Bridge): TQ 171518. Much of the Box Hill estate, including the Victorian Fort, is in
the care of the National Trust, and there is a visitor information centre and shop:
<www.nationaltrust.org.uk/main/w-vh/w-visits/w-findaplace/w-boxhill.htm> Tel:
01372 220642. (LR 187; EX 146).

Drift Bridge (pp128-33). 1.5 miles east of Epsom. NGR: TQ 231601 (LR 187; EX 161).

Sidlow Bridge (pp113-6). 2 miles south of Reigate. NGR: TQ 258470 (LR 187; EX 146).

Waverley Abbey (pp235-41). 2.5 miles south of Farnham. NGR (Waverleymill Bridge):
SU 870455. Waverley Abbey ruins are in the care of English Heritage: there is no
fee for access. (LR 186; EX 145).

SUSSEX, EAST

Barcombe Mills (pp91-6). 3.5 miles north-east of Lewes. NGR: TQ 433148 (LR 198; EX
122).

Cripp's Corner (pp71-81). 4 miles north of Battle. NGR: TQ 777212 (LR 199; EX124).

Cuckmere Haven (pp83-8). 6 miles west of Eastbourne. NGR (beachfront): TV 516977.
The area is best approached from the visitor information centre and car park of the
Seven Sisters Country Park: <www.sevensisters.org.uk> (LR 199; EX 123).

Old Lodge Warren (pp96-8). 2 miles east of Crowborough. NGR: TQ 547313 (LR 188; EX 135).

Pevensey Castle (pp62-70). 4 miles north-east of Eastbourne. NGR: TQ 645048. Pevensey Castle is in the care of English Heritage and there is a fee for entry to the medieval inner bailey. <www.english-heritage.org.uk/server.php?show=conProperty .206> Tel: 01323 762604. (LR 199; EX 124).

SELECT BIBLIOGRAPHY

Alexander, C. 1999 *Ironside's Line*. Storrington: Historic Military Press

Bird, C. 1999 *Silent Sentinels: The Story of Norfolk's Fixed Defences during the Twentieth Century*. Dereham: The Larks Press

Collier, B. 1957 *The Defence of the United Kingdom*. London: Her Majesty's Stationery Office

Dobinson, C.S. 1996 Anti-invasion defences of WWII, *Twentieth Century Fortifications in England,* Vol II. York: Council for British Archaeology

Fleming, P. 1957 *Invasion 1940*. London: Rupert Hart-Davies
Foot, W. 2006 *Beaches, Fields, Streets, and Hills: The Anti-Invasion Landscapes of England, 1940*. York: Council for British Archaeology

Gilbert, A. 1990 *Britain Invaded: Hitler's Plans for Britain, a documentary reconstruction*. London: Century
Gillies, M. 2006 Waiting For Hitler: Voices From Britain on the Brink of Invasion. London: Hodder & Stoughton
Glover, M. 1990 *Invasion Scare 1940*. London: Leo Cooper
Greeves, I.D. 1993 The Construction of the GHQ Stop-Line: Eridge to Newhaven, June-November 1940, *Fortress,* **16**, 52-61

Hylton, S. 2004 *Kent and Sussex 1940: Britain's Front Line*. Barnsley: Pen & Sword Military

Kent, P. 1988 *Fortifications of East Anglia*. Lavenham: Terence Dalton

Kieser, E. 1997 *Operation Sea Lion: The German Plan to Invade Britain, 1940*. London: Arms and Armour Press

Longmate, N. 1972 *If Britain had Fallen*. London: Greenhill Books

Lowry, B. (ed.) 1996 *20th Century Defences in Britain: An introductory guide*. Second edition. York: Council for British Archaeology

Lowry, B. 2004 *British Home Defences 1940-45*. Oxford: Osprey Publishing

Macksey, M. 1980 *Invasion: The German Invasion of England July 1940*. London: Arms and Armour Press

Marix Evans, M. 2004 *Invasion! Operation Sealion, 1940*. Harlow: Pearson Education

Osborne, M. 2004 *Defending Britain: Twentieth-Century Military Structures in the Landscape*. Stroud: Tempus Publishing

Schenk, P. 1990 *Invasion of England 1940: The Planning of Operation Sealion*. London: Conway Maritime Press

Ward, A. 1997 *Resisting the Nazi Invader*. London: Constable

Wheatley, R. 1958 *Operation Sea Lion: German Plans for the Invasion of England 1939-1942*. Oxford: Clarendon Press

Wills, H. 1985 *Pillboxes: A Study of UK Defences 1940*. London: Leo Cooper

INDEX

If you are interested in purchasing other books published by Tempus,
or in case you have difficulty finding any Tempus books in your local bookshop,
you can also place orders directly through our website

www.tempus-publishing.com